Finding Mr. Perfect

Finding Mr. Perfect

· ·

K-Drama, Pop Culture, Romance, and Race

MIN JOO LEE

R

Rutgers University Press

New Brunswick, Camden, and Newark, New Jersey

London and Oxford

Rutgers University Press is a department of Rutgers, The State University of New Jersey, one of the leading public research universities in the nation. By publishing worldwide, it furthers the University's mission of dedication to excellence in teaching, scholarship, research, and clinical care.

978-1-9788-4157-4 (cloth)
978-1-9788-4156-7 (paper)
978-1-9788-4158-1 (epub)
978-1-9788-4159-8 (web pdf)

Cataloging-in-publication data is available from the Library of Congress.
LCCN 2025012743

A British Cataloging-in-Publication record for this book is available from the British Library.

References to internet websites (URLs) were accurate at the time of writing. Neither the author nor Rutgers University Press is responsible for URLs that may have expired or changed since the manuscript was prepared.

∞ The paper used in this publication meets the requirements of the American National Standard for Information Sciences—Permanence of Paper for Printed Library Materials, ANSI Z39.48-1992.

rutgersuniversitypress.org

Contents

Finding Mr. Perfect

Introduction

● ●

The large ballroom was packed with hundreds of people, mostly young women, seated close to each other at long conference tables, eagerly awaiting the South Korean (hereby Korean) television drama-related event to begin. The event was hosted by a popular East Asian media streaming website. The company logo was presented around the elevated podium. The spacious ballroom was abuzz with excitement, but the crowd quickly became quiet when one of the two women sitting on the podium facing the crowd finally picked up a microphone to announce the rules of the event: "We'll display a picture of a Korean male celebrity's body without the face. If you know who the body belongs to, raise your hand and shout out the answer." The other woman on the podium said, "The winner will win prizes, including Korean television drama posters signed by the actors, mug cups, and tote bags!" She waved her hand toward the adjacent table, filled with rolled-up posters and other goodies. The participants sat on the edges of their seats, ready to jump up and shout out the answers. I participated in this event with some hope that I could win a prize, but now, after sensing everyone's zeal, even before the event began, I knew that I had no chance of winning. Although I was a fan of Korean television dramas, my passion for them seemed infinitesimal compared to the love other fans participating in the event had for them. As one of the women shouted dramatically, "Let us begin!" the screen facing the audience flashed a photo of a man's body in a black suit with a white dress shirt and black tie. I was stumped, but clearly, the woman with curly brown hair sitting across from me was not. Her hand shot up into the air, as did dozens of other hands around the room. The woman on the podium pointed to one of the women sitting across from me, and she answered with confidence, "That's Lee Min Ki's body. I know that

1

body from the drama *It Is My First Life*." Around the room, there were mur-murs of agreement, and the woman on the stage said, "Yes! You are correct!" With a tap on her laptop, she revealed the face of the actor whose suited body we were just looking at. Some women in the crowd oohed and aahed while looking at the photo.

After the winner went up to the podium to pick up her prize, in a state of bewilderment, I wondered aloud, "How did you know that was Lee Min Ki's body?" Many other women around me were also asking similar questions: "How did she know so quickly?" "How did you know?" Questions poured onto the prize winner as she walked back to her seat. She sheepishly smiled, tucked her hair behind her ears, and responded to these women's queries by saying, "If you watch as many Korean television dramas and are in love with Korean men as much as I am, then this game is very easy." The game continued at lightning speed, with the participants' hands shooting up as soon as they saw a new photo of a male body part on screen. They correctly guessed who the body in the sweater belonged to as well as who the muscular torso belonged to. The difficulty increased with each question. Near the end of the game, the screen in front of the crowd revealed one muscular arm that, in my eyes, looked nondescript. However, after some deliberation, one participant was able to successfully guess that the arm belonged to the Korean actor Song Joong-Ki; she won a signed poster of him. Many women who won prizes were non-Korean white, Black, Latina, or Asian. They clapped and whooped when they won a television drama poster signed by their favorite celebrity; they oohed and aahed at the photos of the Korean male celebrities on screen; and, as the woman sitting across from me proclaimed, many of them expressed their love for Korean men.

Orientalism and Race

These women's desires for Korean male celebrities and, more broadly, Korean men are not surprising in themselves. Just because they are non-Korean does not mean they would not be attracted to Korean men. However, what was surpris-ing to me about these women's desires for Korean men was that, until recently, in the United States, Asian men have been racialized through discourses of gen-der and sexuality in ways that stereotyped them as physically unattractive, phys-ically weak, bad at romantic and sexual relationships, traditionally patriarchal, and unromantic (Wong et al. 2012; Nemoto 2009). Their race and gender inter-sected to construct an Orientalist and unflattering stereotype.

Orientalism is the West's "Othering" of the East to create a sense of hierar-chy. It inextricably connects race with gender and sexuality to identify Asians as racialized sexual subjects whose race predetermines their sexual proclivities. The stereotype of Asian women as domineering and sexually alluring dragon ladies, innocent damsels in need of Western saviors, or mysteriously seductive femme fatales abound in popular discourse. These harmful caricatures of Asian women portray them as sexually appealing partners due to their racial and ethnic identities that supposedly make them innately feminine and sexual. Orientalism is so resilient that even as some Asian American and Asian women consciously attempt to defy it or co-opt it for their financial benefit, they occasionally end up unintentionally perpetuating the harmful stereotypes (Pyke and Johnson 2003; Hoang 2015).

There is less work that examines Orientalism's racialized sexualizing and gendering of Asian and Asian diasporic men compared to the abundance of work that critically analyzes Orientalism's impact on Asian and Asian diasporic women. The existing research on its impact on men primarily analyzes Orientalist racialized sexualizing of Asian American gay men (Nguyen 2014; Eng 2001; Han 2021). A few scholarly works examine how heterosexual Asian American men perform their racialized gender and sexuality by co-opting popular racist stereotypes of Black masculinity in order to escape the Orientalist stereotypes of Asian masculinity (Jun 2011; Chon-Smith 2014). Similar to the scholarly works that examine the resistance of Asian American women against the monolithic Orientalist racialized gendering of them, these works critically examining Asian American men's resistance also demonstrate the resilience of Orientalism. For instance, in discussing Asian American gay porn actor Brandon Lee, Nguyen Tan Hoang (2014) argues that the actor rather futilely employs "yellow yellow face," an ironic and purposeful donning of the racist yellowface caricature to satirize and disrupt Orientalist racism. While the performance serves as a parody and a critique of essentialism that Orientalism is rooted in, it ends up perpetuating the stereotype for many viewers who are watching the performance for sexual pleasure and not for political commentary. In such ways, Orientalism is hard to escape.

In this context, the Hallyu fans, whom I mention at the beginning of this introduction, with their seeming defiance and rejection of such pervasive Orientalist stereotypes that have racially gendered and sexualized Asian men for centuries, surprised me, precisely because I am aware of the difficulty of escaping such Orientalist legacies. How did they manage to escape Orientalist epistemologies? Did they truly succeed? Or is it a farce? These are some of the questions I address in this book.

Thus far, I have examined Orientalism in the United States, which begs the question, does U.S. Orientalism have any bearing outside of the country? How is it relevant in the Korean context? I contend that Orientalism is not just resilient; it is pervasive. It travels transnationally to other parts of the world, including Asia. In examining Japanese intellectual men's relationship to Orientalism, Chizuko Ueno (1997) argues that the concept entered Japan during the European imperialist era, thereby implying that it was not just the United States but also Europe and the West more broadly that adopted Orientalism in their efforts to expand their imperial power. She coined the term "reverse Orientalism" to explain a strategy deployed by elite Japanese men to reform their racialized masculinity in relation to the Europeans. Ueno defines the concept as some Japanese men's acceptance of their feminized stereotype as the "Other" to European masculinity in their attempts to take advantage of such positionality to peacefully reform Japanese national identity while avoiding the possibility of engaging in violent altercations with Western forces. Such practice paradoxically served to internalize Orientalist racialized sexualizing of Asian men in the minds of some Japanese women who would echo Orientalist assumptions about Japanese men in comparison to white and Black men to claim they prefer the latter as sexual partners over the former (Kelsky 1999).

There is less scholarly work on Korea's relationship to Orientalism than Japan's relationship to the concept. However, the few existing scholarly works on the topic contend that Korea experienced two types of Orientalism: Western Orientalism and Japanese Orientalism (Chung 2006). After all, as Laura Hyun Yi Kang (2020) observes, the West is not the only imperial force that many Asian countries had to contend with; intra-Asian colonialism and racism mark the history of various Asian countries, including Korea. According to Yong-Hwa Chung (2006), both forms of Orientalism were introduced to Korea during the late 1800s, at the onset of Japanese colonialism. Scholars analyzed archival records of newspapers and diaries from the time to argue that U.S.-educated Korean elites such as Seo Jae-pil and Yun Chi-ho brought Western Orientalism back to Korea and proclaimed in widely disseminated newspapers that in order for Korea to become civilized, it had to become Westernized (Chung 2006; Cho 2021a). In prototypical Western Orientalist logic, they equated civilization with Westernization. Jinhyun Cho (2021a) interprets such discourse as Korean elites' "self-Orientalism."

However, I interpret the situation differently. Instead of viewing this rhetoric as Korean elites' blind adoption of Western ideology, I interpret it as a response to Japanese Orientalism that attempted to position Japan as the "West" of Asia, which would civilize the rest of Asia through imperial governance. The Japanese colonial government, which tried to find ways to distinguish Japanese from Koreans, whom they considered to be inferior, turned to race to find the answers they wanted. Since distinguishing "race" was difficult to achieve phenotypically, they resorted to emphasizing "blood," literally and figuratively, as the factor that determined the two groups of people as separate "races" (Diederich 2021).

To fight against the sense of ethnic precarity formed throughout the periods of Japanese colonialism and the Korean War, some Korean intellectual elites adopted the eugenicist theory of social Darwinism and its derivative, Orientalism, and brought the ideas to Korea to use them for Korean nationalist purposes (J. K. Kim 2015). Concurrently, Korean intellectuals attempted to form a sense of ethnic solidarity and used blood as a means to generate such a sense of unity (Diederich 2021; Hyun 2019; J.-Y. Jung 2012). Both the Korean and Japanese efforts were deeply problematic and built upon the belief in one's supposed pure-bloodedness and innate superiority over the cultural and the racial "Other." Rather than creating their own conception of race, Koreans utilized the same tool—serology—and the same logic as the colonizers, only interpreted differently, to define their racial identity.

Granted, race as a conceptual framework existed in the Korean peninsula hundreds of years before the Japanese colonization. For instance, the intense social stigma that *Sokwannyeo* [속환녀]—Korean women during the Joseon Dynasty who were abducted and presumably raped by the Qing Dynasty soldiers and made their way back to Joseon—experienced relative to those raped by Korean men hint at a society that believed Qing soldiers were somehow inferior to Korean men and that women whom they raped became, by proxy, inferior (J. Y. Park 2020).[1] However, I agree with some scholars who argue that the stigma for those women had more to do with a mix of the nation's sense of cultural superiority over the non-Confucian Qing Dynasty and patriarchal policing of women's sexual purity than race (M.-H. Lee 2020). While the concept of race may have existed back then, it may not have been the overriding factor that dictated social standards. Therefore, I subscribe to Gi-Wook Shin's (2006) argument that the Japanese colonial era was the point in the nation's history where race, or *injong* [인종] in Korean, became symbolically important and was systematically mobilized by Koreans.

Post–Korean War racial formation demonstrated Korea's continued adoption and adaptation of Western Orientalism and racial ideology as thousands of U.S. soldiers stationed in Korea "exported" their racism and Orientalism to Korea en masse. For instance, the segregation between white and non-white soldiers created a segregated Korean sex work industry (M. Lee 2008). While some Koreans internalized the Western racism and Orientalist racialized gendering system (N. Kim 2006), others attempted to resist such stereotypes by claiming themselves to be more educated and cultured than Westerners to feel a sense of superiority over the supposedly hypermasculine and "brutish" U.S. soldiers (Gage 2013).

Scholars have been divided about the legacy of Orientalism in Korea. Some scholars contend that contemporary Korea suffers from internalized Orientalism that makes Koreans believe they are still inferior subjects to the West (S. Choi 2005; Cho 2021b), while others contend that Korea now enacts its own version of Orientalism to demean and subjugate others (J. K. Kim et al. 2018; Fedorenko 2022). It is within this context that I find Hallyu to be an interesting cultural phenomenon. More specifically, I believe that the interracial relationships between my Hallyu tourist informants and their Korean male dates demonstrate that the binary framework of Korea as either the

"Orientalized" or the "Orientalizer" fails to accurately capture the nuanced ways in which my informants—both the tourists and Korean men—navigated and negotiated Orientalism and race. Rather than operating through the predetermined category of the subjugator and the subjugated, the positions were constantly flipped between my tourist informants and Korean male informants. I argue that my tourist informants attempted to rework Orientalist stereotypes of Korean masculinity by using Korean television dramas. However, their efforts had ambiguous liberating potentials due to their constant alternation between debunking Orientalism and affirming it based on their day-to-day experiences in Korea. Likewise, my Korean male informants rarely fell within the neat binary category of "Orientalized" or the "Orientalizer" and constantly repositioned themselves somewhere within or beyond the spectrum based on their different encounters with the Hallyu tourists.

The Korean Wave (Hallyu)

So, what is Hallyu? Beginning in the early twenty-first century, Korean television dramas gained transnational popularity. This phenomenon, called Hallyu, consists of many components, including Korean television dramas, K-pop, K-entertainment, Korean beauty products, fashion, language, and food. Reports by the Korea Trade-Investment Promotion Agency (KOTRA 2017) suggest that the direct and indirect profits from Hallyu make it one of the fastest-growing industries in Korea. As a case in point, the Korean romance drama *Descendants of the Sun* (2016) was exported to twenty-seven countries, including China, France, Romania, Sweden, Spain, Saudi Arabia, Iran, Myanmar, Cambodia, and the United States. The Korea Creative Content Agency estimates that in the United States alone, more than eighteen million viewers regularly stream Korean television dramas on their digital devices (KOCCA 2014). According to the report, these viewers devote as much as ten hours weekly to watching the dramas online.

The Hallyu fans are not just couch potatoes who passively consume popular culture. They mobilize their fandom, sometimes in unexpected ways. As Jonathan Gray, Cornel Sandvoss, and C. Lee Harrington claim, "Fandom has emerged as an ever more integral aspect of lifeworlds in global capitalism, and an important interface between the dominant micro and macro forces of our time" (2007, 9). Hallyu fandom is indeed a sociopolitical and economic force. In 2020 fans hijacked Donald Trump's presidential campaign rally in Tulsa, Oklahoma, by reserving hundreds of tickets that they had no intention of using so that his actual supporters could not attend the event. They also took over the racist hashtags on Instagram so that searching for the posts with those racist hashtags would not lead to racist posts but would instead lead to random images of Korean celebrities. By appropriating the racist hashtags, they disrupted the community of racists on Instagram who were communicating and bonding on digital platforms. They serve as a political force around the world, including in countries like Chile, Thailand, Indonesia, and Poland (Trzcińska 2020; Diaz Pino 2021; Andini and Akhni 2021). In such ways, the Hallyu fans are reshaping and rearticulating cultural practices on and offline. Their deep engagement with social justice paints a portrait of them as open-minded, anti-Orientalist, and antiracist crusaders for a world filled with love and acceptance. Hallyu fandom's public images as fan activists separate them from the stereotype of popular culture fans as brainless and immature youths.

Not only do the Hallyu fans stream the dramas and engage in online activities, but some also invest an extensive amount of time and money to travel to Korea in a practice called Hallyu tourism. Approximately twelve million tourists visit Korea annually (Korea Tourism Organization 2013). Granted, not all of them are Hallyu tourists, and tourist travel to Korea existed prior to Hallyu. For instance, during the 1960s–1980s, Japanese businessmen traveled to Korea to engage in business during the day and to visit sex parlors at night in a form of tourism known as *kisaeng* tourism (Graburn 1983). Many factors contributed to the rise in tourism to Korea in the 2010s, including the increase in women's expendable income and transnational mobility in different parts of the world as well as Korea's dramatic rise in economic standing since the 1980s.

However, I attribute the popularity of tourism to Korea, in significant part, to Hallyu because even though Korea's most dramatic economic rise occurred throughout much of the 1980s and 1990s, the most dramatic increase in foreign tourism to Korea did not occur at that point in history. Instead, the steepest increase occurred in the 2010s, which many scholars attribute to the "Hallyu 2.0" era that mobilized transnational collaboration and digital media platforms to garner a global fan base beyond Asia (Y. Kim 2013; Lee and Nornes 2015; Jin 2016). While six million tourists visited Korea in 2005, the number rose twofold, to twelve million in 2013, and peaked in 2019 at seventeen million (Korea Culture and Tourism Institute 2023). The steep increase in tourism in 2013 coincides with the global popularity of Korean singer Psy's song "Gangnam Style" in the second half of 2012, which took the world by storm through its meticulous use of social media and YouTube to make the song a viral hit around the world (Song 2015). Learning from the song's global success, other K-pop singers and the Korean television drama industry started using social media and digital platforms more extensively, thereby also presumably contributing to the popularity of Hallyu tourism. At the time, there was also a demographic shift among tourists: they have become much younger. Whereas the largest age group for tourists in the early 2000s was those in their thirties, the largest in 2019 was those in their twenties (Korea Culture and Tourism Institute 2023). During this time period, there was a gradual decline in the number of older travelers in their forties and above. Such a demographic shift also coincides with the overall demographic of the Hallyu fan base. Although Hallyu fandom comprises folks from all age groups—most notably, in Japan, middle-aged women are the primary consumers of Korean popular culture—those most active nowadays at venues such as concerts tend to be younger fans.

Many Hallyu scholars have written about Hallyu tourism (Han and Lee 2008; S. Kim and Nam 2016; Molen 2014; Ya 2005), focusing on the relationship between spaces and tourists' emotive experience with those toured spaces. I find scholarly works by Youngmin Choe (2016) and Youjeong Oh (2018) that closely examine the driving force of Hallyu tourism and its effects on Korean landscapes to be especially generative for this book. Choe looks at representations of travel in Hallyu films and the travel that emerges from consuming such films. She focuses on the relevant sites as assemblages of their own cultural production to examine how cultural flows are suffused with affective flows so that cultural exchanges are also exchanges of affect. Building on Choe's work, Oh examines K-pop and Korean television drama-inspired tourism while looking at the entertainment industry and the government's systemic efforts to facilitate such mediated tourism. Choe and Oh have a different focus, but their research has a similar theoretical framework: affect. Choe claims that Hallyu is an affective phenomenon that fosters affective tourism whereby people travel to affective sites in hopes of experiencing the similar affects they observed in the films. She contends that people are not traveling from their countries of origin to Korea but to the films. Oh also uses affect as a framework to examine the different geographic spaces in Korea that are reconfigured into tourist sites, arguing that the tourists do not visit those sites for their visual aspects but because of their affective qualities and the tourists' investment in such affect. According to Oh, Korean cities experience the "creation of place" through television drama production and consumption. Building from Oh's assertion, I contend that my tourist informants facilitate the "creation of people" through their racialized erotic desires for Korean men.

My work diverges from Oh and Choe's research in several ways. First, while I also examine the infrastructures of mediated tourism, my primary focus is on the erotic relationships that form between a subset of young Hallyu tourists and Korean men and the racial politics surrounding the formation of such intimate transnational encounters. I incorporate race as one of the key frameworks to examine such interracial relationships. I posit that Korean television dramas are cultural artifacts symbolizing Korea's attempts to reject Western Orientalism as a racial framework and to establish its own racial framework. I analyze the trajectory of how the Korean entertainment industry disseminates its own racially gendered and sexualized images of Korean masculinity that reject Western Orientalist conceptions of Asian masculinity. I examine how the media's attempt to reform transnational perceptions of Korean masculinity is experienced by my Hallyu tourist and Korean male informants who grew up with Western Orientalist conceptions of Asian masculinity.

Second, while Choe and Oh utilize affect as the primary theoretical framework for analyzing the Hallyu industry and spaces, I center emotion—racialized erotic desire—as the central theme of my work. Although some scholars encourage using emotions and affect interchangeably (Ahmed 2014), others emphasize the difference between the two due to their different scopes. For instance, Oh states that affect is a "bodily function that arises in a particular context; it is something that is difficult to present in linguistic terms and lies beyond consciousness" (2018, 16). Even so, there are specific emotions that can be presented in linguistic terms, such as "desire, despair [. . .] joy, loneliness, longing, love" (Pile 2010, 6).

In particular, desire is an ambivalent emotional state that some identify as emotion while others identify as affect. For instance, Steve Pile defines desire as emotion, whereas in the book *Regimes of Desire*, which examines gay identity formation in Tokyo, Thomas Baudinette refers to desire as an "ideological and affective system" (2021, 24) that is neither conscious nor rational. I believe desire can be both affective and emotional. In this book, I use the term "desire" as both affective and emotional, but more so the latter because I do not view my informants' desires as being "neither conscious nor rational." Their racialized erotic desires were conscious decisions they made. Although their desires may look irrational from the outside, they had their rationale, which I will examine in more detail in chapters 3, 4, and 5.

While some scholars may be interested in focusing on the *origins* of desire, that is not necessarily the scope of this book. Instead, I focus on the *trajectories* of desire and their effects, following in the footsteps of theorists of desire such as Gilles Deleuze and Felix Guattari (1983), who encouraged scholars to focus on the directions in which desire flows and to map out such desires rather than trying to trace the desires back to their origin. Examining the flow of desire and its impact is especially important in matters of race because as Robin Zheng, a philosopher of race theory, argues, "Whether or not some particular case of racial fetish is *caused by* an individual's harboring racial stereotypes at some level, it inevitably has the *effect* of reinforcing racial stereotypes" (2016, 410). Intentions are hard to decipher, and even if intentions—or the origins of desire—are "good," this does not mean the end-result as experienced by the desired subjects would also be a liberating experience. Hence, rather than focus on deciphering whether my tourist informants have racist/Orientalist intentions, I focus on what the outcomes of the pursuit of their racialized erotic desire are as they pertain to new formations of racialized sexual portraits of Korean masculinity.

Desire and the Melodramatic Convergence of Reality and Fantasy

It is not my intention to argue that my Hallyu tourist informants from various nations and cultures all interpret Korean dramas in the same way or desire Korean men in a monolithic manner. Instead, I ask, what is it about Korean television dramas' depiction of romance and masculinity that cuts across various cultural backgrounds of these tourists to move them to seek intimacy with Korean men in their real life? What are the consequences of their racialized erotic desires for Korean men?

I contend that desires produce realities. It is beyond the scope of this book to examine the long history of psychoanalytic and philosophical debates surrounding desires that include the likes of Jacques Lacan (Lacan, Miller, and Grigg 1993), who, simply put, describes desire as producing a sense of "lack" that individuals try to satisfy through fantasy, or Slavoj Zizek (1992), who claims that desire's goal is to reproduce cycles of desire. I borrow from Gilles Deleuze and Felix Guattari's conception of desire because I find their focus on the relationship between desire and reality to be especially generative. They claim: "If desire produces, its product is real. If desire is productive, it can be productive only in the real world and can produce only reality. Desire is the set of *passive syntheses* that engineer partial objects, flows, and bodies, and that function as units of production. . . . Desire does not lack anything; it does not lack its object. It is, rather, the *subject* that is missing in desire, or desire that lacks a fixed subject; there is no fixed subject unless there is repression" (2004, 28). Although Deleuze and Guattari discuss desire in relation to capitalism and individuals' desires for class mobility, their theorization about the power of desire to generate reality is applicable and essential to understanding my informants' racialized erotic desires. According to Deleuze and Guattari, the desiring subjects believe that the realities they produced through their desires are "real." While scholars like Lacan (Lacan, Miller, and Grigg 1993) argue that people fulfill desires through fantasies, I do not believe such an association between desire and fantasy applies to my Hallyu tourist informants. From my understanding, Lacan's argument relies on the assumption that desire is based on a "lack" that can only be satisfied by an escape into the fantasy world. However, as I analyze in the book, my Hallyu tourist informants were not escaping into fantasy worlds that were dissociated from reality. Their racialized erotic desire drove them to rework Western Orientalism's racialized gendering and sexualizing of Korean men through the use of Korean popular culture. Whether such reworked portraits of Korean masculinity are liberating and better reflective of the "reality" of how Korean men conceptualize their masculinity is an issue I critically examine in this book.

I discuss desire's power to produce reality to emphasize that the phenomenon I examine in this book is not built around a group of gullible and naïve women. Instead, I want to emphasize how their desires were generated by design through the thoughtfully planned articulation of masculinity in Korean television dramas. The melodramatic qualities of romantic Korean television dramas stimulate the convergence of reality and fantasy. I define a majority of romantic Hallyu dramas as melodramas. Melodrama is a concept that refers to entertainment pivoting around emotions. Through emotion, it facilitates the convergence of reality and fantasy. I find Christine Gledhill's observation that melodrama "demands that the real world match up to the imagination" (1992, 108) to be especially generative for examining my informants' interpretation of this entertainment genre to rework their conceptions of Korean masculinity. Using Deleuze and Guattari's theories on desire producing reality, I interpret Gledhill's argument to mean that the viewers' desires, derived from melodramatic entertainment, produce "realities" that they overlay onto the "real world." In the case of my informants, it would refer to their reworking of Korean masculinity through melodramatic television dramas and using their desire for such masculinity to produce realities about Korean masculinity that they superimpose on the real-life Korean men they encounter once they travel to the country.

In the context of the U.S. contemporary popular media genre, melodramas tend to be trivialized as focusing on emotions derived from "insignificant" situations: "The tears produced by the woman's film or soap opera, on the other hand, are considered unjustified by their trivial domestic or personal content and explainable only in terms of a "feminized sensibility" (Gledhill 1992, 106). Since melodramas are defined as "women's genres," melodramatic entertainment is popularly assumed only to portray "feminine issues" such as domestic and "trivial" personal travails.

In Korea's case, melodramas are far from trivial; they are an integral genre of entertainment that explains the nation's turbulent history and the equally tumultuous emotional rollercoaster that people living through that history experienced. In a way, they symbolize the modern Korean ethos. Both Kathleen McHugh (2001) and Nancy Abelmann (2003) have examined modern Korea through the framework of melodrama. According to McHugh, Korean melodramas are imbued with the emotions and experiences of Korea's rapid modernization. She claims that Korean melodramatic cinema is different from its Hollywood counterpart in that the melodramatic storylines are not just about personal fights for morality but are about the Korean national dilemma within a global neoliberal context. As briefly noted above, U.S. critics have frequently derided Hollywood melodrama's proclivity for converting political and social problems into easily solvable and "trivial" personal problems. In contrast, McHugh argues that in Korean melodramas, personal problems become the basis for discussing the larger familial, social, and political problems that Korea faced during modernization. Likewise, in Abelmann's (2003) research on Korean women's experiences with Korea's modernization, her informants constantly drew on Korean soap operas and melodramatic cinema to describe their experiences. Abelmann points to melodramatic entertainment as one of the most popular forms of entertainment in Korea and says that they are popular because melodramas dramatize issues prevalent in modernizing societies undergoing rapid change. Melodramatic stories' ability to emotionally communicate the nation's ethos is perhaps why the nation supports and celebrates the popularity of melodramatic Korean television dramas overseas (Oh 2018). This is a topic that I examine further in chapter 1.

While Abelmann and McHugh focus on melodrama's resonance with Korean viewers, I argue for expanding the scope of influence of melodramas beyond Korea. I go beyond the time frame of the Korean modernization period to show how melodramas are relevant to Korea (and beyond Korea) in the twenty-first century in the form of Hallyu. More specifically, I contend that the Korean television dramas shaped my tourist informants' erotic desires so that they developed favorable images of Korean masculinity and traveled to Korea to form intimate relations with Korean men in real life.

Melodrama as a genre is a debate between the possible and the real that collapses the dichotomies between the real versus unreal and social projections versus reality (Abelmann 2003). Both the Korean television drama producers working on creating appealing depictions of Korean masculinity and my Hallyu tourist informants who were using those popular cultural images to rework the Orientalist racialized gendered and sexualized perceptions of Korean masculinity were working through social projections to rearticulate reality. As a result, my tourist informants' social projections resulted in real-life transnational intimacies between them and Korean men. In that regard, they collapsed the boundaries between social projections versus reality and between the real and the unreal. As Deleuze and Guattari assert, desires produce realities; the disparate desires of the respective groups of people who were working on and through social projections of Korean masculinity generated real-life erotic encounters. In this regard, I find melodramas to be influential entertainment genres.

However, some feminist scholars are critical of melodramas' potential to impact their viewers' lives. In an especially strong critique, Lauren Berlant (2008) claims that some people engage with fantasies because of their desires to escape reality: "For many people, sentimentality and the fantasy of a better proximate world so close that one can experience it affectively without being able to live it objectively produces art that does, that transports people somewhere into a *situation* for a minute" (31). Berlant's critique stems from her dissatisfaction toward certain women who view melodramas due to their dissatisfaction with their lived realities but do not utilize their fantasy-driven rages back in real life to subvert the social conditions that cause social inequality. Hence, Berlant critiques such viewers as espousing only "half-truths"; they register the failure of the status quo but do not channel such awareness into dismantling such norms.

Berlant's critique against the types of fantasies that melodramas generate is much more critical compared to the stance taken by feminist media scholars, who are more sympathetic yet also critical of such media's influence on their viewers. For instance, Tania Modleski (1982) and Ien Ang (2007) are sympathetic in evaluating such entertainment and viewers' motivations for consuming them. Nonetheless, even these feminist media scholars do not entirely dismantle the binary conception of the "real world" and the fantasy, and they assume that the viewers consume particular entertainment to "escape" from reality. For instance, Ang says the "pleasure of fantasy lies in its offering the subject an opportunity to take up positions which she could not do in real life: through fantasy, she can move beyond the structural constraints of everyday life and explore other situations, other identities, other lives" (2007, 241). Here, fantasy is construed as an alternative world from the realness of "everyday life" and its structural constraints.

I disagree with these critiques of melodramas. I argue that romantic Korean television dramas and their fantasies create racialized erotic desires in my informants that, in turn, produce realities. In that regard, fantasy and reality are not binaries, and my informants were not escaping into the fantasy to avoid reality. Instead, they used their desire for Korean masculinity to produce realities that satisfied their desires. Therefore, I agree with Choe's (2016) claim that Hallyu tourists travel from their home countries to the films (rather than to Korea). However, I contend that such forms of travel are not escapes; they are a reworking of reality.

More specifically, my Hallyu tourist informants were using Korean television dramas to rework Western Orientalism's racialized gendered and sexual formation of Korean masculinity to generate an idealistically romantic, emotional, and gentlemanly perception of masculinity. As one of my informants said, "Being in Korea is like being in my own Korean television drama!" Her travel to Korea is a journey into her version of a romantic Korean television drama in which she is the protagonist. However, such discourse surrounding her travel does not mean that she sees Korea as a land of fantasy. Instead, I interpret her statement as her seeing Korea as the place where she is finally experiencing the "reality" she produced through her media-inspired desires for erotic relationships with Korean men. The racialized reworking of the gendered and sexualized Korean masculinities is central to such convergence between fantasy and reality. The question of whether the "reality" that my Hallyu tourist informants produced through their consumption of Korean melodramas is a more liberating and more accurate reflection of reality than the traditional Western Orientalism's racialized gendering and sexualizing of Korean masculinities is one of the questions that I examine in depth throughout this book.

Tourism: Negotiating Different "Realities" and Power Differentials

My Hallyu tourist informants' physical travel to Korea culminated in months of planning, imagining, and researching. Prior to their travel, they already spent months using Korean television dramas to rework the Western Orientalist stereotypes of Korean masculinity and to produce differently racialized and sexualized conceptions of Korean masculinity that were more desirable to them. However, international tourism does not often play out precisely as planned; their "produced realities" about Korean masculinity may differ from the reality they encounter during travel. In that regard, I view my Hallyu tourist informants' tourism to Korea as a confrontation between their "produced realities" and "experienced realities." Furthermore, I contend that the tourist experience is also the moment of a showdown between Western Orientalism's racialized gender and sexual formations of Korean masculinity versus the tourists' drama-inspired reconfiguration of Korean masculinity.

One of tourism's fundamental objectives is to experience the "authentic" culture of the "Other." Such desire for authenticity lends itself easily to prototypical tropes of Orientalism, including cultural relativism and cultural essentialism. After all, my informants presumably believed they would find some kind of "authentic" masculinity in Korean men only in Korea. Otherwise, they would not have traveled to Korea to find real-life Korean boyfriends. Without the belief in "authentic" experiences they will have in Korea, they would have probably chosen a more accessible option of trying to look for men of any race and ethnicity who display the characteristics of ideal boyfriends that they observed in the Korean television dramas, such as being romantic, emotionally attuned, and not being sexually assertive. Instead, they spent a substantial amount of resources to travel to Korea to find Korean boyfriends, assuming that only they would display the "authentic" masculinity that my informants deemed ideal.

From a particular simplistic feminist perspective, the Hallyu tourists whom I worked with can be seen as the vanguard of feminist empowerment because they have the means and the power to travel around the world to fulfill their erotic desires transnationally. Rather than "settling" for the men and romantic relationships that are available to them in their home countries, they decided to actively seek their erotic fulfillment through transnational travel. However, the racial power differentials and hierarchies of transnational travel and tourism, more specifically, limit such a rosy portrait of my informants' transnational travel.

Many scholars warn against the over-appraisal of transnational travel. The over-celebration of transnationalism obfuscates its inherent inequality (Tsing 2000). Tim Cresswell (2010) foregrounds the unequal politics of mobility. According to Cresswell, mobility is a resource that is differently accessible to individuals; the politics of mobile practice make the same travel route feel vastly different for two people with different identities. Caren Kaplan (2001) critiques Western feminists' embrace of cosmopolitanism. More specifically, Kaplan argues that some contemporary Western feminists embrace women's transnational travel as a mode of practicing feminism and a justified means of self-discovery. Travel, transnationality, and cosmopolitanism are neither inherently feminist nor egalitarian.

Tourism highlights such inequality even further than other forms of transnational travel because the financial and sociopolitical disparity between the tourists and those working in the tourist destinations is especially stark. Furthermore, the industry revolves around a problematic sense of cultural relativism and cultural essentialism whereby the tourist destination is assumed to have a fundamentally different culture and people from the tourists' home countries. Those supposed differences are essentialized as cultural practices that have never changed over centuries. Kaplan (1996) is particularly critical of tourism's role in perpetuating "imperialist nostalgia." She argues that Euro-America experiences imperialist nostalgia through the intersection of transnationality and modernism: the global "periphery" is assigned to the status of the "past" while Euro-America, in comparison, is assigned to the status of modernity and futurity. Such practice solidifies a temporal-spatial distinction between the so-called center and the periphery. According to Kaplan, only middle-class Euro-Americans, privileged enough to be culturally myopic, utilize tourism as a quest for self-discovery and a sense of superiority compared to the "periphery."

I partially agree with Kaplan in that I also see the discourse linking tourism with "authentic" experiences and the notion of self-discovery as problematic. Some of my Hallyu tourist informants and Hallyu fans in online forums echoed such problematic sentiments by claiming that consuming Korean television dramas and traveling to Korea made them realize their true erotic desires and that they were expecting a racialized "authentic" experience in Korea. They were assuming and perpetuating Western Orientalist assumptions about Korea.

However, I disagree with Kaplan's argument that Euro-American tourists experience a sense of imperialist nostalgia about traveling to a place in the "periphery" that they view as less modern and less financially well-off than Euro-America. Although most of my Hallyu tourists were Euro-American, they did not view Korea as in any way less modern or less well-off. Korea's status as a member of the OECD (Organization for Economic Co-operation and Development) and as the twelfth-largest economy in the world, which outmaneuvers the economic size of some of my informants' home countries, makes it nearly impossible for the tourists to affirm their sense of superiority through an assumption of their superior modernity and superior financial status. Both voluntarily and involuntarily, they are forced to forfeit that Western Orientalist nostalgia. This does not mean that my informants did not buy into other problematic traits of tourism, such as cultural relativism and essentialism. However, it would be misguided to argue that they were practicing a Western Orientalist sense of imperialist nostalgia while traveling in Korea. Instead, they were reworking such old and clearly problematic assumptions through Korean television dramas.

I want to further complicate the already complex power dynamics between my Hallyu tourist informants and their Korean male dates by thinking about the media's role in facilitating tourism. Both Choe (2016) and Oh (2018), as well as other media tourism scholars (Couldry 2007; Iwashita 2008; Torchin 2002; S. Kim 2010), argue that media-inspired tourists are not seeking a sense of "authentic" experience related to Korean traditions; instead, according to these scholars, the tourists prioritize authenticity in affects or emotions. Some of them go as far as to argue that the supposedly different priorities of the media tourists debunk one of the critical tenets of tourism that symbolize the power differentials between the tourists and the local people: the tourist gaze (Urry and Larsen 2011).

John Urry argues that in traditional tourism, through the tourist gaze, the tourists used to eagerly pine for the authenticity of other cultures. Their sense of authenticity revolved around culturally relativist and essentialist notions of the tourist destination. Their "gaze" would impose the tourists' cultural assumptions and standards onto the toured spaces and people. Such gaze, combined with the monetary powers of the tourists, would force the tourism workers at the destination country to have an "on" and "off" performance whereby, in the former, they would perform the type of "authenticity" that the tourists expect to see. In the latter, when the tourists were not present, they would "turn off" their performances of "authenticity" (Desmond 1999). However, Urry argues that nowadays, there is less sense of cultural relativism and essentialism attached to the tourist gaze due to media that allow easy access to cultures and people from other parts of the world (Urry and Larsen 2011).

I disagree with Urry and other media tourism scholars who argue that because they prioritize emotional authenticity, media tourists are less interested in seeking culturally essentialist or relativist conceptions of authenticity. I believe media tourists also impose their cultural assumptions and standards on the country they tour. For instance, my Hallyu tourist informants, while not abiding by traditional Western Orientalist assumptions about Korean men as emasculated, unromantic, and sexually weak, imposed new assumptions about Korean men based on what they thought to be "authentic" Korean masculinity they saw in the romantic Korean television dramas. They expected to feel the "authentic" emotions of romance and unconditional love that they assumed Korean men were prepared to give. As I argued in the previous section, melodramas help tourists converge reality and fantasy. Such convergence formulated new expectations and desires of "authenticity" for my informants. Such expectations were as equally culturally essentialist and relativist as traditional forms of tourist practices in that my informants utilized culturally relativist discourses to refer to Korean men as fundamentally different from men of other cultures or races. Furthermore, they utilized culturally essentialist understandings of such supposed differences to claim that being romantic and sexually restrained was a "natural" part of who Korean men were. While their reworking of Orientalist racialized gendering and sexualizing of Korean masculinity through Korean television dramas debunked the problematic racist assumptions about them, the practice perpetuated new assumptions that failed to dissociate Korean men's race with gender and sexuality. They were still being desired as racialized subjects whose race predetermined their gender and sexuality.

While the relationship between my Hallyu tourist informants and their Korean dates did not fit into the normative purview of sex tourism or romance tourism, I still find the literature on sex and romance tourism generative for my analysis of my informants' racialized erotic desires and their relationships to Korean men. Normatively speaking, romance and sex tourism doubly emphasize the geographic inequalities and power hierarchies between the tourists and the local people, perhaps more so than any other types of tourism, such as media tourism and religious pilgrimages. Often, the tourists are from a more affluent country, and the romantic or sexual relationships they form with local partners are founded on monetary exchange to satisfy their racialized erotic desires. Many researchers have examined the financial dynamics and geopolitics of desire in Western men's sex tourism to non-Western countries (Hoang 2015; Brennan 2001; Rivers-Moore 2016). However, women engage in similar activities as well. Research on romance tourism of European and U.S. women to the Caribbean highlights the women tourists' economic advantage over the local men, combined with the tourists' geopolitical advantage of being a tourist from the West, which gives them power over the local men (Taylor 2001). Their financial and geopolitical privileges allow them to disavow local gender norms and be treated as women with men's privileges (Pruitt and LaFont 1995; Jeffreys 2003).

In that regard, tourists of both genders can be predatory and demanding in terms of satisfying their racialized erotic desires. Granted, some scholars argue that men's and women's tourism are fundamentally different in that they claim the former primarily seek sex and perpetuate imperialist power dynamics fueled by their gender privileges while the latter seek emotionally intimate relationships and are not as implicated in perpetuating imperialist power dynamics due to their gender (Pruitt and LaFont 1995; Törnqvist 2012). They claim that due to such gendered differences, women's and men's tourism should be labeled differently as romance tourism and sex tourism. I disagree with this view because, apart from such argument problematically adhering to gender binarism, it disregards the similarity that underlies all of such tourism: racialized erotic desires. The tourists have racialized erotic desires and fantasies they assume they could satisfy when they travel to particular countries. The tourists justify their erotic desire for the locals by stating that the locals (usually men from places like the Caribbean or women from Southeast Asia) are just doing what is natural to them: being sexual (Hobbs, Na Pattalung, and Chandler 2011). The tourists' desires produce realities that they impose on their local partners. The gender and sexual diversity are erased by the tourists' racially and culturally essentialist assumptions that entwine the local folks' race with their gender and sexuality.

My Hallyu tourist informants shared similarities with other sex or romance tourists in that racialized erotic desires also fueled them. However, they were dissimilar from other sex tourists in two fundamental ways. First, other forms of sex tourism usually comprise a tourist who is more financially and geopolitically powerful than their local partner and who directly offers that partner payment, including money or an opportunity to live abroad and gain citizenship in the tourists' home countries. However, such is not the case with my Hallyu tourist informants, who did not always come from countries that are simultaneously more geopolitically and economically powerful than Korea. For instance, Sweden, Switzerland, the Netherlands, and Denmark, where some of my informants came from, have lower nominal GDP than Korea while having higher GDP per capita. There was no direct financial exchange between the tourists and their Korean partners. As I discuss in chapters 4 and 5, I observed my Hallyu tourist informants often being wined and dined by their Korean partners, rather than the other way around. Furthermore, even if some of those tourists did come from more geopolitically and economically powerful nations such as the United States, that did not mean that they always experienced the privileges that sex/romance tourists to places like Jamaica experienced. Some of my informants' skin colors prohibited them from finding boyfriends who were willing to fulfill their racialized erotic desires. I discuss such dynamics by discussing my Black American informants in chapter 4.

However, I still use sex tourism as one of the frameworks to analyze my informants' tourist activities because even without direct financial exchange between individuals, there was a financial component to my informants' tourism. Money did not directly exchange hands between my informants and Korean men. However, the tourists on the net "gave" much money to the

Korean nation and businesses by purchasing flights, hotel rooms, food, clothes, and other expenses involved in transnational travel. Recently, there have been emerging studies in sex tourism that examine the nation-state's facilitation of sex tourism due to the financial incentive it has for the nation, not just for individuals in the sex work industry (E. Williams 2013). Likewise, I suggest that even if the Korean nation is not purposely promoting sex tourism to Korea, through its commoditization of ideal Korean masculinity, it is figuratively operating and promoting an infrastructure that helps the nation reap financial benefits from my Hallyu tourist informants' racialized erotic desires and tourism to Korea. In contrast, the individual Korean men whom my informants dated were unable to experience any financial net benefit.

Furthermore, my informants' tourism to Korea is different from other forms of women's sex tourism due to their disparate expectations of racialized sexualities. Existing research on women's sex tourism focuses on women's tourism to places like Jamaica, Egypt, or Argentina, where the tourists' racialized gender and sexual assumptions of their men revolved around them being hypersexual. However, compared to such stereotypes, Western Orientalism has historically caricatured Asian men as undatable, unromantic, and sexually weak. Nonetheless, my informants reworked those stereotypes through Korean television dramas to reconfigure Korean masculinity as sexually "restrained" due to their prioritization of emotional connections rather than being sexually weak, as romantic rather than unromantic, and as ideal intimate partners rather than undatable. In this book, I parse through such racialized erotic desires to examine whether such reworking of Korean masculinity against the grains of Western Orientalism is truly as liberating as it appears on the surface.

Relatedly, I find that the interracial relationship between my Hallyu tourist informants and their Korean dates as "equals" in a financial and geopolitical sense provides an interesting disruption to the existing scholarship on interracial relationships in Korea that primarily examine the relationships that occur through skewed economic and geopolitical power dynamics. Thus far, oft-studied interracial relationships in Korea have been rooted in unequal power dynamics. For instance, the forcible rape of Korean women by Japanese soldiers during World War II (Min 2003) was marked by the geopolitical inequality between the colonizer and the colonized. In the 1950s interracial relationships between Korean women and U.S. soldiers stationed in Korea were also, to some extent, marked by financial and geopolitical inequality (G. Cho 2006; M. Lee 2008). As a result, mixed-race children and Korean women bore most of the consequences of such unequal power dynamics in relationships (Doolan 2021; Jodi Kim 2009; C. Lee 2021). More recently, emerging social practice of men living in rural parts of Korea marrying marriage migrants from overseas is also marked by geopolitical and economic inequality (M. Kim 2014; E. Lee, Kim, and Lee 2015; Lim 2010). On the contrary, my tourist informants and their Korean dates did not exhibit such inequality. Their relative geopolitical and economic parity provides an interesting case study to examine how culturally different and opposing conceptions of race—Western Orientalism and Korean conceptions of race—that fuel their racialized erotic desires for each other are negotiated between "equal" partners in intimate relationships.

Racialized Erotic Desires

I use the concept of "erotic" derived from the ongoing debate in feminist scholarship regarding its potential to complicate social norms of race. Black feminist scholars in the United States, such as Audre Lorde (2006), Angela Jones (2019), and Sharon P. Holland (2012), spearheaded critical debates regarding whether erotic desires and performances are liberating acts of resistance against racial and sexual stereotypes or whether they inevitably are inflected by such stereotypes and end up perpetuating them. To this debate, Asian American critical race theorists, such as Leslie Bow (2021) and C. Winter Han (2021), have made essential interventions to examine how, in the United States, popular discourse of racialized erotic desires for Asians are built on Orientalism's racialized gendering and sexualizing of Asians that paint essentialist portraits of them that erase the nuances and complexities of their identity. In examining my Hallyu tourist informants' racialized erotic desires for Korean men, I agree with Bow, who claims, "To be in racist love implies a different scale: it reduces worldliness to a consumable fixity, ingestible and small" (2021, 199). In line with Holland, who argues that erotic desires have the potential to entrench assumed differences rather than to undo them, my Hallyu tourist informants and the Korean men whom they dated mobilized racialized erotic desires to highlight the supposed differences between them rather than to examine whether those "differences" were real or, to borrow from Deleuze and Guarrati's theory, "produced realities" stemming from their desires. Therefore, while I do acknowledge the liberating potentials of erotic performances and desires in certain instances, for this book, I agree with the theorists who are critical of erotic desires' potential to usurp racist stereotypes.

Building on these feminist debates on erotic desires' relationship to either the formation or the undoing of "differences," I conceive of erotic desires as articulations that are structured by social differences and tensions. I find Purnima Mankekar and Louisa Schein's definition of the erotic as "politics of difference, shaped by the imagination, and fueled by fantasies. Extending beyond sex acts or desire for sex acts, they are often flashpoints for multiplex social tensions" (2013, 9) to be especially generative for my analysis of the interracial encounters between my Hallyu tourist informants and their Korean dates. Granted, in popular and some scholarly discourse, the term "erotic" is used interchangeably with the term "sexual." While I agree that erotic desires have sexual components, I use a more expanded conception of the term to examine my informants' desires because their desires were not merely sexual; they were a mix of sexual, racial, and geopolitical desires. Furthermore, while erotic desires may often be considered personal, I suggest they are not simply personal but also "public" in that they are "the result of the development of an 'erotic habitus,' where some traits, and some people, are believed to be desirable and other traits, and other people, as undesirable" (Han 2021, 20). My informants were using Korean television dramas to rework their conceptions of Korean masculinity against the grains of Orientalism. In that regard, their desires were shaped by an "erotic habitus" formed by Orientalism and that Korean popular culture contests.

I complicate and contribute to this ongoing debate on eroticism by examining racialized erotic desires from a transnational framework. The existing debate focuses primarily on intra-cultural erotic desires and their racial consequences. However, through media, heterogeneous genealogies of erotics converge and influence one another. I borrow the term "mediated erotics," coined by Mankekar and Schein (2013), which they define as the ways erotic desires reconfigure spaces, boundaries, and cultural differences as well as facilitate physical and imaginative travel for consumers. Hence, I go beyond a single cultural context and analyze the literal and figurative transnational "clash" between the racialized erotic desires of my tourist informants and their Korean dates that occur due to the mediated erotics of Korean television dramas. Through a close examination of the clash between the different racialized erotic desires, I highlight how these desires are built on and emphasize the supposed cultural, gender, racial, and sexual differences between each other rather than attempt to undo those differences.

The concept of "racialized" has been conventionally used to shed light on the power hierarchy between the racialized and the racializing and to characterize the marginalization of racial minorities by the dominant racial group (Hesse 2007; Cartwright 2022). In such context, my use of the term to refer to both the erotic desires of my white tourist informants and Korean men may appear somewhat unconventional because, from a Western racial perspective, Korean men may not appear to be the racially dominant ones who are in a position to racialize white tourists. However, Korean men's racial status in Korea differs from that in the Western racial hierarchy. The issue of whether and to what extent Korean racial hierarchy emulates that of the West or is distinct is still a topic of debate among scholars. In nuanced analyses of the Korean racial dynamic, scholars such as Yeon-Hwa Lee and Jae Kyun Kim (2024) have observed how global white supremacy takes different shapes in different cultures and that it would be misguided to cast Koreans as empty vessels that passively follow the racial dynamic of the West. As a case in point, Sue-Je Gage's (2013) work demonstrates how Korean soldiers subvert white supremacy by positioning themselves as superior to white soldiers, while Sojin Yu's (2023) work demonstrates that being white does not prevent one from being racialized in Korea based on one's other identities such as nationality and class status. By referring to both my white tourists and the Korean men's desires as racialized, I am acknowledging that Western models of racism and white supremacy are not the only ones being practiced around the world. To clarify whose racialized erotic desire I am referring to, when I use the term, I pair it with the appropriate noun, such as white tourists, non-white tourists, Korean men, or the Korean government.

By referring to the Korean nation-state and the entertainment industry's racialized erotic desire, I mean their use of certain visual images of Hallyu fans—young, non-Asian, and ecstatic—to "prove" the transnational popularity of Hallyu. Furthermore, I refer to the ongoing debate in the Korean entertainment industry that attempts to figure out whether the adage, popularized by a former Korean president, "What is most Korean is the most global," could work to sustain the popularity of Korean television dramas or whether they need to reconfigure their production system and storylines to cater to a more diverse audience beyond the domestic audience. These issues are closely tied to the nation's desire for soft power, which refers to the theoretical assumption that a country can attract foreigners and global capital through positive images associated with the country (Nye 2008). Soft power relies on the notion that cultural exchanges and encounters influence individual perceptions about a nation. Such soft power affects the number of tourists visiting the nation and the tourism profits of the place, and indirectly, it also impacts the nation's political and economic standing on the global stage. Media images are essential to the formation of soft power. Thus, the Korean government supports and promotes Hallyu not only because of its economic value but also because of its cultural value in reshaping the nation's global image (Oh 2018; Choe 2016). In describing a larger industry and the nation-state having erotic desires, I contribute to the ongoing feminist debates that examine the scope of erotic desires beyond the realm of individual choices and actions. Moreover, by examining the nation and the industry's racialized erotic desire, I emphasize that they are not passive recipients of my Hallyu tourist informants' and, more broadly, Hallyu fans' racialized reworking of Korean masculinity and the national image. They are active agents who attempt to predict, facilitate, and engage with the global audience to transnationally disseminate a specific "brand" of Korea as a nation.

Likewise, by examining my Korean male informants' racialized erotic desires, I highlight that my Korean male informants were not simply passive recipients of my Hallyu tourist informants' racialized erotic desires. Inferring as such would problematically perpetuate Orientalist stereotypes of them as "objects" that could be judged and categorized by the West without resistance.

Instead, throughout chapter 2 I analyze the depiction of masculinities in transnationally popular Korean television dramas while situating them in relation
to historical contexts that shaped Korean hegemonic masculinity.

Here, in discussing "Korean hegemonic masculinity," I am referring to
Raewyn Connell's (1995) claim that there is a particular form of masculinity
that pervades different historical moments and that legitimizes patriarchal
structures and justifies the subjugation of individuals, including women and
others who do not conform to the embodiment of such masculine gender
performance. Connell received critique from many feminist scholars who
wanted to nuance the formation of masculinity from the binary of hegemonic
versus non-hegemonic masculinity she established in her work that only
accounts for internal hegemony (the formation of hegemony within a particularly myopic Western imperialist national context) and discounts the role of
external hegemony (the formation of hegemony in relation to other races, cultures, and nations) (Demetriou 2001). I agree with the critique of Connell's
conception of hegemonic masculinity. Therefore, when I refer to "Korean
hegemonic masculinity," the concept does not imply the nation's masculinities
formed in a vacuum without dialogue with the non-hegemonic masculinities
and encounters with those from other cultural contexts. Instead, my use of the
term refers to the formation and systematic uplifting of certain forms of
masculinity—such as militaristic and breadwinner masculinities—by the government and popular discourse throughout Korean history, which I analyze
in detail in chapter 2. I examine the ways that television dramas portray masculinity that directly contest hegemonic Korean masculinities but are misun-
derstood and decontextualized by my Hallyu tourist informants. Furthermore,
in chapter 5 I examine how my Korean male informants conceptualize and perform their masculinity while navigating the difference between Western Orientalism and Korean television dramas' reworking of Korean masculinity.

The Process of Examining the Stories of Desire

I argue that the anecdote I described at the beginning of this introduction and
the stories I share in the following chapters are stories of desire. More specifically, they are stories of racialized erotic desires. The different erotic desires of
the Korean nation-state, the entertainment industry, a segment of the Hallyu
fans, and a number of Korean men in their twenties intersect to create transnational connections that complicate the binary of fantasy versus reality and
Orientalism versus reverse Orientalism. The phenomenon I examine is a somewhat cyclical story of desire without a specific beginning and an ending. The
Korean nation-state and entertainment industry's aspirations to create and disseminate their own system of mediated race, gender, and sexual performances
that are in dialogue with, but ultimately independent of, Western Orientalism's

racialized gendering and sexualizing of Asian men produce Korean television dramas that portray distinct forms of Korean masculinities. Such mediated depictions, in turn, fuel the racialized erotic desires of some Hallyu fans from around the world who visit online fan forums and streaming sites where they communicate their desires with each other and produce "realities" through their desires. Such produced realities encourage some, like my Hallyu tourist informants, to physically travel to Korea to seek Korean boyfriends. My Korean male informants react to my tourist informants' desires with their own racialized erotic desires. This, in turn, impacts the discourse of Korean national pride, which, in a cyclical fashion, influences the Korean nation-state's sponsorship of Korean television drama production, and so on.

To adequately examine such a mixture of desires that feed off each other, I find it imperative to mobilize different methods to examine different sites where desires are formulated and manifest themselves. Furthermore, I structured the book so that each chapter introduces the reader to different forms of racialized erotic desire that culminates in the erotic encounter between my Hallyu tourist informants and their Korean dates.

Chapters 1 and 2 provide context for the transnational popularity of Korean television dramas. In chapter 1, I examine racialized erotic desires on a national and infrastructural scale. More specifically, I analyze the Korean government policies and initiatives intended to foster the popularity of Korean culture around the world and the government's racialized erotic desires to attract foreign fans to Korea. I analyze these Hallyu-related policies as a subset of the larger government initiative meant to rebrand Korean national image and identity from one bound in ethnic homogeneity and "purity" toward that of the cosmopolitan, "modern," and inclusive nation. I contend that the policies and discourses surrounding Hallyu are representative of the racialized erotic desire that the nation has for foreign tourists and fans of Korean popular culture and its aspiration to create and disseminate its own mediated gender, sexual, and racial images of Korean men that counter Western Orientalism. Furthermore, through textual analysis of archived interviews of television scriptwriters who partook in creating some of the transnationally popular Korean television dramas, I examine the potential pitfalls that appear in Korean television dramas as they attempt to formulate and disseminate their own conceptions of race, gender, and sexuality around the world. Through analysis of several notorious incidents when the dramas offended a large swath of its transnational viewers for their insensitive depictions of non-Korean "Other," I suggest that these instances demonstrate the limitations of the Korean model of mediated race, gender, and sexuality that aspires to rework the Western Orientalist conception of Koreans.

In chapter 2, I use media analysis to examine the romantic Korean television dramas that played central roles in my Hallyu tourist informants' emotional and physical travel to Korea. More specifically, I examine three types of masculinity portrayed in these television dramas. I suggest that these three masculinities—militaristic masculinity, breadwinner masculinity, and flower boy masculinity—represent the change in ideal masculinity that occurred throughout Korean history following the Korean War. This chapter provides a historically contextualized analysis of televisual depictions of Korean masculinity so that they can be juxtaposed with the racialized ways in which some transnational Hallyu fans interpret such masculinities.

Chapters 3 and 4 analyze the racialized erotic desires of the Hallyu fans and tourists. These chapters are based on data I collected through digital ethnography and ethnographic field research I conducted in Korea between 2017 and 2018. Chapter 3 focuses on the digital Hallyu spaces and the "labor of love" that the Hallyu fans engage in these spaces to share their racialized erotic assumptions and queries with other like-minded fans. Analyzing popular Korean television drama streaming websites and fan websites such as Rakuten Viki, YouTube, and Soompi, I argue that the fans experience a form of digital intimacy with other fans and with the mediated images of Korean men. I contend that the Hallyu fans' and tourists' racialized erotic desires that are fomented in these online fan spaces are closely connected to the ways they engage with Korean men in real life. Therefore, I examine how racialized assumptions and desires are experienced and disseminated in online spaces to produce "realities" that fit some of the site users' racialized erotic desires.

In chapter 4, I analyze the experiences of the Hallyu fans who traveled to Korea as tourists. I conducted interviews and participant observation of Hallyu tourists, their Korean dates, foreign tourists who were not Hallyu tourists, and Koreans who had their interpretations of Hallyu tourism that they wanted to tell me. Except for several Black American and Caribbean women, all my informants identified as white or could pass as white in Korea. They all identified as heterosexual and ranged in age from nineteen to late twenties. They claimed to be from Australia, Denmark, France, Germany, Sweden, Switzerland, Russia, Canada, and the United States. Most of the initial interviews of my informants were group interviews followed by one-on-one interviews and participant observation. While most of my interviews comprised gauging my informants' interpretations of Korean televisual masculinities, sometimes, they would voluntarily discuss their romantic lives and experiences during interviews, in which case I did not deter them. I followed them to clubs and bars to observe how they engaged with their Korean dates. I examine my informant's utilization of their reworking of Korean masculinity through popular culture and digital fan forums in real-life encounters with their Korean dates. Furthermore, I analyze how the Hallyu tourists' racial identities shaped the experiences they had in Korea. While they racially eroticized Korean men, some Hallyu tourists were racially eroticized by Korean men. I follow the trajectory of such racially charged relationships from the first encounters to when the tourists returned to their home countries.

Chapter 5 examines my Korean male informants' perspectives of Hallyu and the Hallyu tourists. Furthermore, during my ethnographic research with my Hallyu tourist informants, I organically had the chance to talk to my Hallyu tourist informants' Korean dates, foreign tourists who were not Hallyu tourists, and Korean workers at hostels frequented by my Hallyu tourist informants, who had their own unique interpretations of my informants' racialized erotic desires for Korean men. I did not actively recruit these groups of people for my research. However, some of them volunteered to participate in my research project after observing me with my Hallyu tourist informants and hearing about my project. As a result, they provided interesting perspectives that sometimes reinforced and sometimes challenged my Korean male informants' accounts of their racialized erotic desires. I analyze how my Korean informants comprehended their sudden popularity among the Hallyu tourists. I analyze how these men engage in interracial relationships with white Hallyu tourists because of their own racialized erotic fantasies about white women. In this chapter I examine how my informants in their twenties living in twenty-first-century Korea used interracial relationships to contend with the discrepancies between the Western Orientalist caricatures of them and the reworked images of them in Korean television dramas. They utilized interracial relationships to disrupt the history of emasculation that Korean men faced due to Western Orientalism. Concurrently, I analyze the discourses of foreign male tourists who were not attuned to Hallyu and its reworking of Korean masculinity, who were befuddled by my Hallyu tourist informants' desires for Korean men and observed them with not only contempt but some amount of fear.

By organizing the book as thus, I hope to have told a complex story of desire through which Western Orientalist racialized gendering and sexualizing of Korean masculinity is problematized and reworked through Korean television dramas. However, rather than narrating a hopeful story of Orientalism's replacement with a less problematic framework, I portray a story of intersecting racialized erotic desires that demonstrate the pervasiveness of Orientalism's impacts in the attempts to rework transnational conceptions of Korean masculinity.

1

Mouth Agape and Ecstatically Screaming

• •

National Media and Industry
Personnel's Conception
of Foreign Hallyu Fans

In 2021 the K-pop group BTS's music topped the American Billboard charts, and the band won three awards at the American Music Awards (AMA), including the Artist of the Year Award. Then-president Moon Jae-In tweeted: "I congratulate and thank BTS for winning major awards at the American Music Awards" (President Moon Jae-in's Blue House 2021).[1] In a prolonged tweet, Moon said, "Korean culture is dominating the world, and it is raising Korea's national prestige and diplomatic power. BTS's winning the AMA this time confirmed that fact once again." Moon's message used nationalistic phrases such as "domination" [석권], "exerting power" [힘을 발휘], and raising "prestige" [명성]. During her presidency, former president Park Geun-Hye addressed Song Joong-Ki, the male actor who starred in the transnationally popular Korean television drama *Descendants of the Sun*, and said, "I think that both Captain Yu in the *Descendants of the Sun* and Song Joong-Ki the actor represent Korean patriotism" (A. Cho 2016).

When I initially read these statements, I found it curious that the Korean presidents would congratulate and thank Korean celebrities for their achievements and hail them as patriots. In the two presidents' speeches, the celebrities' individual achievements were treated as symbols of Korea's achievements. These two presidents were saying that Hallyu was not simply a transnational media phenomenon; in their minds, it was a transnational diplomatic and nationalist phenomenon that elevated Korea's power and influence worldwide. Upon further reflection, I found that the Korean mantra, "What is most Korean is the most global" [가장 한국적인 것이 가장 세계적인 것이다] was the underlying theme in both of the presidents' accolades for Hallyu.

The mantra became popular in the years leading up to Hallyu and, in my view, came to define it. President Kim Young Sam popularized the mantra beginning in 1993 to urge the nation to take pride in Korean culture and strive to globalize it. During his presidency, the nation-state claimed globalization as one of its key agendas (K.-Y. Shin 2006). The specific term the nation-state used was *segyehwa* [세계화], which, literally translated, means globalization. However, the government distinguished the term from that English definition by claiming that the Korean term inferred a more proactive method of globalizing that would make the nation one of the most powerful nations in a globalizing world, as opposed to a country that passively accepts globalization forced upon it (H. Park 1996). Perhaps owing to the desire to proactively globalize Korea that persisted after Kim's presidency, nowadays even a cursory search of Korean news and government discourse reveals that "K" is attached to every exportable item, including relatively conventional cultural items such as K-drama and K-pop as well as some things not conventionally considered cultural, such as the K-excavator and K-atomic energy. This practice begs the question, what could be so different about Korean atomic energy or Korean excavators from that of other countries that they merit the particular title "K"? The question reveals the irony of the mantra "What is most Korean is the most global" and the Korean version of globalization.

Superficially, the mantra promotes the idea that Korea does not need to discard or change its unique traditions, culture, and characteristics to become global. However, it disregards the Western influence that has already shaped what "Korean" means. Many Hallyu scholars have called into question what the "K" in K-pop and the "Korean" in the Korean Wave stand for in the first place (Lie 2012; Jin 2020). As Kyung Hyun Kim claims, cosmopolitan Korean popular culture "in no way differs from other cosmopolitan neo-American aesthetics and styles" (2021, xi). Furthermore, many scholars have critiqued Korea's *segyehwa* policy, which built itself on an Anglo-American model of globalization and failed to account for whether such a foreign model would be applicable to Korea (C. Park 2015; Mimiko 2013). In spite of much critique and concern, the policy continued after the 1997 Asian financial crisis due to the guidance of the International Monetary Foundation (IMF), which recommended the nation's globalization (Kim, Bae, and Lee 2018).

The driving force and the logic behind the call for Korea's globalization was the interchangeability of three concepts: globalization, modernity, and desirability. According to such logic, globalization was a means to achieve modernity, and the nation that successfully became globalized and modern became desirable (Appadurai 1996). President Kim Young Sam and the IMF seemed to have shared similar sentiments based on how vigorously they attempted to globalize Korea.

I argue that while the Korean mantra that "what is most Korean is the most global" appeared to debunk Western Orientalist stereotypes that associate modernity with the West, the mantra's seemingly liberating qualities were only superficial. Western Orientalist stereotypes locate the West as the center of modernity and situate the "Orient" temporally and geographically in the anti-modern periphery. The mantra failed to debunk this Western Orientalist conception of modernity. As many scholars have pointed out, the Korean conception of modernity is still associated with the West, and Korea's method of proving its modernity relies, in part, on Western approval (A. Lee 2019; D. Oh 2020). Such fixation with Western approval is correlated with the nation's complex relationships with whiteness. Korea's racial system is a paradoxical coexistence of Korean superiority and white supremacy. While the two concepts seem to contradict each other, they nonetheless coexist in the Korean racial system, where they compete for dominance over one another (J. K. Kim 2015; Ahn 2015; M. J. Lee 2022). The question of whether Hallyu and the mantra "what is most Korean is the most global" contributes to Korean superiority overpowering white supremacy is called to question, especially when in places like Southeast Asia, Koreans have garnered an honorary white status due to the transnational popularity of Korean pop culture (D. Kang 2017). Instead of disrupting white supremacy, Koreans are designated an honorary white status that equates concepts such as modernity and desirability with whiteness. What does this status mean for Koreans? Is it a status that the nation and its people aspired to? Or is it an unexpected and unwelcome status for a nation that is trying to assert its nationalistic claim that Korean people and culture are superior above all else?

While plenty of literature examines Korean American and Korean immigrants' aspirations to garner the status of honorary whiteness (J. W. Kim 2022; J. Shin 2016), there is limited research on what that status means for Koreans residing in Korea. In one of the few studies that examines how some Koreans aspire to honorary white status, Alex Jeong-Suk Lee observed, "While the stakes are lower than for the Korean soldiers seeking to prove their superiority over other physiognomically similar Asian (Vietnamese) men, Korean men can now ascend a globalized hierarchy of cisheteronormative masculinity by corroborating their manhood via the validation of higher-ranking white (and sometimes what Mia Tuan calls "honorary white") Western men" (2019, 207).

Lee's argument highlights the tensions surrounding whiteness in Korea: even as Korea espouses the notion that it is superior to other ethnicities and races, it seeks approval from white or honorary white people who must give their blessing—so to speak—for Koreans to obtain racial superiority.

As I will demonstrate throughout this chapter, the nationalist discourse surrounding Korean popular culture's global success uses foreign—particularly Western—fans' presence at Korean cultural events and in Korean tourist spaces as proof of Korea's globalization, modernization, and desirability. It does not generate a new mode of thinking about modernity that departs from the problematic Western Orientalist conception of it that designates the West as the standard. Therefore, although the Korean model of *segyehwa* claims to subvert the Western Orientalist version of globalization and modernity by centering Korea instead of the West, to this day, it focuses on Western approval and limits its liberating potential.

I define the Korean nation-state and the mass media's desire to rebrand itself as global, modern, and desirable through Western bodies as a form of racialized erotic desire. I define it as a concept that is similar to Orientalism and Occidentalism in its fascination for the "Other" but also fundamentally different from the preexisting concepts in that racialized erotic desire focuses on the mutuality of the desire whereby the power difference and the hierarchy between the desired objects and the desiring subjects are more nuanced than in Orientalism and Occidentalism. Here, my use of the phrase "racialized" to refer to the subject positions of some Western Hallyu fans and tourists may seem counterintuitive because it is a phrase often used in the West to refer to a racially dominant group ostracizing racial minorities by using race as a tool. However, as I noted earlier, Western ontologies are not the only acceptable worldview (D. Kang 2017); through racialized erotic desires, mutual interactions and worldviews clash with each other. Though whiteness plays an important role in the Korean racial system, white supremacy is by no means the only standard that dictates racial dominance in Korea (J. K. Kim 2015). From the nation's and the entertainment industry's perspective, the Western white fans are subjects who are in positions to approve of Korean culture but also in positions as objects to be utilized by the national media and the entertainment industry to pursue their goal of cosmopolitanism.

In referring to foreign fans as subjects of racialized erotic desire, I abide by Sharon Patricia Holland's definition of the erotic as "the personal and political dimension of desire" (2012, 9). My definition of the erotic goes beyond the scope of sexuality to refer to the desire and allure that one group of people have for another. While I engage with various forms of racialized erotic desires in later chapters, in this chapter I focus on the Korean government, news media, and television drama production staff's racialized erotic desire for Hallyu fans that provides systemic and cultural backgrounds that facilitate Hallyu tourism. To satisfy its desire to become modern, the nation-state "uses" the Hallyu fans to produce a reality that superficially satisfies such desires for modernity. I find parallels between such production of realities and Arjun Appadurai's (1996) concept of "social imaginary," which he refers to as the focal point for imagining a new global order beyond national borders. However, while the emotion of "desire" is only hinted at by Appadurai in his theorizing of the social imaginary, I focus on erotic desire as one of the critical components driving the Korean government and mass media to describe Hallyu's success in nationalist rhetoric and that promotes financial investment and support for the industry.

I suggest that the nation's racialized erotic desire for foreign Hallyu tourists and fans focuses on the desire for superficial multiracialism, whereby the country achieves the appearance of globalization, modernity, and desirability, rather than considering whether Korea is truly a modern globalized nation of cosmopolitans that fully embraces all the consequences of globalization, such as multiculturalism and multiracialism. In the following sections, I examine how the Korean mass media, government, and industry use Hallyu tourists and fans to satisfy their desire to achieve a sense of global ascendance while not accepting the responsibility of multiculturalism and multiracialism that comes with it.

The Korean Government and Hallyu

The two aforementioned former presidents were not the only ones who treated the Hallyu celebrities' success as equivalent to the national success and the global popularity of Korean popular culture as indicative of the nation's success in ascending to the upper level of globalization, modernity, and desirability. The Korean government—both federal and municipal—initiated various pop culture–related projects to enhance Korea's desirability. For instance, around 2015, the Korean government proposed the construction of a "Hallyu complex center" and "Hallyu experience facilities," both of which were meant to facilitate an increase in Hallyu tourism (S. Kim and Nam 2016). Furthermore, the government introduced ambitious plans to build a "Hallyu star street" and "K-pop concert halls" to increase the number of Hallyu tourists. The government proposals regarding Hallyu go beyond just building Hallyu-related infrastructures. For instance, in 2020 the National Assembly introduced a bill nicknamed the "BTS Mandatory Military Service Extension Bill," which, if passed, would allow male Hallyu stars to postpone their mandatory military service. Politicians who introduced the bill legitimized it by arguing, "Ranking number one on the Billboard chart is equivalent to contributing to Korea's national prestige [hence it is their right to be allowed to postpone their mandatory military service]" (J.-W. Jung 2020). On the surface, many of these government policies and plans seem to have the potential to fuel the transnational popularity of Korean popular culture. However, in my view, these government initiatives are populist rather than practical and realistic in their attempts to facilitate the sustained popularity of Hallyu.

In this regard, Youjeong Oh's (2018) argument that municipal governments' investment in drama production is a speculative business seems accurate. After all, the financial benefits of the investment are indeed speculative at their best and destined for failure at their worst. However, I tentatively disagree with Oh that such investments are only speculative ventures. From a political perspective, they are less speculative and more definitive ventures that will renew the voters' belief in their elected politicians' efforts to make the nation global and cosmopolitan. Granted, I do not have exact data on the percentage of elected officials who succeed in being reelected after they invest in Korean television drama or other Hallyu-related productions. Nonetheless, many elected officials promote their part in launching the Hallyu-related infrastructural plans as the focal point of their career during election season. I doubt the lawmakers would be self-promoting their Hallyu-related efforts if doing so was ineffective in maintaining their popularity and being reelected.

Despite ambitious goals to contribute to Hallyu's sustained success, these government projects take a long time to be completed, which raises the question as to whether and to what extent these plans are contributing to Hallyu. For instance, in 2015, the year before the 2016 Korean general elections, the government proposed the construction of a Hallyu complex center, which would enhance Hallyu tourism in Korea by giving tourists a one-stop immersive experience on all aspects of Hallyu. The project was renamed partway through as the K-Culture Valley project and began construction, intending to open in a few years. However, the Goyang city newspaper reported that only 20 percent of the construction had been finished during the three years between 2015 and 2018 (S.-O. Lee 2018). Newspaper articles published in 2020 show no indication of the project being finished any time soon; instead, they indicate that the new deadline for completing the construction project was anticipated to be 2024, nearly ten years since the government first proposed the project (K.-J. Lee 2020). Perhaps coincidentally, 2024 is the year that another Korean general election was scheduled. The project seems reinvigorated during every election season but forgotten otherwise. Around the same time, the government proposed the Hallyu Culture Center; it also proposed constructing a K-pop arena solely dedicated to hosting the concerts of K-pop stars year-round. However, according to a 2018 newspaper article, the K-Pop Arena (also known as Seoul Arena) was still only in its developing stages, with no concrete timeline regarding when the project would come to fruition (Seo 2018). In 2020 the executive officer of Dobong-gu, where the arena is supposed to be built, said that they were in the process of designing the Seoul Arena. He

FIGURE 1 The construction scene from the K-Culture Valley project when the author visited it in January 2024. Through the broken fence, one can see that no construction has been done yet. Photo by author.

anticipated construction would begin around 2021 and be ready for use in a few years (Ok 2020; J.-Y. Park 2020). During the decade since the government proposed these building projects, Hallyu's popularity and significance have grown. Since these government plans have not been carried out expediently, they did not contribute to Hallyu. However, the projects are constantly brought to the limelight by politicians who want voters to renew their sense of national pride and belief that, through these infrastructural projects, their part of town will become a centerpiece of Korean culture's newfound global popularity.

Korea's elected government officials seem to consider Hallyu-related investments as a means to bring foreigners to their municipalities. In that regard, I suggest that these ventures are fueled by politicians' racialized erotic desires for the foreign bodies of Hallyu fans, which they believe will make their municipalities appear, in the eyes of Korean voters, global and modern. In these instances, Hallyu tourists function as racialized subjects whom Korean politicians desire for their ability to affirm Korea's supposed prestige in the global context. The Hallyu-related infrastructural projects are so successful in garnering local people's pride and hope for their town that many elected government officials in small rural cities around Korea spend large amounts of tax revenues to build Hallyu-related infrastructures in their villages. Most of these projects

FIGURE 2 A scene from *Descendants of the Sun* depicting a building collapsing in the fictional Middle Eastern nation called Urk because of an earthquake. Screen grab from YouTube channel KBS Drama Classic.

FIGURE 3 The *Descendants of the Sun* filming set in Taebaek, where the scene of the Urk earthquake was filmed. Photo by author.

fail to attract Hallyu tourists. Still, they temporarily make the local folks envision a future where Korea's globalization does not leave them behind and they become the epicenter of it. For instance, the local government of Taebaek, a city in Gangwon Province, used government funds to preserve the drama set where the Hallyu drama *Descendants of the Sun* was filmed (Bang-Hyun Kim and Park 2019). Before the drama was filmed in that city, it was a small rural

FIGURE 4 A scene from *Descendants of the Sun* where Kang and her medical crew prepare to treat the soldiers in the medical bay in Urk. Screen grab from YouTube channel KBS Drama Classic.

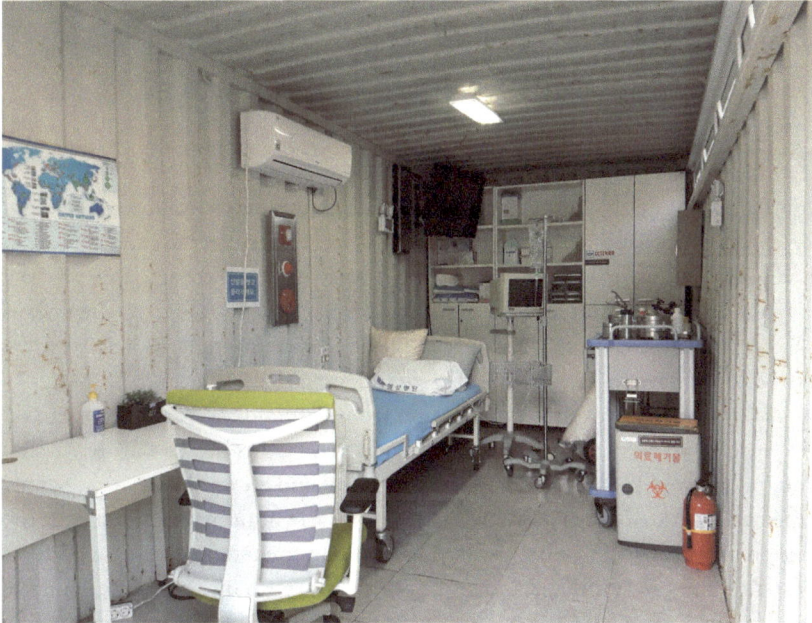

FIGURE 5 The *Descendants of the Sun* filming set in Taebaek, where the scene of the Urk medical bay was filmed. Photo by author.

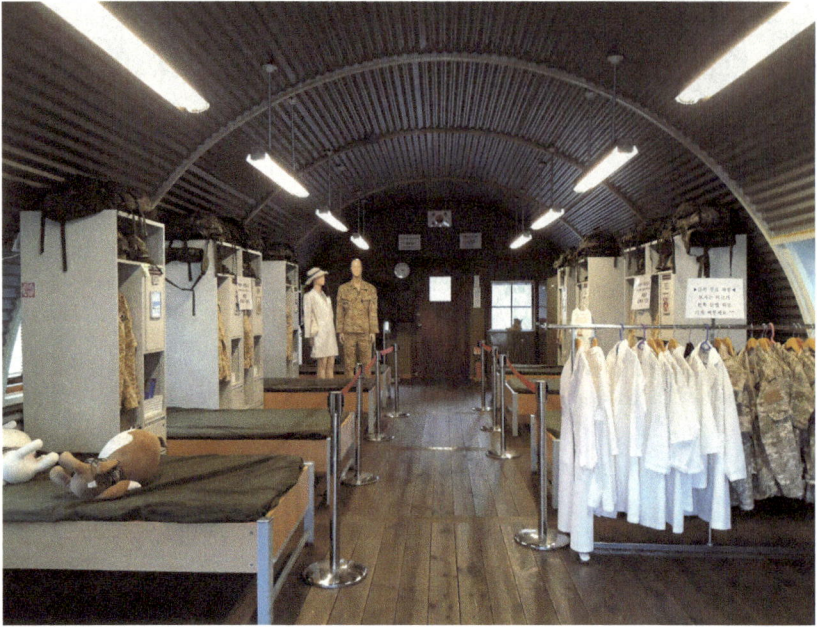

FIGURE 6 The *Descendants of the Sun* filming set in Taebaek, where the scenes involving soldiers' living quarters were filmed. Photo by author.

mining town rapidly declining financially and in size. It is similar to many rural cities in Korea that have been left behind by the country's rapid modernization and globalization. However, the Hallyu drama appeared to suddenly give the city a chance to rebuild itself as the center of Hallyu. In reality, the dream was short-lived because one drama could not resurrect a mountainous, remote town that did not have sustainable industries and jobs.

Many rural cities around Korea suffer from a fate similar to that of Taebaek. From 1997 to 2012, thirty-five drama sets were built around Korea, using roughly $170 million in municipal tax revenues and $4 million in national tax revenues (S.-H. Kim 2015). Many of these sets were built in remote cities at the peripheries of Korea's global economy. Since they are remote, they are hard for Hallyu tourists to visit, and thus, many of these sets go into ruins without garnering much profit from Hallyu tourism, and some of the sets, after being built, garner zero revenues until they are demolished (KOCCA 2011). Jaechun—a small provincial city—devoted approximately $1.4 million to building two drama sets; administrators used tens of thousands of dollars in tax revenue annually as maintenance fees for the sets (S.-H. Kim 2015). In the beginning, Jaechun's investment of millions of tax dollars seemed to be paying off as fans from all over the world traveled to the city. However, after a few years, very few tourists visited (Y.-H. Bae 2019). The sets were closed years later when all hope of garnering tourism was lost.

When investing thousands of dollars in tax revenues in Hallyu-related projects, government officials almost always mention turning their municipalities into "global" spaces. For instance, the director of culture, tourism, and sports in the city of Gwangju said that he was creating a K-pop Star Street in the town to make the city a "K-pop tourism city." Furthermore, he claimed that he plans to rebrand existing cultural venues and artifacts in the city into a "global" cultural space (Jang 2021). The mayor of Goyang, where the K-Culture Valley is undergoing construction, claimed that he hopes to make the city a "global self-sufficient city" [글로벌 자족도시]] (K.-J. Lee 2022). "Self-sufficient city" refers to places where residents can care for their needs, such as shopping, entertainment, and education, within the city rather than traveling to other cities. By using the term "global," the mayor implies that tourists from different parts of the world will be able to satisfy not only their desires for Korean culture but also their nostalgia for their own cultures because the city will be cosmopolitan and multicultural.

These "global" cities are aspirational realities produced by the government rather than accurately representing people's experienced realities. Tourists who only stay in the country for a few days to a few months can only do so much to make a city "global" in the economic and political sense. Instead, as Youjeong Oh (2018) points out in her book, the reworking of a city through Korean popular culture to make it appear global distorts and veils the existing racial and geopolitical reality of these spaces. There is geographic stratification whereby Gangnam, one of the areas in Korea with the most significant number of global corporation offices and wealthiest residents in the nation, uses what Oh calls "established hegemony" and easily overlays it with the sense of global place by building a few landmarks associated with Hallyu. In contrast, cities outside of Seoul have to strive harder to achieve the label of a "global place" by proactively launching campaigns and using their tax money to host television drama filming in their city (Oh 2018). The problem is, as I have noted thus far in this chapter, many of these efforts fail, the gap between Gangnam and the rural cities is further widened due to the latter having spent too much tax revenue on futile attempts to globalize when the money could have been spent elsewhere. Oh contends that Hallyu "reduces the realities of the place to fantasized images that are entirely entertainment-oriented and . . . exploits the presence of fans and the emotional investment that they make in the area" (2018, 137). I agree with Oh's argument that Hallyu overlays spaces with fantasized images of globalization and cosmopolitanism that often ignore the realities regarding the discriminatory politics in Korea that many foreign laborers in the nation experience in their everyday lives.

FIGURE 7 A scene from *My Love from the Star* where Chun's car is about to fall off a cliff, and Do saves her with his magical powers. Screen grab from YouTube channel SBS Drama.

FIGURE 8 The cliff in Incheon where scenes from *My Love from the Star* were filmed. The area next to the cliff was repurposed into vegetable gardens. Photo by author.

Disregarding such realities, the government and media use Hallyu to center Korea as a global cultural powerhouse and use Western fans as tools through which to justify such nationalist pride. The paradox is that even as the government attempts to rework Western Orientalism through Hallyu, it fails to redefine globalization and modernity in ways that significantly deviate from Orientalist and neoliberalist ideologies. For instance, when foreign celebrities

FIGURE 9 A faded poster of the drama *My Love from the Star* attached to a fence erected to prevent people from walking up the cliff shows the desolation of the filming location that was once brimming with tourists. Photo by author.

visit Korea to promote their new films, it has become a widespread practice for Koreans in the audience or those hosting the event to ask these foreign celebrities questions about their knowledge of Hallyu during interviews. When Hollywood actor Matt Damon came to Korea to promote his new movie, the Korean host facilitating the movie premier asked him: "Do you know Gangnam Style?" Although the film had nothing to do with the song "Gangnam Style," the host asked such a question to affirm Korean narcissistic nationalism (H. N. Kim 2019). In such a performance of nationalism, Damon's positionality changes from someone who is desired and idolized for his stardom to someone who is desired for his ability, as an influential white Westerner, to affirm Korean culture's supposed desirability. Figuratively speaking, in this nationalistic performance, he is no longer a Hollywood superstar; he is a supporting actor whose role is to affirm Korea's modernity and desirability. White supremacy is still in operation here, as can be seen in Matt Damon, a white celebrity, being exclusively picked to justify Korea's supposed desirability and given the power to declare it. However, white supremacy is also being challenged here by Korean superiority because Damon is merely an object playing his part rather than a subject who can take control of the situation at hand.

Nonetheless, I disagree with some assertions that Korea "exploits" fans' bodies and emotions (Oh 2018). Exploitation makes the relationship between Korea and the Hallyu tourists sound like the former has the power to exploit while the latter naively gets exploited. I do not believe such a clear hierarchy exists between the government and Hallyu fans and tourists. As I discuss later in this book, my Hallyu tourist informants are by no means indoctrinated by Korean popular culture to adopt a Korean nationalist version of its supposed modernity and desirability. They reinterpret and rework their understanding of Korea—particularly Korean masculinity—through popular culture. I suggest that the relationship between my Hallyu tourist informants and the Korean government and entertainment industry is built on mutually beneficial relationships whereby the nation's desire to appear global, the entertainment industry's desire to earn money, and my Hallyu tourist informants' desire to travel to Korea to find romantic partners finds each other mutually beneficial. I define such mutually beneficial relationships built on desire as "racialized erotic desire" for the cultural and the racial "Other."

Despite finding the nation-state's superficial pursuit of globalization, modernity, and desirability through Hallyu highly problematic, I understand why Koreans are motivated to make such a big deal of Hallyu. The phenomenon is entwined with Korean national identity and success because of its financial and political implications. Hallyu is a multi-billion-dollar industry that contributes to the national economy by bringing in foreign currency and creating jobs. In 2017 the Hallyu industry generated more than $110 billion in profit; $8.8 billion was from exporting Korean cultural products (Ministry of Culture, Sports and Tourism 2019). According to the government report, the industry is growing exponentially: between 2015 and 2016 the profits from exporting Korean cultural products increased by 15.8 percent. The following year, the profits increased by 46.7 percent. Furthermore, as of 2017 the industry employed 640,000 people and generated new jobs yearly. The entertainment industry and the Hallyu phenomenon are essential to the Korean economy, which wants to experience a second rendition of the "Miracle on the Han River" [한강의 기적].

The first miracle on the Han River happened in the decades following the Korean War when the nation experienced a dramatic financial rise by selling cheap labor overseas. On the one hand, it offered cheap labor for Western companies that built factories in Korea. On the other hand, the nation exported its citizens as laborers to developed nations such as Germany, where Korean migrant workers were deployed to take jobs that Germans shunned in the fields of mining and nursing. These migrant workers would send remittances back to Korea. The news coverage during that time emphasized these migrant laborers' sacrifice, sorrow, and hardship. Widely circulated news footage of then-president Park Jung-Hee and his wife visiting Korean miners and nurses in Germany shows the first lady constantly wiping tears from her eyes as she is greeted by six hundred Korean migrant laborers waving the Korean flag (Channel A 2014). In turn, migrant women, dressed in their best Korean traditional attire, also shed tears, presumably due to a complex mixture of emotions, including joy at being recognized by the president for their hard work, sorrow at being citizens of a weak nation, and nostalgia for family back in Korea that they were unable to see for years. In his speech, the president tells the migrant workers they are working hard so that future generations of Koreans can live better lives (Channel A 2014). The event is solemn, with the Korean national anthem and sad tunes playing in the background as everyone sobs and vows to make the nation stronger through hard work. The video denotes the Korean government's and individual laborers' desire for political and economic ascendancy. According to the video, such ascendancy can be achieved through the hard labor of individual Koreans who were forced by the nation's circumstances to sacrifice their happiness for the well-being of their family and nation.

In the five decades between 1960 and 2010, Korea's financial and political position changed dramatically. Roughly fifty years after Park Jung-Hee held back tears in front of a sobbing crowd of Korean migrant workers, his daughter, Park Geun-Hye, who also became president, partook in a series of events filled with joy and pride in Korea. For instance, in 2016 Park traveled to foreign countries on a diplomatic trip where she visited a Korean cultural event. The newsreel shows Park sitting alongside many foreign women (SBS News 2016). She asks one of them, "How are your Korean pronunciation and speaking skills so good?" The woman responds in fluent Korean, "In the past two years, I've been learning Korean at the Sejong Language Institute." The woman expresses her love for K-pop idols and dramas as Park smiles at her and expresses amusement at local women being up-to-date on their Korean drama-related knowledge. While the news from the 1960s focused on tears flowing down migrant workers' faces in Germany because of the nation's weakness as they vowed to make the country stronger through hard work, the newsreel in 2016 includes close-up shots of people smiling and enjoying Korean culture. In the latter video, the notion of sacrifice and sorrow is nonexistent.

While the 1960s news clip shows only ethnic Koreans gathered under the auspices of Korea, the contemporary video clip shows foreigners also enjoying Korean culture. The Koreans in the 2016 news clip do not solemnly plan for the future because Korea is portrayed as already global, modern, and desirable. The 2016 newsreel cuts to another Hallyu event Park Geun-Hye attended in Seoul, Korea, where she made delicate Korean desserts as people laughed in the background (SBS News 2016). At the event in Seoul, rather than the president asking citizens to sacrifice themselves for future generations of Koreans, Park said the K-Style Hub—one of the government's Hallyu-related initiatives—would *reinforce* Korean culture's popularity around the world, implying Korea is already a mighty nation. If the newsreel from the 1960s denotes a desire for ascendancy, the clip from 2016 reflects a sense of ascendance. Such ascendance is visually denoted by the presence of foreign fans who invest their emotions and fan labor to share their love for Korean culture with the rest of the world. If, in the 1960s clip, Korean bodies were depicted as those needing to engage in labor for the nation and the only ones who have the best interest of the country in their hearts, the 2016 clip shows the foreign fans as the bodies engaging in "labor" to consume Korean popular culture and to demonstrate its supposed global appeal and superiority that attracts foreigners to the culture.

Korea incurred a dramatic change in a relatively short period of time from the father Park's presidency to that of the daughter Park's. I believe the driving force, whether it be political, nationalist, financial, or cultural, of such change in the nation's global status would have been strong enough, in theory, to effectively usurp Western Orientalist conceptions of modernity and desirability that center the West as the center of the world order to establish a new model that is more egalitarian than hierarchical and that decenters the West and acknowledges the multiple nodes of globalization and modernity around the world. Here, I specifically refer to "Western Orientalism" because, as I have analyzed at length in the introduction to this book, Korea has been influenced by both Western and Japanese versions of Orientalism that locate either the West or Japan as the powerful center of the world that could decide the worthiness of Korean culture and people. Japan could act as the Orientalizer, so to speak, because while Orientalism is about the West's perspective of the East (Said 1985), the essence of its problematic nature is about the fundamental power bestowed on one group of people in relative power to deem another part of the world as the "Other" who are inferior to them (Ueno 1997). In that regard, any group that is in a position of power over the "Other" can be the one asserting such hierarchies—including Japan, which colonized Korea. In Hallyu tourism, the Korean nation and entertainment industry have that power over the tourists to the extent that they create the structure and the system within which the tourists and the fans have to operate while they are consuming Korean culture.

However, the revolutionary potential of Hallyu's ability to problematize the Western Orientalist ideology has been tempered by the nation-state's zealous nationalist rhetoric to describe Korean popular culture's global popularity. Instead of problematizing the Western Orientalism that revolves around the West as the geopolitical and cultural entity with the ultimate power to dictate other countries' and cultures' worth, the Western fans' approval became central to the nationalist discourse of Hallyu's transnational success. In the process, a hierarchical understanding of modernity and globalization was reinforced. Korea claimed it was as modern and globalized as the West, as opposed to decentering the West. Such sentiment is disseminated by news media as well.

Foreign Fans in Korean News Media

As I watched how Korean news media covered KCON (the Korean popular culture convention), I found it intriguing that many of the official photos of the event posted by the hosting company and the Korean news appeared to focus on fans who are not conventionally phenotypically Asian. For instance, Bibigo, a Korean food company that is a subsidiary of the larger Korean conglomerate CJ, has been KCON's sponsor for several years. Bibigo runs a food stall and Korean food-related events at the convention. Of the ten images the company used in its newspaper regarding its participation in the 2014, 2015, and 2016 KCON held in the United States, very few, if any, centers on an Asian attendee. The photos depict smiling white women and men holding Korean food to the camera or signs saying "enjoy K-food" (Bibigo 2015). The Asians who appear in these photos are either rendered to the periphery of the image or appear as the Korean "experts" who are teaching the white attendees how to make and enjoy Korean food (Bibigo 2014). These photos rely on superficial and phenotypic conceptions of race and racially eroticize white bodies—bodies that become visual symbols of Korean culture's supposed desirability and modernity. The company newspaper's agenda was presumably to use the white participants' bodies to demonstrate Korean culture's desirability. However, in racially eroticizing their bodies, the photos perpetuate Western Orientalist conceptions of modernity. In other words, modernity and desirability are still associated with the West and Western white people, while the global conglomerate's method of achieving desirability is by using their bodies and the modernity and desirability supposedly attached to them by virtue of their Western identities.

An examination of photos that various Korean media used in their news coverage of KCONs held in New York City and Los Angeles reveals that many of them also used images of non-Asians, particularly white women. The photos center on the ecstasy of white fans while women of other races serve as backdrops. For instance, in one photo that appears in the *Korea Economic Daily*, which regularly is within the top-ten ranking of news media in online readership, women are raising their arms in the air with satisfied looks on their faces while all staring at something beyond the photo (H.-S. Kim 2019). The photo centers on a group of white women surrounded by Black women, with some Asians along the periphery. Another photo in the same newspaper that exalts KCON's eighth consecutive year of success depicts four white women clapping their hands or raising their cellphones, flashing a Korean celebrity's name on the screen (D.-U. Choi 2019). Another newspaper article, titled "KCON, an enthusiasm-filled event where you can see Hallyu's race-transgressing influence," depicts two white women, one of whom is screaming with her eyes closed and hands to her mouth. The other woman has her hands clasped in front of her with tears in her eyes and a smile on her lips (K.-T. Lee 2016). Interestingly, just to their left, most of the fans appear to be Asian. However, this crowd of Asians is rendered into a dark background as the photograph focuses on the two white women's happiness at being immersed in Korean culture. The relative absence of Asian fans in these archived images of KCON in Korean newspapers is bizarre because Los Angeles has the most prominent Korean diasporic population outside of the peninsula and the most significant Asian population outside the Asian continent. When I attended KCON in Los Angeles, I saw many Asian attendees. The non-Asian attendees at the event are overrepresented in Korean news media. I suggest that such discrepancy in the actual attendees and those represented in Korean news media is yet another indicator, along with the municipal government politicians' discourses, that represents the white-washed "global" image the nation wants to highlight for its citizens. The Asian fans do not serve as ideal models to represent the image of globalization that the news media want to project regarding KCON.

In these photos, Asians appear in one of two categories: the all-important Korean celebrities, or ethnic Asian fans who remain on the margins. In other words, they are either the Korean celebrities, at the center of attention and the subjects of everyone's affection, or Asian fans who raise the body count at these events but whose presence cannot be visually represented in the images that appear in the news because their phenotypic similarity to Koreans means that they cannot contribute to the Korean agenda of superficially rebranding itself as a global, modern, and desirable nation. There is an exceptional irony in the ambition to use event participants to make the nation appear global and desirable. After all, the participants, similar to tourists, are, by nature, only visitors to a place who do not represent the true effects of globalization such as multiculturalism and multiracialism (Edensor 2009; Werry 2011). The use of Western white fans to manufacture the image of globalization and desirability indicates that the type of globalization that the nation is pursuing is not one comprising a multidirectional flow of goods, ideas, and people that integrates the world (which includes both white and non-white fans) into one economic space (Gibson-Graham 1996). Instead, it is one that, as Alex Jeong-Suk Lee argues, is used as a metonym for modernization and a "certain ways of seeing places and people in the world as desirable or undesirable" (2019, 203).

The selective visual use of foreign—mainly white Western—bodies to mark the success of overseas Korean cultural events and to emphasize Korean culture's desirability and supposed modernity provides a stark difference to how Southeast Asian marriage migrants and migrant workers are conceptualized in Korean public discourse. The difference in how they are portrayed symbolizes the distinction drawn by national media between desirable globalization and less-desirable multiculturalism, with the former being marked by white bodies and the latter marked by non-white bodies. Korean documentaries featuring these groups of non-white foreigners in Korea depict them through the colonialist lens as destitute people whom the nation has the moral imperative to help as a developed nation (Shim 2012; Cha, Lee, and Park 2016). The assistance comes at a price: they must erase their foreignness and fully assimilate into Korea (Cha, Lee, and Park 2016; Kim 2017). Especially for marriage migrants who come to Korea to marry Korean men, their potential failure to assimilate will stigmatize not only them but also their children (E. Lee, Kim, and Lee 2015). Such discourse derives from implicit fear that inadequate multicultural Koreans are going to populate the peninsula in the near future. The underlying xenophobia in these discourses indicates that the problematic mantra—"What is most Korean is the most global"—is still latent in the national sentiment, and that it abides by a very strict and myopic definition of what "Korean" means when it comes to judging the migrants' "Korean-ness."

Oh (2018) also points out the paradox of Korea distinguishing between globalization and multiculturalism. According to Oh, there are parts of Korea where working-class foreign migrants live together. However, those places, such as Daerim, composed of many migrant workers from Eastern Europe, Russia, and China, are never defined as global places even though they are global by virtue of their inhabitants' multicultural and multiracial backgrounds and their factories' contribution to the global economic market. They are not deemed global because Korea does not deviate from the Western Orientalist definition of modernity that associates Western bodies with modernity. Since non-Western migrant workers are not deemed modern, the spaces they occupy are not hailed as global spaces. Instead, the government and news media identify spaces like Gangnam, which the Hallyu tourists fleetingly visit, as global spaces because the Hallyu tourists are marked as modern and desirable subjects. The tourists become racially eroticized bodies desired for their ability to bring immediate globality to the nation without putting much effort into fully grasping the meaning of globalization.

This is not to say that marriage migrants and migrant workers in Korea are not racially eroticized in their own way. Media depictions of marriage migrants and migrant workers racially eroticize them, but in vastly different ways from the Hallyu tourists. While the latter's foreignness reinforces the mantra "what is most Korean is the most global," the former's foreignness raises fundamental problems for the mantra. Therefore, while the Hallyu tourists' foreignness is valued, the marriage migrants' foreignness is something to be expediently erased. The tourists' foreign appearance and cultural background supposedly contribute to Korea's rebranding. In contrast, marriage migrants are valued for their foreign appearance, but their cultural backgrounds become negligible. In other words, their foreign-looking appearances and bodies are valued for making Korea appear diverse, but their bodies become detached from their cultural backgrounds. Women with darker skin colors or those from countries poorer than Korea, particularly from Southeast Asia, become racially eroticized as marriage partners and reproductive vessels. Unlike marriage migrants, the Hallyu tourists are racially eroticized as eclectic consumers whose presence around Korea indicates Korea's rising sociocultural status in the global hierarchy.

Granted, the binary of marriage migrants and the Hallyu tourists is not exclusively about race, although race is a significant factor in why the two groups are treated in different ways. For instance, some marriage migrants from Eastern Europe are white, and some Hallyu tourists are non-white. Hence, the different racialized eroticism that the marriage migrants and the Hallyu tourists are subjected to in Korea occurs at the intersection of race, nationality, and class. This is an example of *injongchabyeol*, which is a Korean discriminatory practice of perceived different human categories loosely based on race, culture, nationality, and religion (D. Oh 2022). I would also like to include class as a factor of *injongchabyeol* because women who come from the same country but with vastly different class statuses, whereby one has to undergo marriage migration while the other could afford to be a Hallyu tourist, would be treated differently in Korea. I expand more on the class issue in chapter 4 in my analysis of Russian Hallyu tourist informants.

In the following section, I examine Korean television dramas and the production industry and how they partake in the strategy to rebrand Korea as a global, modern, and desirable country. I suggest that tracing the chronological change in the production environment and the big controversies that arose throughout the 2010s and the 2020s reveals that television dramas, like national media and the government, embrace the idea of globalization yet attempt to dismiss its effects, such as multiculturalism and multiracialism.

Korean Television Dramas' Conception of Foreignness

To a certain extent, Korean television dramas perpetuate the popular discourse of *segyehwa* that superficially attempts to rebrand Korea as global, modern, and desirable in ways that conform to Western Orientalist conceptions associated with modernity. Such an attitude is most poignantly captured in an infamous incident that occurred in 2017. The first episode of a Korean television drama entitled *Man Who Dies to Live* (2017) caused a massive outcry from the transnational audience because of its insensitive depiction of Islam. The episode depicts a Korean male protagonist who lives in a fictional Middle Eastern nation and converts to Islam. However, he is shown imbibing alcohol and putting his feet next to the Quran—both of which are offensive to Islamic teachings. The drama also portrays Muslim women lying poolside while wearing nothing but bikinis and hijabs. The episode overtly stereotypes and sexualizes Muslim women as if to recreate a scene from racist pornography. The drama perpetuates Western Orientalist stereotypes of the Middle East and Islam as anti-modern, showing Muslims comedically engaging in acts that defy their cultural and religious beliefs. The comedic effect was intended to come from the disjuncture between conventional Muslim propriety and the characters' impropriety. It is as if the drama takes a page out of the U.S. First Lady Laura Bush's speech during the war in Afghanistan, wherein she argued that the United States needed to modernize Afghanistan and liberate its women so they could act like the supposedly empowered Western women who can wear bikinis and nail polish (Abu-Lughod 2002). The underlying assumption in Bush's speech is that the Middle East is anti-modern and needs to be "saved" from itself by the modernized United States. Although *Man Who Dies to Live* does not echo Bush's Western saviorism, it nonetheless perpetuates Western Orientalist conceptions of modernity that center the West.

These depictions resulted in Muslim Hallyu fans' movements to boycott this specific program and Hallyu dramas at large for their insensitivity toward Muslims. If the producers and writers of the offending drama considered the transnational audience of their drama—or, for that matter, multiethnic viewers who live in Korea—such depiction would have been edited, or never even filmed in the first place. Some non-Muslim Hallyu fans I observed also expressed their disdain for such racism in Korean television dramas. This televisual depiction is yet another example of Korean *segyehwa* policies' perilous relationship with Western Orientalism.

The controversies surrounding the depictions of non-Koreans in Korean television dramas primarily focus on their depictions of non-Westerners and illuminate the racial and ethnic prejudice latent in Korea in the form of *injongchabyeol*. For instance, *Racket Boys* (2021), a drama about high school badminton players, garnered controversy among Indonesian viewers for its supposedly negative portrayal of the country and its people. In one episode, the protagonists travel to Indonesia to compete in an international badminton competition. However, they find a dirty and decrepit building at the practice facility. The drama depicts the Indonesian audience loudly booing and heckling the Korean player during the competition. Indonesia and its citizens are portrayed as anti-modern and unprepared for globalization. After the episode aired, some Indonesian viewers criticized the drama's depiction of the country and demanded an apology from the drama production staff. The situation became so severe that the relevant personnel in Korea had to apologize to Indonesian viewers formally. In a similar vein, *Narco-Saints* (2022), a Netflix series, garnered backlash from the Suriname government for its negative depiction of the country as a hub of drug cartels and corruption. The Korean name for the show is *Suriname*, but it had to change its English name to *Narco-Saints* because of the Suriname government's protest. One minister from Suriname said that the government was considering suing the production company. While I cannot verify whether such strong sentiments were a few Surinamese government officials' grandstanding or whether ordinary Surinamese citizens were genuinely offended by the media depiction, the Korean government took the situation seriously. The Korean embassy in Venezuela, which is the closest one to Suriname, sent an official announcement to Koreans living in Suriname to be careful of potential hate crimes against them by the angry people of Suriname. The drama's portrayal of the country and, to a lesser degree, the Korean embassy's warning to the Korean community in Suriname indicate an underlying assumption that the government is anti-modern, corrupt, and prone to violence. The characters from the Global South in these television dramas serve as subjects of racialized erotic desire that, because of their supposed anti-modernity, "prove" that Korea has ascended to the level of globalization, modernity, and desirability.

As an exception to the long list of Korean television dramas that garnered controversy due to their Western Orientalist conceptions equating modernity with the West and the anti-modern with the non-West, several dramas caused controversy for how they depicted non-white Westerners. For instance, *The Penthouse: War in Life* (2020), a drama about a group of wealthy Koreans, garnered international backlash because one of the Korean male characters, who has a violent and impulsive personality, appeared on screen while sporting dreadlocks, facial tattoos, and mannerism that seemed to emulate and make fun of the style of American Black rappers. Granted, not all cultural emulations are offensive appropriations. Crystal S. Anderson (2020) examines the influence of Black culture on Korean popular music and argues that the analysis should go beyond the binary of appreciation and appropriation. She recommends the framework of "citational practices" to understand how K-pop challenges the homogenizing force of globalization. I tend to agree with Anderson that K-pop's relationship to Black American music cannot simply be explained through the framework of cultural appropriation. However, I suggest that television dramas have less nuance than the music scene. *The Penthouse* used racist tropes of Black hip-hop artists to portray the character as outlandish, materialistic, violent, irrational, and, therefore, anti-modern.

Korean television drama's incorporation of insensitive scenes hints at the industry's lackadaisical attitude toward multiculturalism. In a majority of the cases of controversy that I have identified here, the main excuse that Korean media made on behalf of the dramas was that first, the depictions (e.g., a rude Indonesian audience at an international sporting competition and Suriname's drug problems) are supposedly inspired by real-life events at the 2018 Jakarta-Palembang Asian Games and the real-life corruption of the former president of Suriname, Dési Bouterse. Even if this is true, the excuses neglect to consider how viewers from those nations would feel when a foreign television drama critiques their country. Even as the production companies for *Racket Boys*,

Narco-Saints, and *The Penthouse* reached out to global viewers by making them available on Netflix, they disregarded the perspectives of foreign viewers. I suggest that such disregard is, in part, due to the racialized erotic desire for the "Other" that drives Hallyu, which sees foreign viewers as tools to demonstrate Korea's supposed modernity and desirability rather than as people who have their own desires and worldviews.

Although their consumption of Korean television dramas is appreciated, such appreciation does not extend to being more inclusive of foreign viewers in Korean television dramas. Observes Kathleen McHugh, "I consider South Korean cinema as an instance of a national cinema from this perspective: as complex and contradictory, identified and affirmed in encounters with and negations of that which it is not" (2001, 1). McHugh writes about Korean cinema, but her argument can be extended to Korean television dramas. For instance, through racist cases like that in *Man Who Dies to Live*, Korean television dramas are "identified and affirmed in encounters with and negations of" Muslim women. In this sense, Hallyu is a phenomenon where discourses of the global and the national work apace to rearticulate one another. Although Hallyu fans are integral to Hallyu, they are also construed as "outsiders" who mark the boundaries of "Korean." In that regard, attendees at events like KCON and the Hallyu tourists who are temporary visitors to Korea are celebrated because they not only provide a facade of modernity and desirability to Korea but do not fundamentally change the meaning of "Korean."

The Korean form of prejudice and insensitivity that has an eerie resonance with Western Orientalism detracts from Hallyu's global popularity. Contrary to "What is most Korean is the most global," what is Korean is *not* the most global. In other words, foreign viewers did not unquestioningly accept Korea's desire for its version of "globalization" that perpetuated the exclusion and marginalization of the non-West (e.g., Indonesia and Suriname) from the possibility of being imagined as modernized, globalized, and desirable. As I analyze in the following section, the problematic depictions were not created by a few xenophobic workers in the television drama production industry. Instead, the problem was more systemic.

Netflix and the Shifting Drama Production Environment

Before Korean television dramas became truly global and were offered for streaming on global platforms like Netflix, their production and export largely revolved around the mantra that "what is most Korean is the most global." While the dramas were being exported, foreign fans' approval was not something the producers actively sought—rather, that approval was considered something that serendipitously followed the drama's domestic success. This is because the production system in Korea at the time only allowed producers to profit from the dramas' domestic success. At the time, in gauging the success of a television drama, the broadcasting companies used Nielsen ratings, which consider only the viewership of the dramas in the domestic market. The ratings were the mechanism used to convince foreign broadcasting companies to buy the streaming rights to the dramas. The logic in such a tactic was that the drama that succeeded in Korea would also likely succeed elsewhere because what is most Korean has the potential to become the most global. In other words, Korean culture (whatever it means at a given time) is globally appealing in its original form, and Koreans should not alter Korean culture to cater to foreign tastes. Therefore, the producers focused on garnering domestic success rather than global success. In that regard, during the first Korean Wave in the late 1990s and 2000s, Korea's desire for approval by Western white fans factored less in the creation and dissemination of Korean television dramas.

A remnant of the early era of Hallyu's adherence to "what is most Korean is the most global" could be seen in some drama scriptwriters' sentiments even in the late 2010s. The defiance of the idea that Korean cultural products need affirmation and approval from foreign consumers extended to that of all foreign fans. For instance, *Saimdang: Memoir of Color* (2017) is a drama about one of Korea's most famous and talented female scholars. The drama was expected to be popular because it starred the actress Lee Young-Ae, who played the heroine in *The Jewel in the Palace* (2003), which experienced resounding success in Korea and worldwide. Lee's come-back to television after her decade-long hiatus following her performance in *The Jewel in the Palace* was expected to make her new drama a Hallyu sensation.[2] The drama was scheduled to air simultaneously in Korea and China. However, according to the show's scriptwriter, to make the drama appeal to foreign viewers, the production staff had to pay excessive attention to anticipating the assumed desires of Chinese viewers. Eun-Ryung Park, the scriptwriter for the drama, claimed that these futile efforts to cater to Chinese viewers even before the drama began broadcasting ruined it:

> The drama was pre-produced with an ambitious desire to broadcast in two countries simultaneously. However, editing the script without viewer feedback was like walking in darkness. Moreover, the THAAD missile crisis worsened China and Korea's foreign relations, and the simultaneous broadcasting schedule was pushed back. Many people anticipated this drama was going to be profitable. The problem was that so many people saw this drama as a figurative lottery to turn their fortunes around. It was tough to write scripts that I wanted to write. During the filming and editing process, all the essential lines and scenes were cut to cater to the whims of all the business interests who invested in the drama, anticipating that it would be a Hallyu drama. Scripts that I never wrote were dubbed into the drama. . . . I just let it slide, but I begged the production company to keep the ending the way I wrote it, and the

producer gave me his word, but in the end, the finale was different from the script I wrote. I am the writer with my name attached to the drama, and I tried really hard to write a good drama, but some unknown ghostwriter was ripping up and editing my scripts. In these cases, the viewers cannot find the drama appealing because the drama's emotional (*gam-jeong*) tone is inconsistent. (E.-R. Park 2017)

Park claimed the drama's failure was mainly due to the production staff and sponsors paying too much attention to catering to the assumed desires of Chinese viewers when they should have been paying more attention to emotionally connecting with domestic viewers and satisfying their emotional needs. The assumption in the scriptwriter Park's comment is that if she had feedback from domestic viewers, she would have been able to make a better drama that could have succeeded overseas. She adhered to the mantra that "what is most Korean is the most global." However, unlike the current trend of Hallyu that seeks foreign—particularly Western white—approval for proof of its global appeal and desirability, Park, along with many other drama scriptwriters at the time, rejected the idea that the mantra implied the need for foreign approval. Rather, they believed that by purely existing in its Korean-ness, the global popularity would follow automatically.

Despite the early era of Hallyu's seemingly unadulterated confidence and national pride in its television dramas, I find this period to be very straightforward and somewhat liberating in its pursuit of globalization on its terms. It did not primarily abide by Western Orientalist conceptions of desirability and seek affirmation from Western white fans. Comparatively, now that Korean television drama production has become a multi-million-dollar global industry, there has been more intervention of Western Orientalist ideologies in that the Western conglomerates and fans were granted more power to dictate the desirability and success of Korean television dramas. In response, the question of what exactly is Korean about K-dramas became a persistent topic of debate among scholars and Korean government politicians.

The increasingly sizeable financial role that Netflix and other online streaming platforms have played in the transnational dissemination of Korean television dramas since the late 2010s has changed the production environment. Production companies no longer focus only on domestic viewers; more is at stake in pleasing the global audience. Hence, "what is most Korean is the most global" is no longer about the serendipitous popularity of Korean popular culture but about the need to actively seek approval from the "global" about whether they approve of the version of "Korean" that is being produced through the television dramas.

The global streaming platforms brought production fees that were several times more than what the local broadcasting companies could offer the production companies. In 2023 Netflix reported spending a whopping $2.5 billion exclusively to produce Korean television dramas. Even before then, Netflix-funded Korean dramas *Mr. Sunshine* (2018) and *Kingdom* (2019), dramatically changed the Korean drama production environment. *Mr. Sunshine* was initially supposed to air on SBS, one of Korea's three major broadcasting companies. However, it was a massive historical drama that required approximately $1.5 million in production fees per episode—more than double the average Korean drama. SBS did not want to invest more than $20 million in a drama that may not succeed. The drama appeared to be on the brink of being unable to be produced. However, Netflix stepped in and paid the majority of the production fee in exchange for copyright. *Mr. Sunshine* was a resounding success both in Korea and abroad, and it demonstrated a new paradigm of Korean television dramas, with each episode filmed like a high-quality film. The following year, Netflix produced the first Netflix original series Korean television drama, called *Kingdom* . The drama's Korean production company bypassed Korean broadcasting companies, decided to sell the drama's copyright to Netflix, and made it exclusively available on the platform. It was larger in scale than any Korean drama that came before. Netflix fully funded the production fee, which amounted to over $3 million per episode. Up to that point, it was the most expensive series that Netflix produced in any country. Like *Mr. Sunshine*, this drama was a huge success, artistically and commercially, and resulted in the production of a second season and a spin-off movie, all funded by Netflix.

After the success of these two dramas, more Korean production staff focused on the global audience rather than drawing the boundary between the domestic and the global audience. Such change occurred because the profit structure in the Korean television drama industry changed. Sang-Baek Lee, the CEO of the production company that produced several globally acclaimed television dramas, recounted the evolution of the Korean television drama production industry. According to Lee,

> Cable and broadcasting networks prioritize getting their hands on the copyright because they can profit greatly from selling advertisement slots during a popular drama's airtime. On the other hand, the production companies that sold the copyright to the drama cannot earn additional income even if the dramas are hugely popular because they no longer own the rights. . . . We made *Kingdom* (2019) to make it into the OTT market, so we sold the copyright to that drama to Netflix. . . . When it came time to decide what to do with *Extraordinary Attorney Woo* (2022), . . . I only sold the international broadcasting rights to Netflix. Now, the drama has been a global success. Because the company owns the copyright, we plan on creating an animation and musical about the drama. We are also in conversation with companies from

dozens of countries about selling broadcasting and remake rights to the drama. (Y.-M. Jung 2022)

This interview indicates that this highly successful production company's focus is no longer on the domestic audience but on receiving approval from the global streaming platforms that could decide the company's future financial profitability. Other production staff also shifted their views to prioritize the global audience as much, if not more, than the Korean audience. For instance, Heekyung Noh, a famous Korean television drama scriptwriter, had a suggestion for drama scriptwriters-in-training: "When you're writing a script, try not to overthink about the specific dialogue you want to write but about what kind of story you want to tell. The dialogue can be simple and will get simpler in the future because in the increasingly OTT-dominated world we live in, each dialogue will just be translated into different languages" (Y.-Y. Kim 2022). OTT refers to streaming platforms such as Netflix that bypass cable, broadcast, and satellite to reach the audience directly via the internet. In the 1990s, Noh's dramas were known for their beautiful and poetic use of the Korean language. Therefore, Noh's saying that she no longer thinks about the literary aesthetics of her script because more accessible lines make for more straightforward translations indicates a significant paradigm shift for her.

Some entertainment industry personnel expressed concern about the global streaming platforms' near monopoly of Korean television dramas and how it may erode their cultural uniqueness. The topic was even addressed during a government audit meeting whereby lawmakers discussed the consequences of Netflix's intervention in the Korean television drama production environment (S.-J. Choi 2021). Furthermore, between 2020 and 2023, in Korean online and newspaper discourse, there were lively discussions about Korean television dramas produced as Netflix original series and how, even though all the characters are speaking in Korean, the lines are either so badly pronounced or challenging to hear that even Korean viewers have to watch the dramas with subtitles (B.-S. Kim 2022). Some production industry personnel wondered why the actors, previously known for their excellent pronunciation and vocalization skills, appeared to have inferior articulation skills when they appeared in Netflix movies and series. They attributed it to the changing production environment that prioritizes visual effects that foreign audiences will appreciate more than the auditory aspects of the dramas (B.-S. Kim 2022).

The underlying fear in such discourse is that "what is most Korean is the most global" has not only been utterly disproven but also that the Korean-ness of Hallyu has become questionable because now, the industry and the nation are turning to non-Koreans to receive approval for what is an acceptable form of Korean culture and what is not. However, as I have argued in this chapter, the mantra was already a paradox that did not define the "global" beyond the

Western Orientalist discourse that associated the West with modernity and globalization. Therefore, the racial and geopolitical depictions in the dramas echoed Western assumptions and put Western white supremacy as the standard. Likewise, the Korean government and news media's Western Orientalist and neoliberalist claim that Korean cultural events and localities filled with tourists and Western fans symbolize Korea's global power, while refusing to call spaces filled with migrant workers from the Global South as global spaces, indicates the paradox underlying the nation's attempt to use Korean television dramas to rework its image. Nonetheless, the mantra seems to be hard to discard, because discarding it would mean that the "Korean-ness" of Hallyu would be fundamentally questioned. That would lead to questions about whether and to what extent average Koreans can take pride in the global popularity of Hallyu, and whether politicians can use the phenomenon as an example of their successful method of globalizing and modernizing Korea.

My discussion of the Korean government, mass media, and drama production industry's racialized erotic desires for foreign fans and tourists highlights (1) the extent to which the images depicted in Korean television dramas and the visual images of their global fan base are manufactured through the collective efforts of the three groups to enhance Korean nationalism, and (2) how my Hallyu tourist informants' racialized erotic desires and those of the government, mass media, and drama industry coexist with each other in a mutually beneficial relationship.

My Hallyu tourist informants were not simply naïve and gullible women who could not distinguish between fantasies and realities. Instead, as I have mentioned in this chapter, Hallyu fans actively interpret the dramas rather than unquestioningly accept Korean cultural norms portrayed in the dramas, and they make their voices heard by boycotting certain dramas until the drama producers issue an apology. Furthermore, their motive to travel to Korea for love is not based on their naïve conflation of fantasy and reality. They were attracted by the idealized depictions in Korean television dramas carefully manufactured by the industry and government alike. As Youjeong Oh's (2018) interviews with industry personnel reveal, they invest a lot of time, money, and effort into depicting specific geographic locations in Korea as ideal tourist destinations and in depicting the romantic emotions associated with those places as achievable for tourists who emulate the dramas' characters and visit those locations in search for love and happiness. Such carefully mediated images of Korea inspired my informants to believe that travel to the country would allow them to make their produced realities become experienced realities.

They are not the only ones who rely on television dramas to produce "realities" that satisfy their desires. The Korean government uses the dramas to rework specific spaces and the nation's image into that of an ideal global powerhouse. While my tourist informants used the dramas to racially eroticize Korean masculinity, the government and production staff racially eroticize tourists and fans like my informants as phenotypic and ethnic "Others" whose existence at Korean popular culture events and in Korea as tourists indicates Korea's ascended status as a global cultural force. While Western Orientalism used the bodies and cultures of the "Orient" to distinguish the supposed superiority of the West, Hallyu gave the Korean government and news media an opportunity to reverse the Orientalist dynamic and use the Orientalist assumptions *against* the West. In other words, the Orientalist assumption that Western cultures and people are associated with modernity is utilized by Korean popular discourse to show that Korean pop culture events and spaces full of these "modern" Western bodies represent the nation's supposed ascendance to the Western level of modernity. While such co-optation of Western Orientalism to serve Korean nationalist purposes may seem liberating, as I have demonstrated in this chapter, I find the act problematic in perpetuating Orientalist binaries between modern versus anti-modern and desirable versus undesirable that rely on Western standards. In effect, utilizing tourists' and fans' foreignness to assert Korea's supposed globalization, modernity, and desirability demonstrates that Korea is as globalized, modern, and desirable as the West rather than going beyond such a West-centric perspective of modernity and desirability.

2

Romance and Masculinity in Korean Television Dramas

• •

One mid-afternoon during my field research in Korea, I was walking on the busy streets of Seoul with Emma, a tourist from France with a big smile, blue eyes, and long blond hair who spoke English with a thick French accent. She was eyeing the socks and accessories displayed on the street vendors' carts. We were being jostled and pushed by sweaty passersby from all sides. We were in Hongdae, a neighborhood in Seoul that was typically crowded and noisy throughout the day due to a combination of tourists and Korean college students. While edging our way to our destination—the air-conditioned living room of the hostel where we were staying—we conversed loudly in English. I yelled, "So what kind of television do you enjoy watching?" She responded, "Apart from Korean? Not much, really. I sometimes watch some U.S. shows, but that's it." I asked, "What about French television dramas? Are there any good French dramas that you watched or would recommend to me?" Emma stared into space and pondered for a minute before replying, "I think dramas are unique to places like the U.S. and Korea. I don't think other countries have a big drama culture. In France, the dramas are horrible. They are not fun at all, so people watch a lot of imported dramas from other countries, never its own drama. No, French television dramas are really boring. I don't really have any recommendations. French, German . . . I just think they are not interesting. They are so . . . dry."

Contrary to Emma's claims that "dramas are unique to places like the U.S. and Korea," television dramas exist in different parts of the world, as seen in Spanish telenovelas and Indian television serials, to name a few. Nonetheless, I began this chapter with Emma's statement because I found her distinction between "dry" French television and Korean/U.S. television dramas interesting. What did she mean when she described French television as "dry"? More importantly, what was it about Korean television dramas that attracted Emma?

Melodrama—a genre that I use to describe a subset of Korean television dramas—is often associated with the emotion of sadness and the evocation of tears. For example, melodramas are often called "tearjerkers." In film magazine reviews, melodramas are evaluated based on how many handkerchiefs viewers (hypothetically) need when watching melodramatic movies (L. Williams 1991; Hanich, Menninghaus, and Wilder 2017). Therefore, when Emma said French television dramas were "dry," I interpreted her as saying that French television dramas were *emotionally* "dry" (i.e., they do not elicit tearful reactions) compared to the U.S. or Korean television melodramas. The overflow of emotionality is central to melodramas, a genre exemplified by emotional excess (L. Williams 1991). Melodramas evoke more than tears or sadness: they startle viewers and make them smile (Hanich, Menninghaus, and Wilder 2017). However, melodramas are still described by and large as genres that move their audience to tears because tears epitomize emotional "excess."

Due to their emotional "excess," melodramas have often been derided as unrealistic entertainments. For instance, Christine Gledhill writes, "Until very recently, melodrama had been abandoned as a nineteenth-century phenomenon—displaced in modern consciousness by the superior values of realism or modernism and retained merely as a derogatory term to berate the products of mass culture for a backwardness excusable only in women and children" (1992, 105). In these ways, melodramas have often been associated with femininity and critiqued as an unrealistic genre of entertainment that women consume to escape from reality. While some feminist media scholars have problematized the social trend that defined women's entertainment as uncultured and divorced from reality (Ang 1985; Kuhn 1999), that is still the perception disseminated in popular discourse. The argument that these genres are devoid of reality and, therefore, escapist not only maligns the genre's largely women audience but also assumes a strict binary between fantasy and reality that is not applicable when it comes to melodramatic Korean television dramas.

Melodrama has been an integral entertainment genre for Koreans because the emotional rollercoaster depicted in such genres resonated with Koreans who experienced similar emotional turmoil during the Korean War and the rapid modernization of the nation throughout the 1900s and the 2000s (Abelmann

2003; McHugh 2001). They would use melodramatic films and dramas as references to make sense of their lived realities (Abelmann 2003). Melodramatic Korean television dramas have never been able to be explained through the binary of fantasy versus reality because the two were always intertwined in their plot and how Korean viewers interpreted them. The genre is a fantasy embedded in reality either through its reflection of people's lived experiences that enable viewers to feel a sense of connection with the fictional characters or by twisting reality to create a more utopic or idealized reality for viewers to use as aspirational points of reference (Jo 2013; Y. Kim 2009).

Therefore, I problematize a binary understanding of fantasy and reality. I find Eugene Holland's (2002) interpretation of Deleuze and Guattari's theories on the relationship between reality and desire in *Anti-Oedipus* (1983) especially useful in complicating the notion that there is a clear-cut boundary between fantasy and reality. Holland interprets the two scholars to be saying: "Desire produces reality in the same sense that lawyers 'produce' evidence in a court of law: they cannot 'wish' it into existence; they don't make it up, but they do make it count as real. Here too, however, any distinction between what counts as fact, evidence, and reality inside the courtroom and what counts outside it is moot: desire in the schizoanalytic sense produces reality in and of itself, *before* any such inside-outside distinctions can be drawn" (23). Desire does not manufacture reality but can make certain depictions or narratives be perceived as "real." In other words, strong emotional desire produces realities that cater to those desires. For instance, my informants firmly believed that the desire-driven reality they produced—Korea as a nation filled with soft masculine men who are romantic and sexually restrained—was a reality that they could find once they traveled to Korea. In other words, their desire drove them to fantasy and then back to "reality" instead of just imprisoning them in fantasy. In this regard, my informants' desires cannot be explained through a binary of reality and fantasy whereby they follow a linear trajectory of escape from reality into fantasy. Instead, I suggest that their desires and where such desires lead my informants are much more complex than the binary of reality and fantasy would permit.

My Hallyu tourist informants did not seek melodramas to escape from reality; they did so to find examples of romantic masculinity that they could draw on to formulate their erotic desires and expectations. For my informants, rather than remaining separate from reality, these desires and fantasies served to renegotiate the boundaries between "fantasy" and "reality." Jenny was one of my Hallyu tourist informants who went on dates with Korean men every night. She was from Germany and had long, dyed jet black hair. She wore heavy eyeliner and dark red lipstick. On one rare day when she did not have a date, we sat down on the side of the street to eat some Korean street food for dinner.

While munching on fried sweet potatoes, she stated, "Guys back home just want to hook up without even going on a date. Korean guys actually still want to take me out on a date and get to know me. That's why I think Korean guys are attractive. They make me feel like I am in my own Korean drama." Korean television dramas profoundly shaped her experience of reality. In particular, Jenny's perception of Korean dating culture and men was influenced by Korean television dramas: she referred to dating Korean men as being "in my own Korean drama." In other words, Jenny felt that dating Korean men allowed her to make her fantasy a reality. Her fantasies and realities were not binaries; they were categories that converged on each other through her transnational travel.

As Jenny's case indicates, romance-centric stories of Korean dramas facilitate transnational intimacies between Hallyu fans and Korean men in real life through Hallyu tourism. According to my informants, all of whom were heterosexual women, much of the attraction of the Korean television dramas' representations of romance pertained to their depictions of Korean men. Apart from Jenny, my other informants also stated that they found Korean drama heroes (and Korean men at large) appealing because they are depicted as preferring romantic dates over casual sex. During one such conversation, a Hallyu tourist noted, "The men in the [Korean] dramas are perfect. They would do anything to please their women."

Jenny and many of my informants noted their deep dissatisfaction with masculinity in their home countries. They described Korean television dramas' depictions of masculinity as providing a much-welcomed alternative to problematic masculinity back in their home countries. From a purely gendered and feminist perspective, their actions could be interpreted as both empowering and disempowering. On the one hand, their decision to find alternative masculinities that suit their tastes better than what is available in their cultures appears liberating because they are refusing to settle for the status quo (Lorde 2006). On the other hand, their acts may appear disempowering from a traditional feminist view because these women appear to be abiding by postfeminist ideology. Here, by postfeminism, I am not referring to the ideological "backlash against or a dismissal of the desirability for equality between women and men, in the workforce and the family" (Holmlund 2005, 116). Rather, I am referring to a cultural discourse that rejects feminism and equates empowerment with garnering and manipulating men's desires through the consumption of certain beauty and self-care products (Jess Butler 2013). While postfeminism, in the first meaning of the term, has been widely critiqued for its seeming embrace of patriarchy (Holmlund 2005), the second definition of the term has garnered extensive debate about whether it reverses the progress that feminism has made thus far by seemingly embracing patriarchy or whether it should be interpreted as its own form of resistance against social norms (M. Bae 2011).

Relatedly, the question becomes, are the Korean television dramas a form of postfeminist entertainment genre discouraging their viewers from feminist activism that directly combats patriarchy? In some ways, yes. After all, it would be a stretch to call Korean television dramas liberating tales of feminist empowerment. Furthermore, some feminist theorists argue that even if individual women viewers may feel some sense of empowerment from consuming melodramatic dramas about women and empathizing with such stories, ultimately, this act of media consumption is devoid of true activism (Berlant 2008).

However, to merely say that the dramas are devoid of reality creates a paradox. There is a significant group of people who believe the dramas impact reality for the worse. Often, Korean misogynist and patriarchal communities point to Korean television dramas as causing Korean women to change for the worse by giving women unrealistic expectations of romance and romantic masculinity. In their online communities, they argue that Korean women are not dateable because the dramas "ruined" them (M. J. Lee 2023). The paradox here is that even as some feminist scholars critique melodramas and other women's genres as devoid of real-life activism because they supposedly embrace patriarchy and are escapist, the misogynists are saying that the genre has influenced Korean women's behaviors in real life in ways that bother them. So, which is it? Do the dramas have real-life consequences in gender relations, or are they just inconsequential entertainment? While I do not agree with the misogynists who claim that the dramas "ruined" women, I do agree with them that the dramas have real-life consequences in gender dynamics. This is because the Hallyu dramas utilize various televisual techniques to envision romantic relationships that undermine various archetypes of masculinity. In arguing that television dramas undermine various archetypes of masculinity, I am referring to the archetypes of masculinity as they exist in modern and contemporary Korea. In other words, television dramas disrupted the hegemonic masculinity that was formulated and propped up by the nation as the dominant masculinity, such as militaristic masculinity and breadwinner masculinity. These masculinities became hegemonic due to Korean geopolitics and resultant government policies. Romantic Korean television dramas problematize these forms of culturally contextualized archetypes of Korean masculinity.

In particular, while Lauren Berlant's argument and a lot of critique of the romance genre as postfeminist or anti-feminist may make sense in Hollywood, where men largely direct and produce films aimed toward women, the situation is slightly different in Korea, where the directors may be men but the drama scriptwriters, who are the most foundational components of the dramas, are mostly women (M.-H. Oh 2015). This is not to say that women cannot abide by paternalistic ideology. However, I found during archival analyses of these writers' interviews that they actively sought to disrupt patriarchal ideology through their dramas. As one writer argues:

I despise the term "Chungdamdong daughter-in-law."[1] What on earth is a Chungdamdong daughter-in-law anyway? . . . I thought society would provide women with a fair chance in life if they got enough education. But I realized when I was of marriage age that neither the mothers-in-law, the husbands, nor societal perceptions of women changed one bit from when my mother was growing up. Still, women were objects who had to marry into rich families and be subservient to their in-laws and husbands. I was angry about that and wanted to use the dramas to portray the so-called "Chungdamdong women" and the limitations of that lifestyle on women's happiness. (J. S. Cho 2013)

This writer wanted to problematize the hegemonic patriarchy propped up by cultural norms and enforced on girls by critiquing the lifestyle of women who conform to social conventions. During my archival research of drama script-writers' interviews, I found that other drama writers expressed similar sentiments. Therefore, I approach the melodramatic Korean television dramas not as a genre that should simply be maligned and critiqued but as one that needs more nuanced analysis.

However, when the genre is viewed across different cultures and interpreted in different ways by transnational fans, the issue of whether the dramas are liberating for women becomes murkier due to the racial "cost" that may be incurred by such liberation. In contrast to Korean women scriptwriters who experienced real-life Korean masculinity, found some problems they hoped to change, and turned to television dramas as a medium to express their discontent, my Hallyu tourist informants approached the television dramas from a completely different context. Many of my informants were driven to Korean television dramas not because of their dissatisfaction with Korean masculinity, but because of their dissatisfaction with the masculinity in their home countries. In that regard, while televisual masculinity was an expression of discontent with hegemonic real-life Korean masculinity and patriarchy for Korean women writers, for some tourists it functioned as a way for them to denounce masculinity in their home countries by appraising Korean masculinities. Therefore, while the Korean women whom I talked to and those interviewed in ethnographic works by other scholars (Y. Kim 2009; Abelmann 2003) de facto distinguished between televisual depictions and lived realities, my Hallyu tourist informants comprehended the "alternative" qualities of the drama heroes' masculinities *as accurate reflections of real-life Korean masculinity*, which inspired them to travel to Korea to seek intimate relations with Korean men. Hence, my critical analysis of the fictional drama heroes in this chapter foreground how my informants' drama-inspired desires and the production of "realities," far from being inconsequential, profoundly influenced my tourist informants in real life by helping them reconfigure and reframe their real-life experiences in Korea to fit their racialized erotic desires and needs.

The function of this chapter is twofold. First, I demonstrate, particularly to those unfamiliar with the genre, how the dramas could be read through Korean cultural contexts as disruptions of Korean patriarchal norms. By doing so, I complicate both some feminist discourse that critiques women's entertainment as not feminist enough and misogynist discourse that blames the genre for "ruining" women. As Michel de Certeau (2014) and other fan studies scholars have established, it is the viewers' prerogative to "poach" the original text and derive their own interpretations and meanings (Bennett 2014; Jenkins 1988). Hence, I am not trying to argue that my analysis of the dramas in this chapter is the only "correct" way to interpret the dramas. I merely display my analysis of them through an academic lens to provide a possible juxtaposition between my reading and that of my informants'. Second, by comparing one way that the television dramas could be read by a Korean woman like myself to the ways that my informants interpreted them, I emphasize how racialized erotic desires cut through their interpretations of Korean television dramas in ways that were not embedded in the drama texts.

In this chapter I analyze three popular Hallyu dramas: *My Love from the Star* (2014), *Descendants of the Sun* (2016), and *The Guardian: Lonely and the Great God* (2016). They were the three dramas my Hallyu tourist informants mentioned most frequently as their favorite during my fieldwork with them in 2017–2018.[2] Here, I must mention that not all Korean television dramas are Hallyu dramas. Therefore, the masculine tropes that I examine in this chapter are not present in all genres of Korean television dramas. Granted, online streaming increased the trend of "spreadable media" (Jenkins, Ford, and Green 2013) that are disseminated and viewed around the world. Hence, it would be impossible to clearly distinguish between Korean television dramas that are part of Hallyu and those that are not. Prime-time dramas with huge production funds and well-known actors tend to be more integrally associated with Hallyu than other types of Korean television dramas. For instance, while some primetime television dramas are consumed by millions of viewers around the world, the daily morning soap operas (thirty-minute television dramas that air during the morning time and are geared toward homemakers who are home at the time of the broadcast) are rarely translated and disseminated online for the transnational audience. For this research, I define a television drama as a Hallyu drama if it is a primetime drama exported to transnational digital streaming platforms or broadcasting networks in other countries. Furthermore, I define a television drama as a Hallyu drama if the transnational online Hallyu fandom and most of the Hallyu tourists I worked with during field research appeared to know about the television drama. I argue that the three dramas I analyze in this chapter depict heroes who are in control of their emotions and sexual desires, are loyal, and are willing to sacrifice themselves for the sake of the heroines. Through such traits, these protagonists problematize masculinities that are tied to patriarchal masculine tropes of authority and power.

Descendants of the Sun (2016) and the
Korean Militaristic Masculinity

Descendants of the Sun consists of sixteen episodes, which aired from February 24, 2016, to April 14, 2016. It was allotted a production budget of $13 million—far beyond the average production costs of Korean dramas at the time. The investment turned out to be very cost-effective; within Korea, the Nielsen ratings for the drama reached 38.8 percent, and in the city of Seoul alone, the ratings were as high as 44.2 percent for some episodes (Yonhap News 2016). The drama was sold to twenty-seven countries, including the United Kingdom, France, Italy, and Germany (G.-E. Yoon 2016).

The drama's plot revolves around two couples intertwined through their friendship. It is a melodrama about four people's love lives and personal growth: Captain Yu Shi-Jin, Doctor Kang Mo-Yun, Master Sergeant Seo Dae-Young, and Captain Yoon Myung-Ju. In this drama, the four characters' love stories traverse from Korea to Urk (an imaginary postwar Middle Eastern country to which the characters are deployed on a peacekeeping mission) and back. Each couple faces significant hurdles in their relationships. These hurdles include external factors such as kidnappings, espionage, and parental intervention, as well as internal dilemmas such as doubts about self-worth. Throughout the drama, the couples overcome these obstacles individually to make their love come true. While the couples are going through hardships, the male characters show dependable militaristic masculinity without the hypermasculine and hypersexual traits stereotypically associated with such militaristic masculinity.

In *Descendants of the Sun*, the heroes' gazes are the key to creating romantic emotions in the scene. For example, at the beginning of the drama, Yu and Kang break up after going on several dates because Kang realizes that she does not want to develop deeper feelings for a man like Yu, who would always risk his life on dangerous military missions. She is afraid that if she gets emotionally attached to Yu and he dies during one of his missions, she will not be able to heal from the loss. She relays her concerns to Yu. Despite already having romantic feelings for Kang, Yu respects her concerns and responds, "I understand. I am truly sorry. I wish you well." They separate, and several months pass before they fatefully reunite in Urk. However, on their first encounter, Yu walks past Kang without even acknowledging her presence while Kang stares at Yu's back. Kang speculates, "Did he not see me, or is he just pretending not to see me?"

The scene cuts to inside the building that Yu just entered and shows a full shot of Yu in a combination of Dutch and low angles. The shot highlights the

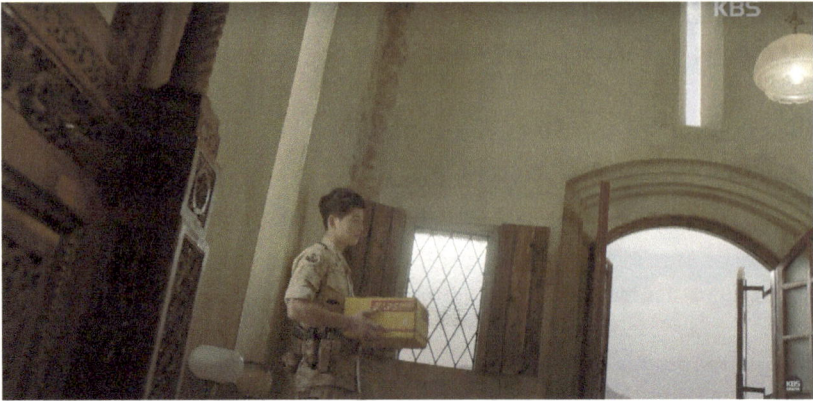

FIGURE 10 Dutch-angle shot of Captain Yu after he encounters Kang. Screen grab from YouTube channel KBS Drama Classic.

FIGURE 11 Captain Yu is intently staring at Kang, who is off-screen. Screen grab from YouTube channel KBS Drama Classic.

bland sandy walls and the empty spaces inside the building that surrounds Yu. He is utterly alone and desolate. He dejectedly leans against one of the walls near the entrance to the building, and we get a close-up of Yu's face. He stares off into space, and the camera follows his gaze to a mirror hanging opposite him that faces the entrance. The mirror shows a reflection of Kang still standing outside the building. She cannot see Yu, but he can see her. The camera slowly pans from the mirror to a close-up of Yu's face as he stares intently into it. We are next provided with a close-up of the mirror, and we see Kang walk off beyond the mirror. The scene shifts to a close-up of Yu's face as he leans back against the wall. The sound of him exhaling dejectedly breaks the monotony of the melancholy tunes playing throughout the scene. Through these sequences

FIGURE 12 A reverse shot sequence reveals that Captain Yu is staring at Kang's reflection in the mirror. Screen grab from YouTube channel KBS Drama Classic.

FIGURE 13 Captain Yu stares off into space dejectedly as Kang leaves and her reflection disappears from the mirror. Screen grab from YouTube channel KBS Drama Classic.

of scenes, the viewers understand Yu's genuine emotions, which are unavailable to the heroine. We find out that he is acting cold not out of indifference but because he is actively restraining himself. Even though Kang rejected him and so many months have passed since the rejection, this sequence of scenes reveals Yu's steadfast feelings for Kang and highlights his emotional loyalty to her. He purposely acts cold toward her to help her not develop feelings for him, yet he steals indirect glimpses of her through the mirror.

Such restrained sexuality was the key component of Korean televisual masculinity for my informants. Due to their aggressive encounters with hypersexual men back home, my informants seemed to find pleasure in

Korean television dramas that depicted romantic heroes who restrained their sexuality and expressed their erotic desires through tenderness and caring acts. Many of my informants compared men back home with Korean men by saying that men they dated before coming to Korea only seemed to be interested in sex, as opposed to Korean men, who were supposedly interested in forming intimate relations beyond just sex. However, the terms they used to describe Yu is noteworthy. My informants characterized Captain Yu and Korean men at large as "gentlemanly," "cute," "romantic," and "weak" while describing men back home as physically and sexually "aggressive." As I discuss further in chapter 3, many fans, while watching the drama through online streaming platforms, would call Yu "weak." Granted, while my informants appeared to echo Western Orientalist stereotypes about Korean masculinity by calling Yu "weak," they changed the connotations associated with the stereotypes from negative to positive. In other words, describing Korean masculinity as "weak" was no longer used as an insult; it was supposedly meant to be a compliment. However, merely changing the connotation attached to specific descriptors does not solve the more significant issue of racialized erotic desires.

Apart from "weak," the other adjectives may appear rather benign. However, I find Leslie Bow's (2021) argument about "racist cute" to be especially generative in parsing through the racial politics of defining certain Asian materials and people as "cute." In describing Western Orientalist fascination with Asian "cuteness," she contends, "Kawaii [cute] things allow for the enjoyment of asymmetry, circumventing the prohibitions placed on racial desires in the twenty-first century" (2021, 73). My informants' use of the concept of "cute" to describe Korean masculinity is not problematic in and of itself. However, it becomes political because, as Bow indicates, the term shrouds the politics and power dynamics surrounding racialized erotic desires. In other words, the descriptor "cute" combined with "weak" and "romantic," which are the terms that some of my informants often used to refer to Korean masculinity, links Korean ethnicity and race with certain forms of gender and sexual performance that limit the possibility of a diverse embodiment of Korean masculinities. In that regard, the newfound "positive" connotation associated with Korean masculinity fails to unchain Korean race and ethnicity from a particular form of sexuality and gender performance.

The use of terms such as "cute" and "weak" to refer to Yu is especially poignant because the drama does not intend for him to appear "weak" or "cute" but rather masculine and strong. After all, he is supposed to be a highly decorated captain who carries out missions that protect Koreans from terrorist activities. For instance, in one of the episodes Yu leads a joint training exercise with a group of American soldiers. When they fail to complete the exercise, a white American soldier angrily throws a pocket knife toward Yu so that it becomes lodged into a wooden box adjacent to Yu's face. The camera turns to show four

American soldiers standing, staring at Yu to see how he would react, while their leader shouts, "Hey man, what's going on? How about you and your Korean Boy Scouts go back home and train with your mamas?" Yu does not back down from the fight. Instead, he dislodges the knife and throws it between the American soldier's legs so that it becomes lodged right underneath his groin. In response to insults aimed against Korean masculinity, Yu symbolically castrates the white soldier by throwing a knife near his groin to emasculate him. They rush at each other and get into a physical altercation. The camera reverts between close-ups and full shots to show them exchanging blows: Yu, although slight in physique compared to the American soldier, can nonetheless fight with him without backing down. The scene ends with the American soldier tacitly accepting Yu's masculinity and capability as a soldier as they share mutual gazes of respect. I interpret the dramas as directly addressing Western Orientalism that characterizes East Asian men as small and weak to assert an alternative view: even if slight in physique, Yu is not weak. The elaborate camera work and the scene's mood indicate that this fight scene is supposed to be an exhilarating moment when Yu, on behalf of Korean men, demonstrates his strength against the white Western soldiers. As I indicated in chapter 1, when Hollywood actor Matt Damon arrived in Korea and was asked questions like "Do you know Psy?" Damon's positionality in relation to Korea shifts from a globally famous Hollywood actor to a person who becomes a supporting actor whose purpose is to verify Korea's supposed globalization, modernity, and desirability; likewise, the foreign soldiers in this scene serve as supporting actors to verify the same message. Rather ironically, many of my informants found this scene "ridiculous" rather than exhilarating or a symbol of Korean masculine power. Many of them laughed when I mentioned or showed them clips of the scene because they rejected the message of Korean masculine strength that the drama was trying to convey to them.

Here, I offer a different, culturally contextualized explanation for Yu's character that departs from some of my informants' interpretations of his character as weak and cute. Rather than weakness, a different interpretation of Yu's masculinity is that he is an idealized version of militaristic masculinity fantasized by women that counters archetypal images of militaristic masculinity throughout Korean history. The drama heroes' sexual restraint is atypical, considering the Korean hegemonic discourse of militaristic masculinity. The mandatory military service in Korea not only tends to separate male soldiers from female civilians physically but also symbolically segregates them into a different class of citizens (Y.-M. Park 2016). Such hierarchy creates gendered pressures for individuals of all genders. Countless scholars have written about the relationship between gender and militarism in Korea (Cheng 2011; Gage 2013; W. Han, Lee, and Park 2017; I. Kwon 2000). Among them, I find Seung-sook Moon's (2005a) scholarship, which closely examines the sociocultural consequences of militarism in Korea, especially generative for my work. According to Moon, while men are pressured to conform to specific ways of manliness, women are expected to sacrifice themselves (particularly their bodies and sexuality) for the brave young men who are sacrificing their time and lives through their military service. In her analysis of a Korean television variety program, *The Youth Report* (2003), Moon (2005b) argues that female lovers' bodies are overtly sexualized and objectified for the pleasures of male soldiers. *The Youth Report* is a popular game show filmed on military bases around Korea. In this show, soldiers appear on stage hoping to win a chance to reunite with either their mothers or lovers. The show makes the soldiers and their loved ones compete in various games to win the opportunity to see each other. Moon notes, "Although the militarized masculinity of a filial son is asexualized, gentle, and even sensitive to the mother's suffering and pain, the militarized masculinity of a lover is indeed sexualized and aggressive" (2005b, 82).

The gendered hierarchy of Korean citizenship based on militaristic masculinity is so pervasive that some Korean men openly make sexist claims that they should have more rights as Korean citizens than Korean women. W. Han, Lee, and Park (2017) analyze Korean men's reactions to a Korean television program, *Real Man* (2013–), depicting celebrities experiencing Korean military life. In analyzing Korean men's responses to the show, they state, "Women were constructed as opportunistic types who abandoned traditional responsibilities and only pursued their own interests. The underlying rationale is that today's women do not take responsibility in the area of social reproduction (e.g., giving birth to babies via marriage). Yet, laws and regulations fully protect their rights. Attributing the low birth rate in Korea to women's selfishness, a few argued that it is the women who do not deliver the children who must serve in the military" (73). In these men's arguments, military service is analogous to pregnancy. While *The Youth Report* objectifies women's bodies for the immediate sexual pleasures of the soldiers, the sentiment that *Real Man* engenders in its male viewers is one of demanding equal sacrifice from women through childbearing. In such ways, the hegemonic archetype of Korean militaristic masculinity demands compensation from women, either through sexual availability or through reproduction. While I find it justified for men drafted against their will into mandatory military service to demand fair compensation from the government, I find it problematic that some of them demand compensation from the women, not from the system that forced them to sacrifice a part of their lives. Their anger toward women in lieu of fighting the larger systemic problem may make them appear weak for picking a fight with those who are easier to beat than the system.

In contrast, the drama argues that restraining from sexually taking advantage of women is the ultimate form of strong and reliable militaristic masculinity.

For example, Yu and Kang reunite in Urk in the middle of an earthquake after another long separation due to Yu going on a mission in another part of the world. Yu and his soldiers are redeployed to Urk to help Kang and the doctors rescue local patients from the earthquake. Instead of running up to each other to exchange passionate kisses or hugs, Yu stares at Kang from a distance. Yu and his company of soldiers are depicted in full shots with light from the helicopter beaming behind them. They appear in slow motion, walking in rank and file amid the dust and rubble. The scene cuts to a medium shot of Kang's dusty face and zooms in on it, and a look of surprise appears on her face as she sees Yu. She tears up, and the scene cuts to a medium shot of Yu in a reaction shot. Everyone around them moves in slow motion as the scene cuts back and forth between a full shot of Yu and one of Kang. People around them constantly cut across the screen, so we see Yu and Kang peering around the moving people to exchange gazes. Close-ups reveal their eyes desperately seeking each other amid the chaos. Only when Kang is called to help an injured person do they break their longing gaze toward each other. Later in the scene, even when they are physically closer, Yu ties Kang's shoelaces for her and tenderly ties her hair instead of kissing or hugging her. Yu expresses his desires for her through his acts of care and tenderness.

As viewers of the dramas, we see male characters who are romantic in ways that are respectful toward the women's wishes and, at the same time, all-sacrificing. Their gaze differs from Laura Mulvey's (2009) conception of the power of the "male gaze." Mulvey argues that popularly consumed visual media centers on the male gaze and heterosexual male pleasure. She claims that there is a power hierarchy between the ability to gaze versus being gazed at, mainly because there is a gender disparity in terms of who is permitted to gaze at others. According to Mulvey, men are often the ones who experience the pleasure of gazing, while women are the ones who are sexually objectified and gazed at by men, both on screen and among the audiences. Granted, many scholars have theorized about the politics of the gaze and attributed the gazer with power (Griffin 2014; Urry and Larsen 2011). I do not deny such power the gazer possesses over the gazed objects. Nonetheless, in melodramatic Korean television dramas, the gaze functions to deemphasize such power dynamics because it replaces acts—forced kissing and other manhandling—that symbolize even more imbalance in power. Furthermore, even though the male characters in Korean television dramas gaze at the heroines, their actions are not rooted in the sexual objectification of the female characters. As the scenes I analyzed above indicate, instead of a symbol that asserts one's affection, the male gaze serves as a request for permission to love. The male protagonists take furtive glances at the heroines so as not to burden them with their affection. When they are overtly staring at the women, it is often a mutual gaze rather than a one-sided gaze. In that regard, the male gaze in Korean television dramas resists the conventions of the gendered politics of the gaze, as remarked upon by Mulvey and other scholars.

Regulating Masculine Sexuality Through Censorship

Apart from the drama scriptwriters' desires to depict ideal masculinity, there is a logistical reason that many Korean television drama characters express their sexual and romantic desires through restrained acts rather than through conventional performances such as kissing, hugging, and having sex. Korea's broadcasting regulations heavily dictate the television dramas' depictions of sexuality. In this section, I briefly interrogate the regulations to contend that Korean cultural stigma against overt sexuality may provide a foundation for the Korean drama heroes' "alternative" qualities, such as their sexual restraint and romantic characteristics. By examining such structural influences that shape televised masculine sexuality, I demonstrate that rather than representing the "reality" of Korean masculinity, televised masculinities are a product of the nation's sexual propriety.

The Korea Communications Standards Commission (KCSC) aims to maintain an ethical and fair media culture in Korea by censoring certain forms of media depictions that may potentially harm the public good. It enforces lengthy broadcasting rules throughout various media forms, including televisual, cinematic, and online media. It has the power to block "harmful" media, compel the producers of the problematic content to erase/edit contentious scenes, and fine individuals involved in creating the problematic media if they do not heed the recommendations of the KCSC.[3]

An entire section of the KCSC's rule book is dedicated to the regulation of the portrayal of sexual activities. According to Section 5, Article 35 of the Broadcasting Rules,

1 Television shows should not portray unethical or inappropriate relationships between men and women. If such a depiction is inevitable for the narrative flow, the program must be especially careful in depicting such relationships.
2 Televised media should not sensationally describe sexuality, nor should they depict sex as a marketable commodity.
3 Television shows are prohibited from portraying sexual activities, including explicit sexual activity with excessive sexual motion and sound, voyeurism, group sex, incest, necrophilia, sexual activities in the presence of a corpse, abnormal and abhorrently explicit sexual acts, sexual organs including a child's sexual organ, rape and sexual assault combined with physical or verbal violence, the depiction of children

and teenagers as objects of rape or sexual pleasure, and any explicit description of the above-banned images. (Korea Communications Standards Commission 2017)[4]

Titled "Maintenance of Dignity," Section 4, Article 27 of the same rule book explains that explicit sexuality on screen is banned because it will arouse discomfort in the viewers and jeopardize Korean morality and ethics. The extensive list of sexual acts that are prohibited from being depicted in media underscores the nation's hypervigilance of sexual propriety.

The results of such extensive limitations on the portrayal of sexuality lead to heterosexual Korean drama heroes who are neither sexually demanding nor assertive. Rather than expressing their love through hugs and kisses, they let their eyes and gaze speak for them. The dramas use various televisual techniques and plot devices to depict heroes who practice sexual restraint yet convey their romantic desires through their acts of loyalty and sacrifice. The Korean television drama heroes provide unconditional love and care for the heroines, as best exemplified by their depictions of the breadwinner masculinity.

Breadwinner Masculinity and Sacrifice in *Guardian: The Lonely and Great God* (2017)

Guardian aired on cable television tvN. The sixteen-episode drama aired on Fridays and Saturdays from December 2, 2016, to January 21, 2017. It made history by becoming the first cable drama in Korea to have ratings beyond 20 percent; it averaged 20.5 percent ratings throughout the series. Within twenty-four hours of airing in Korea, episodes were made available in the United States, Canada, South America, and Europe (G.-E. Yoon 2017). Apart from these countries, it was also exported to Japan, Cambodia, Mongolia, Maldives, and Pakistan (G.-E. Yoon 2017).

The drama is a complicated love story that involves a 935-year-old goblin named Kim Shin, and Eun-Tak, a high school student born with the destiny of becoming a goblin's bride . Kim Shin, the goblin, was a warrior for Goryeo, one of Korea's old kingdoms. He was a great warrior, praised and adored by the citizens, but was murdered by the king, who was jealous of his popularity. For some unknown reason, rather than letting him die, God made him live for an eternity with a sword stuck in his chest. The only way he could die was to have the goblin's bride pull the sword from his chest. Kim Shin wants to die, and so for nearly a thousand years he has been searching for a goblin's bride who could give him a blissful death. Eun-Tak is the chosen one destined to be the goblin's bride. She was almost never born in the first place because her mother got into a car accident while pregnant with her, but Kim Shin saved her life through his goblin magic. Through that connection, unbeknownst to either of them,

Eun-Tak became marked by god as the goblin's bride. Because she was saved from death by magical powers, she sees ghosts and thus leads a miserable life. After her parents' death, she lives with an aunt and cousins who physically and emotionally abuse her. She is even ostracized in school because her peers think she is weird. She is all alone in the world with no one who loves and cares for her. Since her youth, she has always heard whispers from the ghosts that she is the goblin's bride, so she waited all her life to meet a goblin in hopes that she would find the one person in the world whom she could finally call family. These two lonely souls, Kim Shin and Eun-Tak, happen upon each other on Eun-Tak's nineteenth birthday, and hence the romantic rollercoaster of a drama begins.

Eun-Tak's dismal situation is on full display in the first and second episodes of the series, where we witness an ample amount of physical and emotional abuse from her aunt and cousins. They only live with her to steal the small sum of money that Eun-Tak's mother left her before dying. When the television drama first portrays Eun-Tak at her aunt's house, she is busy preparing breakfast for her aunt and cousins in the kitchen. Each shot is very short, and the scene quickly cuts from one shot to another. Within the shots, Eun-Tak's body is only portrayed partially because it is always either cut through with a feature of the apartment or the shot portrays a segment of her body. Such disjointed depictions of Eun-Tak's body highlight not only the claustrophobic environment of Eun-Tak's living situation but also the sense that Eun-Tak is not physically or emotionally thriving in this environment; she is disjointed and cut through with the jagged edges of the house. Suddenly, a bowl filled with rice flies from behind her and hits Eun-Tak in the head. The camera follows the rice bowl as it clatters down the steps, spraying rice everywhere. The scene cuts to a medium shot of the cousins, who are nonchalantly eating breakfast as if nothing happened. The aunt hurls verbal abuse at the heroine. Eun-Tak is now filmed in a close-up from the side to show both her pained face and the rice that is stuck to her hair from the physical abuse. This sequence sets the emotional background for viewers to understand why Eun-Tak is desperate to escape the house by meeting a goblin destined to be her husband.

Granted, some may argue that it is inherently disempowering for Eun-Tak to think that the only mode of escape from her abusive situation is to find a husband, and that she should have thought of a way to be independent. After all, women's financial independence was one of the focal points of the feminist movement (Baxandall and Gordon 2002). However, this interpretation discounts the possibility that for many women, not just in Korea but around different parts of Asia, marriage can feel freeing because it offers them a sense of autonomy and maturity (Bo-Hwa Kim, Lee, and Park 2016; Huang and Brouwer 2018; Pande 2015). For instance, Raksha Pande (2015) uses the term "feminism fit for purpose" to describe how Indian, Pakistani, and Bangladeshi women who are not in positions to take drastic measures to change the gender norm, such as cutting ties with their family or risking social ostracization, can find small measures of empowerment by manipulating the system to their benefit. Marriage is a system that the women in Pande's study manipulate to achieve the modern lifestyle they cannot experience while living with their parents. Likewise, for Eun-Tak, marriage is not her method of conforming to the system but a way to manipulate an already broken system that has failed her.

Kim Shin serves as Eun-Tak's savior and becomes a breadwinner in their relationship. After finding out that Kim Shin is a goblin who is fated to be her husband, Eun-Tak goes to his house to beg him for accommodation to escape from her aunt. She enters his home, and the camera films her in an extremely long shot to depict her in the middle of an enormous apartment with tall ceilings and big, inviting spaces. While the lighting at the aunt's home was blue and dingy, the illumination in Kim Shin's apartment is yellow, warm, and inviting. The camera pans as Eun-Tak makes her way through the house. Unlike the scene in the aunt's house, where shots of Eun-Tak were constantly interrupted by walls or other physical structures of the house, in Kim Shin's house we see Eun-Tak roam freely without such visual hindrance blocking our view of her. This scene symbolizes Kim Shin's role in Eun-Tak's life as a husband, provider, and protector who will give warmth and affluence.

In the drama, Kim Shin does not take advantage of Eun-Tak's desperate situation. Instead of asserting his privilege and power, his love for her is represented in terms of restraint and sacrifice. In the beginning, Eun-Tak relies entirely on him for monetary support; her proclamation of love, rather than an exclamation of romantic feelings, is her method of survival. "I am going to marry you. I love you," she says to him in the first episode, smiling the widest smile that she has so far shown. In the second episode as well, she says "I have every intention of dating you with marriage in mind, I love you" to Kim Shin again. She emotionally and verbally commits herself to him because that is her only option to escape her dangerous living situation. The "I love you" that she utters is her cry for help and a desperate attempt to escape from her abusive home and lonely existence. Kim Shin, although embodying a position of breadwinner masculinity, complicates it by not asserting his authority. While she is a minor, he provides for her like a rich friend or benefactor without attempting to take advantage of her situation. They have a romantic relationship once Eun-Tak becomes an adult, but it quickly ends because he sacrifices his life to save her from a vengeful ghost.

At the show's climax, in a dramatic scene, a vengeful ghost attempts to possess Eun-Tak's body and kill Kim Shin with her hands. In the short moment before the ghost fully possesses her, Eun-Tak pleads with Kim Shin to kill her—along with the ghost that will possess her body—and save himself, but Kim Shin refuses. While wrapping her hands in his, he pulls out the sword stuck in

FIGURE 14 The two protagonists of *Guardian* stare into each other's eyes before Kim Shin's death. Screen grab from YouTube channel tvN D ENT.

his chest in a virtual suicide in order to kill the ghost with the sword so that he can protect Eun-Tak. Kim Shin chooses to commit murder-suicide by killing the ghost as well as himself because that is the only way that Eun-Tak can live a peaceful life without constantly being bothered by the vengeful ghost. After he uses the sword to kill the ghost, the suspenseful music subsides into an ominous tune. Medium shots of Kim Shin capture him in pain while parts of his body devolve into sparkles of fire and float into the air. Music changes into a melancholic song as Eun-Tak fully regains consciousness and runs to him to hold him, as if to prevent his body from turning into ash. The scene shifts between a close-up of their faces as they hold each other and a full shot of them to show his body slowly disintegrating. The camera revolves around them as they desperately cling to each other in the form of shots used often in Hollywood to depict kiss scenes between couples in romantic comedies. However, instead of a kiss, their physical intimacy consists of longingly gazing into each other's eyes. Kim Shin subverts the archetype of breadwinner masculinity by unconditionally providing for Eun-Tak. He miraculously reincarnates after several years, but even after they reunite, we only see them lying next to each other on their first night as newlyweds. The camera shoots them from a high angle as they lie in bed, staring at each other. Eun-Tak tells him that she is sleepy and closes her eyes. The scene cuts to a full shot of them from the side of the bed to show Kim Shin patting her to sleep while lovingly gazing into her face.

Being a breadwinner, or what I call modern "breadwinner masculinity," developed and became embedded in Korea through various historical events that are too long to describe in this chapter. Different terms have been used throughout history to refer to breadwinner masculinity, and the details of what such masculinity entailed were somewhat different. For instance, the concept of *gajang* [가장 in Korean and 家長 in Chinese characters] has been used since the 1600s–1700s. It refers to the male head of the household during the Joseon dynasty, whose responsibility is to take care of the family's wealth (M.-W. Lee 2023). Up to 2008, a system named *hojuje* [호주제] centered men as the leaders of families and made it their responsibility to take care of family wealth and support the other family members financially.

Certain government systems fueled people's support of this unfair system. For instance, in the years following the Korean War, the country came under a long military dictatorship. One of the dictators, Park Jung Hee, focused his efforts on boosting the war-torn Korean economy. One of the fields he encouraged was chemical and mechanical engineering. To facilitate the field's growth, the government instituted a program in which male experts in the field could work in companies related to these fields as a substitute for mandatory military service (Moon 2005a). Furthermore, the government actively recruited male students into higher education programs in engineering by giving them scholarships. This created a systematic gender imbalance in the job market whereby jobs in the lucrative engineering industry were primarily accessible to men (Moon 2005a). Through a domino effect, with men in Korea earning more money through different access to education and jobs, men became de facto breadwinners in heterosexual relationships. Before the 1970s Korean industrialization, Confucian ideology encouraged men to be the head of the household. The particular gendering of the job market during the industrialization period added breadwinner masculinity onto the men's preexisting patriarchal privilege and burden as heads of households (Moon 2005a).

Even though the hegemonic and government-facilitated encouragement of breadwinner masculinity was disrupted through the 1980s labor union movements, the ideology of the masculine breadwinner persisted. Much of the union activities were performed under male leadership, which often marginalized gender issues in favor of labor rights. As recently as the 1990s Korean financial crisis, the ideal type of male breadwinner persisted. This perception of the Korean male breadwinner worked in conjunction with global capitalism to marginalize Korean women in urban areas in this moment of national crisis: "Indeed, the ideology of the male breadwinner has exercised power in everyday discourse. During the IMF period, employers openly said that it was unavoidable to lay off women workers since they were not primary breadwinners. Newspapers, broadcasts, and television programmers eagerly started a 'campaign to restore the husband'" (U. Cho 2004, 33).

Women's plights were deemed unimportant compared to the fear of purported loss of men's masculinity. The breadwinner masculinity in the television drama *Guardian* is distinct from archetypal breadwinner masculinity in that Kim, in the television drama, makes sacrifices to protect the heroine's well-being. In contrast, normative breadwinner masculinity demands certain sacrifices from women in order to uphold the status of male breadwinners.

My informants appeared to latch onto the characteristic of "unconditional love" that Kim Shin exemplifies. Some of my informants pointed to such unconditional love to idealize Korean men. For example, one day, a Hallyu tourist from the Dominican Republic came into the hostel carrying a big bowl of poutine. The rest of the Hallyu tourists who were lounging in the hostel greeted her, and one of them asked, "What's up with all of that poutine?" She said, "I was just walking on the street, and this Korean guy approached me and said, 'You are so pretty.' I don't think he spoke a lot of English, but he kept doing this," she mimed the thumbs-up gesture that the Korean man was doing. "He said he would like to buy me some food and just bought me this poutine." The other Hallyu tourists present there oohed with envy, and one of them asked, "He just treated you to food? Did he ask for your number or anything?" To which she replied, "No, nothing. He just wanted to buy me some food, I guess. Everyone, have some of this poutine. There is too much for me." The other women crooned as they forked through the poutine and said, "Korean men are romantic like that; they just treat women nicely. But shouldn't you have given him your number or something since he gave you food?" She responded, "No, I don't think Korean men are like that." In other words, she said that Korean men did not demand something in return for their romantic gestures. Although there may have been other reasons that the Korean man bought my informant food, she relied on the reality she produced through her racialized erotic desire for Korean masculinity to interpret the situation as emblematic of Korean men's supposed romanticism. In other words, her desire fundamentally shaped how she interpreted the reality she experienced, whereby a Korean man bought her food without asking for anything in return. Her racialized erotic desires produced "realities" that she experienced as very much real during her travel to Korea.

According to my informants, Kim Shin deconstructs the power hierarchy created by the "provider" masculinity, which many of my informants claim to have experienced in their home countries. When I asked my informants about their dating life back home, many of my informants discussed the sexual pressure they felt when their male partners paid for the dates. Helga, a Hallyu tourist from Spain, said, "Most of the time, I pay for my own stuff on dates because I don't like the feeling of a guy paying for my dinner." Helga flicked her short dark hair with her hands as she swiped left and right on Tinder profiles of Korean men. Another tourist from Sweden said, "I agree. Whenever a guy pays for my meal, I feel like he has the right to demand something from me in return. It's like he owns me now and can demand sex [from me] even if I don't want to. That just makes me uncomfortable." When I asked, "What about when you go on dates with Korean men? Do you pay?" Helga looked up from her phone and pondered for a minute before responding, "No, I don't think I pay. At least not as much as I do back home. I don't feel that much pressure with Korean men." Even if the men back in their home countries and Korean men provide them with the same material goods (e.g., dating expenses), they categorize such exchange with men back home as conditional and untoward as opposed to the same exchange with Korean men, which they deem to be unconditional and "purer" in intent.

In the above anecdotes, some of my informants equated unconditional love to material goods given without a cost—particularly a sexual cost. Such materialism attached to the notion of unconditional love indicates the possible influence of postfeminist materialism on my informants in that some of them appeared to associate empowerment with what they could make a man do for them unconditionally. They felt uncomfortable with the supposed sexual conditionality of men back in their home countries while they felt empowered by Korean men's unconditional gestures of flirtatiousness. Many feminist critiques of unconditional love have been premised upon women being expected by social convention to be the giver of unconditional love in their roles as mothers, wives, or caregivers (You and McGraw 2011). In that case, is it subversive to portray a woman as the recipient of unconditional love in a romantic relationship and for my informants to feel as if they are experiencing it with Korean men? I would say no. While unconditional love seems to be touted in popular discourse as the ultimate form of love that everyone should aspire to, many philosophers and feminist theorists have resisted such appraisal of unconditionality by closely examining what entails love, and an unconditional one at that (Wilkinson 2014; hooks 2000). For instance, bell hooks (2000) claims that unconditional love and care stunt a person's growth as a human.

Furthermore, adding a racial component to my informants' comments makes the question of their romantic agency more convoluted. After all, even when two groups of men—Korean men, and men of the tourists' home countries—do similar acts, such as paying for the dating expenses or the bar tab, why did some of my informants in the above anecdote interpret such actions differently and define one group of men as selfless and unconditional in their love while defining the other group as hypersexual? Continuing my analysis from the previous section, could the reason for different interpretations of the same actions also be associated with the notion of supposed "weakness" and "cuteness" associated with Korean masculinity? If so, how can that be reconciled with my observation that my informants often attempted to resist such Orientalist stereotypes? Are all Korean men de facto described as cute and weak due to the influence of Western Orientalism? Or are there certain masculine tropes depicted in the dramas that inspired my informants to develop such assumptions? In the following section, I analyze a type of masculinity that has been the most widely researched in Hallyu studies: *kkonminam* masculinity, which has been attributed by existing scholarship as one of the origins of the cute, effeminate, and "weak" Asian masculine tropes

(Elfving-Hwang 2011). I analyze whether and to what extent such masculinity may have influenced my informants' assumptions about Korean masculinity and how such masculinity could be interpreted differently by examining its origins.

Mature Flower Boy in *My Love from the Star* (2014)

My Love from the Star was highly successful in Korea, earning ratings up to 28.1 percent. The drama aired on SBS, one of Korea's three major broadcasting networks. It consisted of twenty-one episodes and one special episode that aired from December 18, 2013, to February 27, 2014. Internationally, the popularity and impact of the drama was sensational. For instance, on a Chinese-based video streaming website, each episode of the drama raked up to 3.7 billion hits. Not only that, but *My Love from the Star* also popularized *chi-maek* (Korean fried chicken and beer); in the drama, it is the heroine's favorite food. BBQ Chicken, a Korean fried chicken brand, experienced a 50 percent rise in revenue after the drama aired in China. Kyochon Chicken, another Korean fried chicken franchise, saw its revenues around the world increase threefold within the year that the drama aired in Korea (M.-S. Park 2016).

My Love from the Star is a romantic comedy about an alien and a Korean superstar. The drama depicts an alien who goes by the name of Do Min-Jun, who has been stuck on Earth for hundreds of years. At the beginning of the television series, he realizes that he has only three months left on Earth before he can finally return to his planet. He lived in Korea for four hundred years and developed a pessimistic attitude toward humankind because of the multiple bad experiences he had during those hundreds of years. Alien Do is counting the days until he can return to his planet, not only because he is cynical about humanity but also because he will perish on Earth unless he returns this time. Despite his wishes to live a quiet and detached last three months on Earth, he encounters our heroine, Chun Song-Yi. Chun is the most famous actress in Korea. She seems to have everything from wealth to popularity and even devoted friends and a rich man following her, claiming to love her. However, everything she possesses is perilous and ephemeral. She becomes the primary culprit in the mysterious death of another actress who was her archenemy. In one fell swoop, she loses the popularity and the wealth she had before the incident. She becomes the most hated person in Korea, the target of everyone's spiteful jokes. At the lowest point in her life, she meets Do.

The drama depicts Do as a *kkonminam* (flower boy). This term "refers to males with pretty facial features and slim and attractive body shapes" (C. Oh 2015, 63). In the conventional sense, it refers to androgynously beautiful men. As Joanna Elfving-Hwang (2011) states, they also are marked by their invariable youthfulness. *Kkonminam* usually refers to young men such as K-pop idols in their late teens or early twenties before their mandatory military service; they are perceived to be sexually innocent and pure. Flower-boy masculinity garnered popularity by distinguishing itself from more mature forms of archetypal masculinity, such as hegemonic militaristic masculinity and breadwinner masculinity (distinct from those portrayed in the television dramas). The delineation between the archetypal soft and hard (heteropatriarchal) masculinities mainly revolves around sexuality. For instance, Kam Louie describes soft masculinity as not having traditionally manly traits "such as aggressiveness and sexual dominance" (2012, 935). Discussing K-pop idols, Chuyun Oh (2015) argues that a part of the appeal of *kkonminam* is that women fans can imagine engaging in women-dominated relationships with men who embody such masculinity. It is a type of masculinity that has been manufactured by the entertainment industry, arguably to cater to women who were seeking nonpatriarchal masculinity (Louie 2012). However, attributing the emergence of this type of masculinity only to women's desires is heteronormative and disregards the impact that it has on queer men. While this type of masculinity has been coopted to mean slightly different things in different parts of the world (Kang-Nguyen 2019; Baudinette 2021), in Korea it is ephemeral masculinity embodied by some young men who possess androgynous aesthetics and purported "innocence" before they become "tainted" by age and experience.

In the Korean context, flower boys' sexual innocence, rather than being seen as a voluntary condition, is viewed as an involuntary result of their youthfulness. Male celebrities who embody *kkonminam* masculinity have to appear as if they are not "performing" sexual innocence but are "naturally" and effortlessly sexually innocent. In reality, these stars are not prepubescent—they are in their late teens to early twenties—but they have to appear as though they embody prepubescent notions of sexual innocence. Hence, their management companies meticulously plan the male celebrities' gender performances in order to make them appear naturally sexually innocent. Even if the male celebrities who are marketed as *kkonminam* are having sex in their private lives, they have to hide it to maintain their facade of innocence. In more extreme cases, the management companies make some young K-pop idols sign contracts agreeing that they will not have intimate relations, even in their private lives (Zhao 2021), in exchange for fame and popularity. Although great effort goes into creating the *kkonminam* masculinity's image of sexual innocence, everything must appear natural and effortless.

Do, the alien character in *My Love from the Star*, complicates the flower boy's framework of "natural" sexual innocence: instead of being "naturally pure," he is portrayed as being voluntarily chaste. Do's voluntary sexual inexperience is significant because it indicates that men can *consciously* practice sexual restraint. In other words, Do's version of *kkonminam* masculinity is premised on conscious sexual restraint, as opposed to the "natural" and effortless sexual innocence associated with prototypical *kkonminam* masculinity. Physical instincts do not dictate his libido. Instead, they appear to be controlled by his willpower. The colloquial Korean phrase "men's natural sexual instinct" [남자의 성적 본능] is undermined through the depiction of Do's voluntary sexual restraint, which is intertwined with his fidelity to Chun. Do serves as a form of critique toward Korean men who look at *kkonminam* masculinity with a sense of nostalgia about their "innocent" past (Elfving-Hwang 2011). Instead of *kkonminam* masculinity and its sexual innocence being exclusively tied to youthfulness, Do shows that such sexual innocence—or sexual restraint—can be practiced by men of any age. The conscious effort made in the drama to detach sexuality from masculinity counters the hegemonic masculine norms in Korea and, beyond that, associates sexual virility with masculinity to the point that any perceived lack of heterosexual desire is deemed to be a problem that needs to be fixed (Vares 2018; Cheng 2021).

In contrast to hegemonic masculinity, which presumes masculine hypersexuality and indicates one's true manhood, *My Love from the Star* contends that sexual innocence can be an appealing trait. For example, one of the scenes highlights Do's sexual purity by focusing on the aftermath of the kiss and the hero and heroine's different reactions to it, rather than the kiss itself. The kiss scene only lasts for a few seconds. Then, the scene cuts to a split-screen with the words "one hour after the kiss" at the bottom of the scene. One side of the screen shows a medium shot of Do reading a book. On the other side, it shows a medium shot of Chun lying in bed. Each of the split screens cuts to a close-up of their faces, and the sound of heartbeats dominates the soundscape of the scene as Do's heart rate reaches 150 beats per minute (bpm) and increases to an alarming rate as time passes. Meanwhile, Chun's heart rate slowly decreases back to normal. Multiple scenes of them two hours, three hours, and five hours after the kiss are depicted to show that Do's heart rate reaches 300 bpm, and the sound of the heartbeat grows faster until, with a poof, the numbers burst like balloons. Meanwhile, Chun's heart rate monitor has all but disappeared from the screen, indicating that her state of mind has returned to normal after the kiss. The drama uses the split screen, the comedic heart rate monitor, and the sound effects of heartbeats to show Chun's nonchalance about the kiss compared to Do's excitement after his first kiss.

The scene flips the gendered script of sexual chastity that usually requires women to be chaste while not having similar requirements for men (H. Choi 2014). The scene rearticulates Do's sexual innocence not as a sign of his emasculation or weakness but as a symbol of his romanticism and endearing character. According to Elfving-Hwang (2011), the flower boys' supposed innocence is supposed to give women more power and agency to explore and initiate sexual encounters. This is similar to Chun and Do's relationship, where Chun is more eager in terms of seeking sexual intimacy, whereas Do is portrayed as the one who is innocent and profoundly impacted by each sexual encounter. As I

FIGURE 15 A scene from *My Love from the Star* shows Chun and Do on a split-screen after kissing. While Chun is peacefully sleeping, Do is wrapped in a blanket and sipping hot tea to calm down. Screen grab from YouTube channel SBS.

will discuss in chapters 4 and 5, the reality of the dating experience in Korea is not always one where women are in positions of power over men. In my view, such relationships are not aspirational either, since such a desire for more power over the flower boys still results in a problematically hierarchical relationship.

Contrary to Elfving-Hwang's argument that flower boys are popular because they seem to create a relationship where women have more power over men, my informants did not indicate that they wanted a relationship where they had more power over men. Instead, it seemed as if they invoked *kkonminam* masculinity to express the bare minimum that women should expect from their romantic partners: a sense of safety from violence. Therefore, the Hallyu fans I interviewed tended to believe flower-boy masculinity was equivalent to "safe" masculinity. For example, Sarah, a French tourist with long wavy blond hair, said, "Korea is so safe," when I asked her about her impression of Korea and Korean men. Sarah elaborated, "When I am in Korea, I don't have to worry about safety. I just go around wearing whatever I want. But when I am in South America or other places, even South Asia, I have to be so careful. It is so beautiful, but I have to be so uptight and careful that I don't end up enjoying it as much." This notion of Korean "safety" partly derives from the ubiquity of closed-circuit television and police presence in Seoul. It also derives from the assumption that men with "soft" masculine traits do not threaten women with violence or hierarchical submission.

From the framework of gender, the pleasure that my informants claimed to derive from Korean television dramas' depictions of masculinity was upsetting because the bare minimum of human decency shown by the fictive characters appeared to appease them. Granted, the television dramas' male characters are exceptionally handsome and romantic in ways that a real-life man would find difficult to follow. However, my informants did not seem to be expecting average Korean men to look like celebrities or to be ultra-romantic like the drama heroes. Instead, they highlighted the male characters' sexual restraint, unconditional love that did not pressure women to reciprocate a romantic gesture through sex, and a type of masculinity that feels safe to be around. These traits are ones that any decent human should possess, and yet, my informants felt as if they had to travel to the other side of the globe to find such masculinity. From a feminist perspective, my informants' inability to take for granted what should be the norm of masculine behavior points to a larger problem with hegemonic and toxic masculinity (Pascoe and Hollander 2016).

Nonetheless, the racial framework of my informants assuming that Korean men would be "safer" than men in their home countries raises questions about whether the reframing of Western Orientalist stereotype of Asian men as "weak" into a more positively connoted term "safe" is meaningfully disrupting societal racism. Not all Korean men are "safe," but the new framework derived from Korean television dramas also seems to elicit a sweeping generalization about Korean masculinity that may potentially lead to dangerous situations for some tourists.

My informants' desires for Korean masculinity may just be a reactionary desire against the toxic masculinity in their home countries. However, I find that their desires merit further exploration through a racial framework, as many of my informants come from countries that have higher gender-equality rankings than Korea. Based on the rankings, it is counterintuitive for many of my informants to express disdain for masculinity in their home countries and yet idealize Korean masculinity. The behavior indicates that more factors contribute to my informants' desires for Korean masculinity than the desire for more equal treatment from men.

While not within the scope of this book, in the future, it would be interesting to observe whether Hallyu fans and tourists also change their conceptions of Korean masculinity as depictions of gender relations in Korean television dramas change. The dramas I analyze in this chapter aired roughly ten years before the publication of this book. In the past ten years, Korean television dramas have remained consistent in their depictions of romantic and sexually restrained men. In contrast, television dramas have been evolving in their depictions of women. As a case in point, depictions of breadwinner masculinity are less prevalent in Korean television dramas compared to ten years ago. The dramas' heroines are increasingly portrayed as financially well-off women or passionate about their jobs and careers. For example, television dramas entitled *Crash Landing on You* (2020), *Search: WWW* (2019), and *Oh My Baby* (2020) depict successful women who are CEOs of their own companies. They do not have to rely on a male breadwinner; they are often depicted as mentoring and caring for younger men.

My Hallyu tourist informants also appeared to notice the evolution in the gender dynamics depicted in Korean television dramas. Early in my field research in Korea, I overheard a conversation between a Chinese woman in her mid-thirties who did not identify herself as a Hallyu tourist and one of my Hallyu tourist informants. The woman in her mid-thirties said she used to watch some Korean television dramas in the early 2000s but stopped watching them because "they are stories about helpless women waiting for knights in shining armor. None of the female characters in those dramas are strong and independent." My informant interjected and said, "Maybe the older television dramas were like that, but the dramas nowadays are different. Women characters are stronger and fierce." Television dramas have to change with the change in culturally acceptable norms of gender and sexuality. Hence, the female characters in contemporary television dramas tend to have their own careers and are rarely depicted as helpless individuals who need financial assistance from the male characters. I highlight this exchange between the two women to note that Korean television drama is not a stagnant genre.

Korean television dramas may provide the starting point of desires for Korean masculinity, but those desires are perpetuated and invigorated through online fan spaces. Hence, in the following chapters, I examine some popular online spaces where Korean television drama fans convene to share their desires and feelings with each other.

3

Digitalized Intimacies
of Hallyu

● ●

The dormitory at one of the hostels where I was staying while doing field research contained six cramped bunk beds, each with a thin white mattress that was not particularly effective in providing a cushion between one's body and the hard surface of the bed frame. I got bruises on the side of my hips and my knees after a week of sleeping on those beds. The room was dank and smelly from all the unwashed laundry each traveler carried in their bag. The hostel workers attempted to dispel the smell by spraying air fresheners in the room every morning, but that did not help much. Guests' luggage and belongings were strewn all over the floor, so one had to be careful not to trip over the bags when one was making one's way from the door to one's bed. The feat was especially tricky because the room was perpetually dark, as it had to cater to tourists from different time zones who were sleeping in the room at all hours of the day.

One day, I looked out from my bottom bunk to see what my informants were doing. The only light source in the room came from the brightly lit cell-phone screen of one of my Hallyu tourist informants, an American woman named Nicole. She was lying on her stomach on her flimsy mattress, riveted to her phone. When I approached her to ask if she wanted to get out of the room to get something to eat, without taking her eyes off her screen, she murmured that she would join me once she finished the episode. I peered over her shoulders to see what she was watching: a Korean television drama titled *Secret Garden* (2010). The drama was about a wealthy male heir and a stunt woman who were magically forced to switch bodies. They fall in love with each other while attempting to figure out a way to return to their own bodies. Even though the dormitory room was not a pleasant place to stay in, Nicole was so immersed in the television drama world on her phone that she did not mind the dank room or the discomfort of the paper-thin mattress on her bed. Throughout my field research, I frequently observed my Hallyu tourist informants riveted to their cell phones or laptop screens because they were watching Korean television dramas. Their usually chatty demeanors were replaced by silent immersion into the fictional world portrayed on their media screens.

Watching Korean television dramas is an activity that people can do in their respective countries. Even so, many of my tourist informants, who had spent much time and money traveling to Korea from different parts of the world, spent considerable time watching television dramas on their cell phones or laptops while in Korea. From the perspective of the "traditional" tourists who travel to another country to physically immerse themselves in "authentic" and "exotic" cultural experiences, my informants' desires to stay in the hostels and watch television dramas would be incomprehensible. After all, foundational theories on tourism operate under the assumption that the tourists embody the "tourist gaze" that motivates them to immerse themselves in unique cultural experiences they can only experience while they are at the tourist destination (Urry and Larsen 2011; Maoz 2006; Strain 2003). Watching television shows would not conventionally be considered a popular tourist activity.

Although Nicole's actions might appear inconceivable from the traditional understanding of tourism and tourists' desires, emerging scholarly research on "fan tourism" and "media-inspired tourism" that analyzes the critical role that media play in facilitating tourism offers some insight into my Hallyu tourist informants' behaviors (Couldry 2005; Iwashita 2008; M. J. Lee 2020). After all, as Youngmin Choe (2016) argues in her book on Korean film–inspired tourism, the tourists are not simply traveling to Korea, a geographic location; they are traveling into the films that inspired them to travel to the geographic location in Korea. The fictional spaces in visual media and the real geographic spaces in Korea become singular through the tourists' travel. Choe's argument applies to my tourist informants' experiences as well. Their travel began with virtual travel through their screens as they consumed Korean television dramas and virtually experienced the cultures featured in them. The media they consumed and the fans they interacted with online facilitated their racialized erotic desires and their resultant travel to Korea. For my informants, going online to stream Korean television dramas and interacting with other fans online while they were traveling in Korea was an integral part of their tourist experience. Engaging in such activities was as important as engaging in offline activities, such as dating Korean men and sightseeing.

Therefore, I argue that when my informants were watching television dramas on their cell phones in Korea, they were not being lazy or bizarre. Their consumption of Korean television dramas was a continuation of their tourist experience instead of being an antithesis of it. The websites my tourist informants visited to stream Korean television dramas or interact with other fans were essential in motivating their travel to Korea. The websites they frequented slightly differed based on their nationality. Nonetheless, from my observation, many of them centered on fan-uploaded content, provided subtitles created by fans, and had comment sections where my informants could read reviews written by other fans before choosing a drama to watch.

In this chapter I examine online streaming websites and fan communities where some Hallyu fans—my informants included—would visit not only to watch the dramas but to connect with other fans to share their racialized erotic desires with each other. I analyze three online spaces of Hallyu fan activities: YouTube, the K-drama fan forum Soompi, and the television streaming website Rakuten Viki. I suggest that these online spaces generate and legitimate the site visitors' desires to rework Western Orientalism's racialized and gendered perceptions of Korean masculinity through Korean television dramas. Through the process, they produce collective "realities" that conform to their racialized erotic desires for Korean masculinity. Since only a select few Hallyu fans can afford to become Hallyu tourists, these digital spaces are excellent archives to observe a broader segment of transnational Hallyu fandom and their interpretation of Korean television dramas and the masculinity depicted in them.

Before I delve into analyzing the contents of these websites, I must acknowledge that some scholars are critical of websites like the above, which primarily rely on user-uploaded materials, and find them to be exploiting the fans. Gabriella Lukács (2020) argues that websites that mainly profit from user-uploaded data blur the boundaries between production and reproduction, extracting value from users and fans who are not contractual laborers for the company. According to scholars who examine fan labor, noncontractual (and often unpaid) exploitative fan labor becomes repackaged by the websites and the fans themselves as a labor of love that the fans voluntarily engage in for their own pleasures (Lothian 2015; Busse 2015; Dwyer 2012). While I agree that from a financial standpoint the relationship between the Hallyu fan websites and the fans appears exploitative, my encounters with some fans also made me wonder whether it is accurate for me to insist that the fans are being exploited when they reject the idea. For instance, when I asked some of my informants whether they felt exploited by some Hallyu-related companies, they acknowledged that sometimes they felt exploited by the major entertainment companies that encourage fans to consume overpriced products that arguably did not provide much value. However, they rejected the idea that the fan interactive websites were exploiting them.

The question arises, why did my informants distinguish major entertainment companies from websites that primarily rely on user-uploaded materials? In exploitative relationships, one group derives most of the benefits while the other group puts in all the labor without garnering much benefit. Such a lopsided power dynamic is clear between major entertainment companies and the fans because the latter rarely get a say in what kind of products will be sold and at what price. Since many of the products have become increasingly interlinked—for example, where buying a set of overpriced records is a precondition for increasing one's possibility of being selected for meet-and-greet events with their favorite K-pop idols—the fans feel that purchasing an item is less of a choice that they are exercising and more of an imperative that is forced upon them by the companies that are using their affection for monetary gains (Sun 2020). The feeling of being exploited comes from feeling as if their love is one-sided.

Such a lopsided power dynamic is less obvious for fan-interactive websites that rely on user-uploaded content, because the fans interact with each other while the website appears to merely provide space for fans to do so. These websites rely on a form of "affective labor" that "expands sources of value extraction by inviting individuals to invest multiple aspects of their personality simultaneously as the raw material of valorization. That is, affective labor taps into what constitutes a person as a unique individual" (Lukács 2020, 138). Affective labor is closely connected to individuals' strong emotions, passion, and personality and cannot be neatly quantified and translated into financial compensation. At the same time, affect "exists at the cusp of narrativization and lies beyond (or, perhaps more accurately, prior to) semantic articulation. Affect cannot be located solely in individual responses, nor is the individual the source or even the locus of affect" (Mankekar 2013, 605). In other words, affective labor does not simply refer to the form of labor that one fan engages in to create You-Tube videos or subtitles to their favorite television dramas; it refers to the culture of voluntary labor of love that fan communities engage in. From a purely financial standpoint, such affective labor is exploitative because the websites are profiting from the advertisement and membership revenues that would not exist if not for the fans. However, when considering the nonmonetary emotional satisfaction that fans derive from engaging in affective labor—pleasure, fulfillment of desire, connection with other fans who share similar interests and desires—the type of labor that the fans engage in online spaces of Hallyu may not feel exploitative for the fans, some of whom, based on their facial expressions of incredulity when I asked whether they felt exploited, seemed to take offense at the thought. To a certain extent, labeling their fan labor as exploitation feels as if I am discrediting their choice and agency to invest their labor in sharing their favorite pastimes with others.

Instead of debating whether the fans are misguided in denouncing their supposed exploitation by the fan websites, I focus on analyzing the websites through the framework of mutual racialized erotic desire between different parties involved in Hallyu fandom and tourism. More specifically, I focus on analyzing the desires present in the content that some fans upload to the websites and how the various structures of the websites contribute to the creation of such desires. By focusing on desire and tabling the debate on labor exploitation, I am not arguing that the Hallyu fans and their potential labor exploitation are homogeneously irrelevant. For some fans, their labor may feel more exploitative, while for others, it may feel far from exploitation. Nor is it my intent to group them into a monotonous community of "fans" who are stripped of their cultural, racial, gender, sexual, and national identities. Instead, in this chapter I aim to analyze how these Hallyu fans from different parts of the world form transnational connections with each other by sharing their erotic desires about Korean men and by producing shared realities that satisfy their racialized erotic desires for Korean masculinity.

Fan-Made Music Videos as Introductions to Korean Romance

YouTube is one of the many popular websites that rely on user-generated content. Although the website is not explicitly dedicated to Korean television drama fans, they carved out a niche for themselves on the website. Millions of fan-made music videos dedicated to Korean television dramas exist on YouTube. Some fan-made videos have more than fourteen million views (as of 2023). Official videos uploaded by the broadcasting companies for the original drama and its remakes in other parts of Asia amounts to only a few dozen; most of the videos related to Hallyu dramas are uploaded by fans. Accounting for the sheer number, the videos have divergent styles and are made through different mixtures of cultures as well as languages. I ranked the fan-made music videos of the dramas *My Love from the Star, Descendants of the Sun*, and *Guardian* by viewership and analyzed the top ten videos and viewer reactions to those videos. These videos are important because many of the Hallyu tourists I interviewed have told me that these YouTube clips were their first introductions to the world of Korean television dramas.

These music videos reflect various cultural influences. Roughly half of them use Korean songs, while the other half combines drama imagery with English-language pop songs. The creators of the music videos with Korean songs meticulously subtitled the lyrics and the lines from the dramas for viewers who do not speak Korean. Some went one step further by providing different kinds of subtitles (YozohhhCH8 2014). For instance, in one of the most popular videos for *My Love from the Star*, three different subtitles flashed on the screen: first, the typical English translation of the lyrics; second, the Romanization of Korean words to the song so that the viewers could sound out the lyrics and sing along with the music video; and third, the lyrics in the Korean alphabet

(*Hangeul*) (YozohhhCH8 2014). Not only is the music video visually pleasurable, but it also aims to serve an educational purpose through various subtitles. These videos seem to have helped my Hallyu tourist informants learn Korean. Many of them could sing along to the dramas' original soundtracks despite not being fluent or knowledgeable in Korean.

As for the music videos that utilize English-language pop songs, the songs' English audio and Korean imagery mesh together because the emotions running through the songs and videos were similar: mainly, romantic desire. For example, in one of the videos, a Canadian pop star, Kristina Maria, sings longingly of her affection that words cannot convey. At the same time, on-screen, Captain Yu, the protagonist of the *Descendants of the Sun*, hugs Doctor Kang, the heroine, and tells her, "I'm sorry for making you upset" (xFictionShadowMV3 xKBS 2016). In another video, Alex and Sierra, contestants from the show *America's Got Talent*, sing about how love makes them wholesome people as a fan-made music video flashes with a montage of Kim Shin and Eun-Tak (from the Hallyu drama *Guardian: The Lonely and Great God*) lovingly gazing at each other (Rosart 2017). The songs used in the music videos talk of love and missing a loved one, while the Korean drama scenes depict similar struggles of love. The music videos and the lyrics that their producers chose for them highlight the Korean television drama characters' devotion, loyalty, and unconditional love.

These videos symbolize the nonteleological dimensions of transnational media. In other words, transnational media's power is not absolute; media cannot "indoctrinate" all their viewers with the message they want to convey. Instead, the transnationality of media can often lead to unexpected outcomes as viewers from different parts of the world reinterpret and "dub" the media through their own needs and desires. After all, the multilingual and multicultural aesthetics of the fan-made music videos are similar to what Tom Boellstorf (2003) describes as the "dubbing culture" of Western films in Asia. According to Boellstorf, when Western films are dubbed in Asia, the Asian sounds and Western visuals do not perfectly match, and the binarism between import-export, as well as authentic-inauthentic, becomes insufficient to explain the uncanny yet harmonious dynamic between visuals and sound. I see the Hallyu fan-made music videos serving similar purposes. Whereas Boellstorf discusses the relationship between film sight and sound, I find a similar uncanny yet harmonious relationship in the Hallyu fan-made music videos regarding the original dramas' emotional arc and the music video creators' emotional arc.

The videos occasionally use scenes that were somewhat unimportant to the dramas' plot but had emotional resonance with the person who made the music video. For instance, in many of the videos I watched concerning one drama, there was a shot of the characters' hands or arms brushing past each other—this despite that shot having been a minuscule part of the full shot of the characters interacting with each other. In this regard, the drama's storyline and visual aspects were reinterpreted to prioritize the emotional satisfaction and the fulfillment of the video creator's desire. The objective of both the drama and the fan-made music videos appeared to be the desire for loyal and unconditional romantic love. The fans reinterpreted the scenes and plots of Korean television dramas based on their desires.

The YouTube fan-made music video comment sections serve as spaces of romantic expressiveness and affirmation where viewers discuss their emotions and try to find others with the same emotional reactions to the dramas. In particular, the comment sections serve as spaces where fans share their desires for Korean men and romance. For instance, one commenter said, "K-drama actors are beyond perfect. It set the bar high for men of real-world to qualify, so I prefer to [be] lost in da world of K-dramas though I know such a person doesn't exist in [the] real world," to which numerous others voiced agreement: "Omo, and I thought I was the only one!!!" (YozohhhCH8 2014) For many fans, these online spaces are important ways to connect with other fans. After all, even as Korean popular culture is garnering global popularity, in many countries outside of Asia the Hallyu fans are still considered part of a niche culture, and their enthusiasm for Korean pop culture is neither shared nor understood by family and friends (Lyan and Levkowitz 2015). Deemed "weird" for liking entertainment from Korea, online they meet fans who share their sentiments and desires, and they feel a sense of relief and satisfaction from making such digital connections.

My tourist informants' travel patterns indicated that they did not have many people to share their love of Korean pop culture offline. Most of my informants traveled to Korea alone and met other like-minded fans in Korea instead of traveling with friends from back home. Although their tendencies for solo travel were, in some part, attributable to their friends not having the financial luxury to travel, others claimed it was due to their friends from home not being committed fans of Korean popular culture and, thus, having little desire to travel to Korea. However, due to online spaces like YouTube, watching Korean television dramas and desiring televisual subjects have become communal activities. These Hallyu fans realized they were not the only ones fostering desires for Korean men.

These fans used the incognito encounter in online spaces primarily to have lengthy conversations about Korean dramas' portrayal of love:

VIEWER 1 In my opinion, Goblin (*The Guardian*) is better than *Descendants of the Sun*. Anyone agree?

VIEWER 2 I agree 1000000% with you

VIEWER 3 Both are different, one is about love other is about the love you wish to get but never receive

VIEWER 4 That's right, how can one compare one with another

VIEWER 5 In *Descendants of the Sun*, even after I realize that it's a happy ending for both the couples, still my heart aches. They were apart from each other for a long time. Still they waited for each other. Indeed, true love can wait <3 (kpopfan 2017)

One commenter raised the above issue in a fan-made music video on the drama *Guardian*. Even though the music video that sparked this debate was solely based on *Guardian*, the discussion between the fans freely flowed between the drama and *Descendants of the Sun* under the presumption that people who watched one of the dramas assuredly watched the other. My Hallyu tourist informants indicated that the fan-made music videos were their first encounters with Korean television dramas, and that inspired them to watch further dramas. However, the music videos and the comments underneath them were not easily accessible; they did not introduce new fans to the Korean television drama fandom by neatly organizing the dramas' plots for those who have not watched them. Instead, the videos focus on certain emotions that viewers felt while watching the drama, and they encourage viewers who happened to stumble upon these music videos to watch Korean television dramas if they wanted to feel these emotions and desires.

The music videos and the comments idealize love that takes a long time to be fulfilled. For instance, commenters noted that a drama depicts "love you wish to get but never receive" and that "true love can wait" (kpopfan 2017). In other words, they found pleasure in Korean dramas because of their portrayal of love as a long-drawn-out waiting game. Melodramas build on the emotions of longing and melancholy attached to the disjointed temporality of two lovers. Prime examples of such disjointed temporalities would be the stereotypical melodramatic plots about unrequited love or scenes of the hero running toward the bus/train station after the heroine has already left due to a misunderstanding. Romantic melodramas would be short and boring stories if such missed temporalities did not exist.

I point out the commenters' desires for long-drawn-out love to emphasize how their erotic desires were not rooted in fast-paced and sex-oriented eroticism. Instead, their motivation in seeking intimacy with Korean men was based on eroticism that is somewhat detached from quick and casual sex acts. Such desire for romance and the pursuit of it in the Korean cultural context may have some geopolitical reasons and implications. For instance, Ingyu Oh (2011) and Sun Jung (2010) analyze Japanese women's love for the Hallyu drama *Winter Sonata* as nostalgic longing. According to them, Japanese women enjoyed watching this drama because it reminded them of a Japanese "past" where romantic intimacies were purportedly more physically timid than they are in contemporary Japan.

Oh claims that these Japanese women's desires relegate Korea to the temporal "past" and thereby perpetuate a colonially hierarchical relationship between the two countries. According to Oh's psychoanalytic analysis of Japanese Hallyu fans, these fans believe that Japan no longer has slow-paced romance because Japan is too modernized; by such colonialist logic, Korea still retains "slow" qualities of romance because it has not reached the level of modernity that Japan has already achieved. I do not condone such ideologies because they are extensions of the Japanese justification for their colonization of Korea. However, if, as Oh and Jung pointed out, the Japanese fans' nostalgic affection for Korean televisual depictions of romance and masculinity is based on the nation's problematic colonialist past, how can we make sense of the desires of fans who are from countries that did not have direct colonial relationships with Korea? Do they have more liberating reasons for desiring Korean masculinity and Korean forms of romance? I address these questions by examining one of the most popular Korean television drama streaming platforms: Rakuten Viki.

Digital Friends: Rakuten Viki and Timed Comments

Rakuten Viki describes itself as "Global TV powered by fans: Thousands of TV shows and movies. Millions of engaged viewers. Endless possibilities." According to the company's website, it reaches a global audience of one billion viewers. Viki was a U.S.-based company that, according to news sources, was created by Harvard and Stanford graduate students who wanted to remove barriers for viewers who wanted to experience entertainment from other cultures (Swisher 2013). As the website's unique name states, it claims to be the "Wikipedia" of "videos" because it offers an expansive library of dramas and television shows from East Asia. Although it features television shows from various East Asian countries, the original focus of the website during its early days was Korean television dramas. By subscribing to monthly or annual plans offered by the website, viewers can stream television programs and films from various East Asian countries with limited or no commercial breaks. Alongside subscriptions, much like other streaming websites, Rakuten Viki primarily makes money through in-stream advertisement revenues that the website shares with its content providers (Swisher 2013).

The website, which used to be simply called Viki, was bought by Rakuten, the largest Japanese-based e-commerce company, in 2013 and was renamed Rakuten Viki. Rakuten is one of Japan's most popular online retail platforms; however, compared to its size, it hires very few employees, which may indicate that its business model is to "extract value from labor without actually employing workers" (Lukács 2020, 5). It appears the same business ideology applies to Rakuten Viki because one of the unique aspects of this website is that the fans have been tasked with creating the dramas' subtitles.

The website constantly recruits "fan volunteers" to subtitle the shows and manage the television drama fan pages. Only through such minimally paid and voluntary labor of fans can the website provide subtitles in over twenty different languages. However, these fans do not complain about doing all this labor. Instead, they praise the website for its interactive-ness. After all, "Its community of fansubbers is united by passion for specific programs, movies or genres, and the wish to share this content with as wide an audience as possible. As its homepage declares, they 'translate to spread the love'" (Dwyer 2012, 218). Their eagerness to participate in fan labor may be due to their labor not always being recognized let alone deemed legitimate enough for exploitation (Jenkins 2019). Even though the concept of "labor of love" may seem hypocritical and exploitative, as I suggested earlier in this chapter, some fans derive significant nonmonetary benefits from their labor, and some even feel recognized for having their labor be valued. Creating a binary of exploitation/unexploited when it comes to fan labor is unproductive because such a generalized portrait of popular culture fandom risks erasing the geopolitical and class differences among fans (Iwabuchi 2010). The unevenness of transnational cultural flows creates situations where some fans are being exploited for their labor while others are so marginalized by the entertainment companies due to their nationality that their labor is not even being considered for exploitation (Botorić 2022). In other words, some fans from countries that the companies do not deem lucrative enough to target will be utterly ignored and excluded from the possibility of hosting concerts or having certain dramas made available to them for streaming. In that regard, Rakuten Viki and some other Korean pop culture websites I examine in this chapter are unique for being all-inclusive in encouraging fans' participation regardless of national and cultural backgrounds.

I find it important to consider the sense of community that some fans may feel in these spaces that they do not feel otherwise because they are one of only a few in their local communities who love Korean pop culture. After all, the fans can opt to consume the dramas and the subtitles without contributing their labor, but many of them volunteer (Dwyer 2012). As Rhiannon Bury contends, "Participatory fandom has always been premised on making connections and building community with people with similar specific fannish interests, most of whom one does not already know. It is the media text that binds, not prior relations" (2017, 635).

Apart from the diverse subtitles, the website is also known for another factor that attracts the audience to the website, which, I argue, facilitates a sense of collectiveness and convergence of media and reality that aids viewers in producing certain "realities" that satisfy their racialized erotic desires. Unlike Netflix or Amazon Prime, Viki is unique in that it provides a timed comments function. Other streaming sites either forgo viewer comments (like Netflix) or have a comments section separate from the videos (like Amazon Prime).

However, on Viki, viewers' comments appear on the screen, overlapping on top of the dramas. This technology is not novel to Korean dramas; other fandoms have been utilizing similar technologies on their streaming platforms to form a sense of fan community (Xiang and Chae 2022). Jinying Li (2024) argues that these on-screen commentaries are contact zones that sustain communication between fans, as opposed to serving as a space of convergence as Henry Jenkins (2006) argues. According to Jenkins, fans' creative activities are a form of convergence culture that aims to create new derivative content. I find both Li's and Jenkins' arguments applicable to Rakuten Viki's on-screen comments. On the one hand, as Li argues, the on-screen comments are contact zones because fans are still bound by the media text and are overlaying their emotions on it rather than attempting to create new derivative content. On the other hand, there is a form of convergence occurring through the comments in that "as we have seen, the age of media convergence enables communal, rather than individualistic, modes of reception. Not every media consumer interacts within a virtual community yet; some simply discuss what they see with their friends, family members, and workmates. But few watch television in total silence and isolation" (Jenkins 2006, 26).

The on-screen comments and fan-made subtitles create the effect of multiple viewers all watching the dramas together and reacting to the scenes "live." It is as if, instead of having a talkative family member beside you as you watch the drama, you have multiple talkative digital friends with whom you are sharing the viewing experience in real-time. For example, in *Descendants of the Sun*, one of the most popular dramas on the website as of 2018, there were at least four comments per second for all sixty minutes of each episode. At times when something more dramatic happened on-screen, the timed comments section erupted to an average of twenty comments per second. These comments were in many languages, including French, Spanish, English, and Arabic, representing the Korean television drama viewership's diverse cultural and linguistic backgrounds.

Sometimes, the timed comments became entertainment and fostered a sense of collective experience and desire. For example, among the timed comments from Viki's *Descendants of the Sun*: "I CAN'T THESE COMMENTS ARE AMAZING XD" (episode 3, 43:44), "Lol oh mah gad instead of me reading the subtitles I'm reading the comments and damn they are funny!!" (episode 3, 55:57), and "I love the comment section lmaooo" (episode 3, 56:15). On Rakuten Viki the language subtitles appear at the bottom of the screen while timed comments are at the top of the screen. Although the timed comment section can be turned off, some viewers said they elected not to do so because the timed comments were part of the pleasures of watching the dramas on Rakuten Viki.

Viewers actively use the timed comments section to interact with each other and to discuss particularly salient or moving scenes. In so doing, they create a strong sense of shared space, time, and desire. The pleasure they experience on the website is similar to what Laura Marks (1998) calls "haptic visuality," which refers to the multimodal pleasures elicited by visual media: "Haptic images are erotic regardless of their content because they construct an intersubjective relationship between the beholder and the image. The viewer is called upon to fill in the gaps in the image and engage with the traces the image leaves. By interacting up close with an image, close enough that figure and ground commingle, the viewer gives up her sense of separateness from the image" (341).

Viewers "complete" the mediatized image through their imaginations by "fill[ing] in the gaps in the image." In the process, they become intimately and erotically intertwined with the mediatized images. Through timed comments, viewers utilizing Rakuten Viki literally and figuratively merge their emotions with media, so they all become part of the entertainment.

In other words, viewers' comments, desires, and emotions become an inherent part of the experience of consuming television dramas through the website. For example, during a particular scene in *Descendants of the Sun* where the hero appears to die, viewers shared their emotions:

VIEWER 1   am i the only one crying my eyes out? (episode 15, 26:29)
VIEWER 2   my heart is being ripped to pieces. (26:31)
VIEWER 3   no you are not alone (26:33)

They reaffirmed each other's emotions by articulating that the pain was not being felt alone and was an emotion shared by others. By echoing each other's emotions, individual viewers can form a sense of collectivity with other fans and, through their support, affirm that their emotions are not abnormal. The conversations that viewers carry out on the website complicate a theoretical framework provided by Vivian Sobchack (1990), who describes the dialogic and dialectic tension between the forms depicted on-screen, the bodies of the viewers, and the materiality of the cinematic film itself in one's active comprehension and consumption of the film. Sobchack argues that our interpretation of films should not focus solely on the two material forms: the person on-screen and the viewer. She points to the often-ignored materiality of the film itself in dictating viewers' attention. I suggest that the users of Rakuten Viki do not just experience tension between three materialities analyzed by Sobchack; they also contend with a fourth materiality: the presence of other viewers who share similar emotions as oneself. In the case of Rakuten Viki, the presence of the "other viewers" and the comments they leave on-screen also dictate the viewers' focus. When one sees comments such as "my heart is being ripped to pieces" while streaming the television drama, it functions to focus one's attention on the scene and bodily response to the scene. In that sense, it creates connections among Hallyu fans through emotional and corporeal experiences. Digital, human, individual, and collective emotions become inseparable in these instances of haptic connection among transnational fans.

Such a sense of shared space, time, and emotion has been mobilized to establish a shared understanding of the desire for Korean masculinity. During an episode of the *Descendants of the Sun*, a viewer commented, "Where can I find a guy like him?" (episode 1, 48:44) Others responded by saying, "He is bae," "I am in love," and "I find the other taller guy with sad eyes so hot. . . . I'm attracted to him more than the lead not that the lead isn't cute." These desires resonate with the sentiments of some Hallyu tourist informants who visited Korea to seek the answer to the question: "Where can I find a guy like him?"

"Online fantasy" and "offline realities" are not mutually exclusive here. Online discourses on websites like Viki are not just isolated figments of individual imagination—They are thoughts and desires that critically shape transnational erotic relationships. The fantasy-inspired production of "realities" dictated how my informants described and interpreted their encounters with Korean men. In this regard, it is important to make note of some racialized stereotypes of Korean masculinity that run throughout some of the online timed comments I reviewed for this book.

Although the online commenters were mainly in agreement about their desires for Korean men, some of the context and content of their desires was intertwined with Orientalist and racialized formations of Asian masculinity. Amid the celebratory remarks about Korean men's good looks, some fans commented in a manner that seemed to adhere to racist stereotypes about Asian masculinity: "he still looks like a stick" (50:01), "Pretty none aging face, deep manly voice, body hot asf [hot as f-ck] . . . smart and awesome personality how can one person be so blessed" (50:08), and "i don't know who is prettier? song haegyo or song joongki dang." (51:21). Such comments were made in response to a scene in *Descendants of the Sun* where the semi-naked male character Yu exercises at the gym. While shirtless, Yu calls the heroine Kang: one side of the screen shows the muscular, topless, sweaty, glistening male character while the other half shows a close-up of the heroine's face as she talks with the hero on the phone.

In the scene at hand, Yu is depicted as very fit and muscular; his core muscles and arm muscles are laid bare on the screen for viewers to admire. However, those contexts and the objective physical fitness of the actor playing Yu's character are ignored in the comment that claimed he looked like a stick. Other comments were compliments about the hero's good looks, yet some of them also seemed to resonate with stereotypes of Asian men's effeminacy. For example, the male protagonist is described as having a youthful-looking face but "body hot asf." This resembles how Western mainstream critics described Korean pop singer Rain when he made his U.S. debut. Hyunjoon Shin (2009) argues that Korean men's embodiment of masculinity cannot be defined by Western masculine categories. Hence, these Asian men's bodies are interpreted through the Western Orientalist lens as boyish and immature masculinity that aspires to the "mature" and "authentic" masculinity of Western men. In a similar vein, the comment describes Captain Yu as boyish and immature but alluring at the same time.

Apart from the physical features of the drama's hero, his restrained masculine sexuality was a topic of adoration and apprehension for Viki users. For instance, while watching the scene in the *Descendants of the Sun* where the hero and the heroine say farewell to each other before the hero goes on a dangerous military mission, the viewers commented:

VIEWER 1 they should have kissed:((episode 15, 14:51)

VIEWER 2 it is like they sign a contract not to kiss;((14:51)

VIEWER 3 Asian does not depend on "kiss" for every occasion (14:54)

VIEWER 4 I feel like if they kissed, they truly wouldn't be able to part ways (14:57)

VIEWER 5 I love K Drama 'cause they don't kiss in like every single scene like in USA, i always mute/skip it, it's just meh . . . (14:58)

VIEWER 6 isn't there a saying like if u don't need your characters to kiss to know they're in love, it's a good written romance? (15:12)

Some viewers felt that the scene was compromised because it did not depict the couple's passion through physical intimacy, while other fans liked the scene because of its lack of physical intimacy. Having different opinions about the relationship between physical and emotional intimacy is not problematic. However, as is the case with one of the viewers who said that "Asian does not depend on 'kiss' for every occasion," the opinion becomes problematic when viewers draw essentialist binaries between Korean and U.S. culture. As I indicated in chapter 2, the binary understanding of Korean and U.S. culture of physical intimacy not only relies on a decontextualized interpretation of Korean media's lack of depictions of physical intimacy but also contrasts the supposedly Korean norms depicted in fictional media with supposedly real-life normative cultural practices of the United States. I frequently observed such conflation of fiction and reality in the Rakuten Viki viewers' comments as well as in the forums on Soompi.

Online Fan Forum Soompi

Soompi is "the world's largest and longest-running English online media providing complete coverage of Korean popular culture" (Soompi 2024). The site description says it was created in 1998 by a single K-pop fan residing in Los Angeles named Susan Kang to share K-pop news with other fans living in the

United States. According to Kang, she created the website as a hobby and not for profit, so when it grew, she paid out of her pocket for additional servers and enlisted the help of some fans who volunteered their technical expertise (Garcia 2010). However, when the website's popularity grew exponentially and became too expensive to pay out of pocket to sustain it, Kang looked for advertisement sponsorships to maintain the expenses of running the website, which had eighty thousand people visiting it regularly (Garcia 2010). Approximately ten years after its inception, the company was consecutively bought by entertainment companies such as Crunchyroll, an animation streaming website, and Rakuten Viki, the aforementioned Asian television drama streaming website. It is now a multinational enterprise with offices in San Francisco and Seoul, and editors and contributors from around the world. It boasts users from 150 countries, making it a transnational epicenter of online Korean popular culture fandom.

While the website primarily focuses on sharing news related to Korean popular culture, during 2017–2018, when I visited the website to collect data, it also had forums where site users could interact. In particular, several forums were dedicated to discussing dating Korean men. Hallyu fans who personally experienced dating Korean men and others who wanted to experience doing so in the future shared their fantasies and experiences in these forums. Granted, instead of everyone idealizing or essentializing Korean masculinity, some dissenting voices attempted to provide a more critical perspective. For instance, two of the comments on the forum said,

> I know of many girls on Twitter, Tumblr, and in real life that have this view of Korean men, that they're all good looking and they all buy their girlfriend expensive gifts and their all this and that; only good things. Maybe *some* Korean men are like this but from my knowledge, it's rare and it's certainly a huge misconception from K-entertainment fangirls that Korean men are the ultimate boyfriends because men are men. (Oegukeen 2012)

> I wish girls would realize that a Korean guy is a guy before he is Korean. All the douchy things that other guys do, a Korean guy is likely to do too. They're not all sweet and won't run to the ends of the world and back just to cheer up their girl like in the kdramas. They're not all drop-dead gorgeous sons of chaebol owners who are foolishly in love with a plain, down-to-earth girl. So girls, don't be fooled by the kdrama industry any longer!!!! (Oegukeen 2012)

While attempting to dispel certain myths about Korean masculinity, these comments resorted to gender essentialism to claim that "men are men" and that "a Korean guy is a guy before he is Korean." These comments relied on two assumptions. First, they assume that there is a similarity in how all men behave, which makes them predictably disappointing. Second, they disassociated "Korean" with "men" or "guys." I interpret the distinction between "Korean" and "men" to be the commenter's attempt to distinguish between several binaries, such as the fulfillment of desire versus the disappointment of reality, ideal romantic masculinity versus realistic hypersexual patriarchal masculinity, and fantasy versus reality. Through the binary, "Korean" symbolizes the antithesis of the conventional notion of "men." Such dissociation between the two categories could be interpreted as a way that the site users are praising fictional representations of Korean masculinity for defying patriarchal and misogynist practices.

However, the comments risk perpetuating Western Orientalist stereotypes of Asian masculinity that effeminized them when such characteristics are deemed to be facts applicable to all Korean men rather than as one of many facets of Korean masculinity. After all, to say that "a Korean guy is a guy before he is Korean" implies that Korean men are somehow atypically masculine because of their Korean-ness and only conform to the conventional concept of a "guy" when he prioritizes that identity above his identity as a Korean, as if the two identity categories cannot coexist. While the cultural backgrounds of the people who wrote the comments are hard to decipher due to Soompi's anonymity, as I established in the introduction, Western Orientalism is pervasive and spread to the non-West as well. Regardless of the geopolitical and racial identity of the commenter, the comment reflects Western Orientalist stereotypes that presume Asian men's racial/ethnic identities predetermine their gender and sexual performances.

Some of the site's users made more overtly racist claims. For example, one fan on the online forum questioned, "What would I be curious about: Does he have a small penis? You know what they say about Asians, right" (Oegukeen 2012). In this comment, the romantic qualities of Korean television drama heroes are reconfigured to fit into the Orientalist stereotypes of Asian men that portray them as effeminate and sexually incompetent. In some of these forums, fictional stories and Orientalist stereotypes converged to reify the notion that Korean men embody "liminal" masculinity. I observed some of my Hallyu tourist informants echo the queries and discourses that I found on the forum, such as asking about Korean men's romanticism, their penis, and ways to date Korean men. Such resonance between the online forums and my informants' comments about Korean masculinity indicate that my informants were not outliers or aberrations in how they described their desires for Korean masculinity; they were a part of a larger group of fans around the world who occasionally and inadvertently interpreted Korean televisual masculinity through Western Orientalist frameworks despite their attempts to rework such frameworks.

Granted, not all fans have similar racialized erotic desires for Korean masculinity. In the forum, some women claimed they wanted certain masculine traits found most often in Korean men. For example, one commenter stated, "Why do you think women are so shallow? We dream of a guy who is going to be smart, kind, romantic, and treat us nicely. If I find a Korean guy like that, then the fact he is Korean will be an added bonus" (Oegukeen 2012). Others echoed this sentiment, claiming they were looking for particular types of masculinities and that they were not fetishizing Korean masculinity. While this commenter and those who echoed such sentiments may be telling the truth of their desires, I observed that the overarching sentiment in the forums was that the romantic, kind, and admirable masculine traits were inextricably entwined with how the site users conceptualized Korean masculinity.

I suggest that such a strong sense of shared belief in Korean masculinity formed among the site users because of another function that the site serves: fans sharing links to live-streaming of the dramas as they are being aired on Korean television. After all, a site's modality shapes what kind of fan communities the users create (Bury 2017). With few exceptions, official channels of transnational media have varying degrees of temporal lag between the airing of the media in its country of origin and abroad. Such "aesthetics of lag" is fundamental to watching videos online (Starosielski 2015). These periods of lag would be used to dub, subtitle, and edit television shows for the foreign audience. Especially in the case of Korean television dramas, due to their near "live production" style of filming, some degree of the time difference between the dramas airing in Korea and being made available in other countries is paramount.

However, some Hallyu fans use online fan spaces to bypass such "temporal lag," creating increasingly efficient time/space compressions. For instance, demanding immediate gratification of their desires, some of the transnational Hallyu fans utilized forums on Soompi to gain immediate access to the dramas. More specifically, I observed some site users sharing online links where the dramas could be watched as they were broadcast in Korea. While they watched the dramas in real-time, they screen-captured scenes and talked about them in real-time at online forums. This sharing of streaming links is one of Soompi's appeals to transnational Hallyu fans. Still, to the producers and corporations that need to profit from official channels of Hallyu consumption, these fan sites produce quandaries that can neither be abolished nor approved. After all, as Henry Jenkins (2007) argues, producers and entertainment corporations have to navigate the fine line between protecting their intellectual property and, at the same time, using fan labor to promote their films/television programs. Even if the fans initially use illegal streaming websites to access the dramas, they may eventually purchase the drama's DVDs or buy other goods related to the drama. While exploring the financial consequences of fan activities is an important research topic, it is not within the scope of this book.

Rather, the aspect of live-streaming that I find interesting and relevant for the purpose of this book is that it prioritizes viewers' emotions and interpretations of the dramas above all else. I suggest that such priority placed on the viewers' emotions and interpretations gives some viewers the sense of power to "produce" realities about Korean masculinity that satisfy their racialized erotic desires. As a new episode of *My Love from the Star* was about to start airing in Korea, one commenter on Soompi addressed other fans in the Soompi drama forum: "Finally the long awaited ep14 about to start! Happy watching *yorobeun* [Korean word for "everyone"]" (Maetawinz 2013). The fans watching the dramas began live commenting and posting copious screen captures of the dramas. "I too love reading the comments it's like hearing all LIVE," one commenter proclaimed. Indeed, the endless streams of screen captures and minute-by-minute commentary about the scenes made the drama forum read like a form of drama script. The dramas are filmed before they are broadcast, so they are not "live" per se, but the transnational fans refer to watching the dramas in Korean time as "live." Viewing it "live" brought with it the privilege of experiencing emotional tingles and heartaches and sharing those emotions as others around the world were simultaneously experiencing them. Therefore, the sense of "live" in these online drama forums did not just refer to the dramas themselves but also to sharing raw emotions with each other as other fans were concurrently feeling them.

My interpretation of "live" streaming in Soompi forums coincides with Suk-Young Kim's (2020) theoretical observation of what "live" performance means in the K-pop scene. Kim problematizes the conventional way that "live" performances are defined as antithetical to the concepts such as "digital," "mediatized," and "inauthentic" (2020, 13). Instead, she emphasizes the various forms of aural and visual pleasures the fans experience "live." I agree with Kim that expanding "liveness" is necessary, especially when we shift our attention to television dramas, which, technically, in its narrowest sense, cannot ever be "live" because they are filmed before air time. I suggest the aforementioned forum users' excitement about "live" streaming the drama was associated with the excitement of watching the new episode alongside the Korean viewers and also the excitement at being able to share the viewing experience with other fans from around the world who shared similar interests and desires. While websites like Rakuten Viki allow for a figurative sense of watching the dramas together through the timed-comments function, some illegal streaming venues permit a sense of collectiveness in watching the dramas "live."

Live-streaming television dramas, especially without subtitles, causes multiple problems that lead to the prioritization of viewers' emotions and interpretations over what is happening in the dramas. I observed comments where viewers misinterpreted a scene or merely focused on the handsomeness of the male characters and ignored what was occurring on-screen. These issues arose because illegal live-streaming means that global viewers watch dramas without subtitles. Some scholars emphasize that linguistic comprehension is essential to the popularity of transnational media and contend that Francophone countries have their web of transnational media, while Anglophone cultures have their market (Chalaby 2005).

However, in the live streaming of Korean dramas, language was not deemed fundamental to the viewers' deriving pleasure. Some Hallyu fans watched the dramas in real time without subtitles, claiming, "YES, it was AWESOME even though I didn't understand most of it lol. But loving it. Can't wait for subs/recaps," "I don't understand anything . . . but somehow I could understand the whole storyline. The emotion that Min Joon and Song Yi were feeling . . . it was felt by me. It was just wow . . . bravo" (Maetawinz 2013). Emotional connection overrode the linguistic and cultural understanding of Korean television dramas. Even without a detailed knowledge of the plot and the dialogue, the viewers claimed to understand and feel the drama and enjoy it. Despite the language barrier, they formed an emotional bond with the drama by "understanding" it through what they presumed to be the characters' emotional arc.

These viewers' claims to emotionally comprehend the drama's plot despite the language barrier are possible to a certain extent due to the melodramatic qualities of the dramas. After all, not all transnational media can be consumed purely through emotional understanding. For example, one would not be able to claim that one "understood" the news reports without understanding any of the languages in which the news was conveyed. However, this is possible for Korean television dramas because they are melodramas. Linda Williams (1991) describes melodramas as "body genres." Along with horror films and pornography, melodramas are genres of entertainment that are not just visually entertaining but also entertaining by engaging other senses of the body. The emotion-driven quality of melodramas makes Korean television dramas comprehensible to fans even without subtitles or knowledge of the Korean language.

The online fan forums' emphasis on emotions frequently made them targets of critique among other users who visited the fan community. For instance, one commenter said, "I think it's pretty funny that Korean drama watchers complain about plot holes. Like I've said before, if you're looking for realism, watch HBO" (Lollypip 2016). In this comment, HBO serials and Korean television dramas were pitted against each other at opposite ends of the entertainment spectrum, even though both produce fictional dramas with varying degrees of realism. The commenter implied that to be entertained by Korean television dramas, one has to be somewhat "illogical." During my field research, I encountered multiple incredulous people (primarily men) who remarked on how stupid they thought the Korean dramas and their female viewers were. Their sentiment echoed a phenomenon that numerous feminist scholars observed whereby entertainment deemed to cater to women is often denigrated in popular discourse as too emotional and devoid of reality (Radway 1984; Kuhn 1999).

In the context of such patriarchal critique of so-called women's genres, perhaps it is invigorating that the fans who visited Soompi did not attempt to justify the dramas by describing them as logical and unemotional. Instead, they contended that emotions, particularly emotions of love, were important and pleasurable.

> No. (my defence of kdramas, now) I've heard this argument more than I care to, and I think it just ignores the qualitative difference between the media. If kdrama were HBO-style, that subtle thing that makes kdramas what they are would be erased. Every time I've tried to watch an HBO show, after pushing myself through it, I realised I just had to stop, because it was making me die inside. Five seconds don't go by without foul language, innuendo, crass sexual references, violence, gore. The realism I want is not the HBO kind. To me, kdramas have always offered emotional realism, and I find that the more compelling storytelling. . . . I would also argue that what HBO depicts is only a slice of the realism spectrum. Nothing in my world, that I've ever seen or experienced, has ever resembled anything in one of its shows. Sure, I'll agree it's grittier and maybe edgier, but that doesn't really make it better or more realistic. (Lollypip 2016)

Many other online comments echoed the above sentiment: "And I love the subtlety kdramas offer . . . HBO would not do that, or know how to do that. I could go on and on, but I will stop here," and "HBO caters to a mostly male American audience, who is so far removed from their emotional core, that shock and awe is the only thing that gets them" (Lollypip 2016). To critique melodramas and their emotional pleasures would risk echoing some misogynist argument that pits logic against emotion and places more value on the former than the latter under the misguided assumption that logic is associated with masculinity while emotions are associated with femininity.

My reservations about the viewers' claims to have "understood" the dramas they watched without subtitles are not meant to perpetuate the misogynist discourse that discounts emotions and prioritizes logic. Instead, my reservation of the online fan forums' emphasis on viewers' emotional interpretations of the dramas is that they may create and justify decontextualized comprehension of the dramas and the masculinity depicted in them. Decontextualization creates space for Western Orientalism to assert itself in how the viewers interpret the dramas. For instance, while many viewers on Soompi condemned sexuality on American television programs, they claimed to enjoy sexual scenes in Korean television dramas. One viewer commented, "I was screaming like crazy when they [Korean television drama characters] kissed. My mum must have thought I'm crazy" (Maetawinz 2013). Others echoed similar sentiments. The viewers, who presumably had limited Korean proficiency, were unable to decipher the nuances of the dramas' scenes because they were watching the episodes "live" without subtitles. Some of the sexually intimate scenes that some viewers claimed to be "screaming like crazy" about were not romantic scenes per se but sad and melancholic scenes that did not merit the screams of joy and pleasure. Even as some viewers claimed that HBO shows lack emotional nuance and Korean television dramas are abundant with it, during "live-streaming," they could not fully catch the emotional nuances of Korean television dramas. If that is the case, what distinguishes the sexually intimate scenes on Korean television dramas from that of HBO to the point that the viewers scream with joy at the former but claim to detest the latter? Based on the sentiments in other comments, I deduce that the fan preference for sexual scenes in Korean dramas may have been related to the audiences' assumptions about "safe" Korean masculinity. Due to the assumed "safety" of Korean masculinity, their sexuality is disassociated with patriarchy or misogyny and, therefore, is more palatable than some sexual scenes on HBO that overtly objectify women (Elfving-Hwang 2011).

The online fan forum's interpretations of Korean masculinity in television dramas as "safe" could be interpreted as a positive note for change. For instance, Celine Parreñas Shimizu (2012) argues that instead of critiquing Hollywood films for depicting Asian American men as effeminate, such depictions should be reinterpreted through a more optimistic and oppositional lens as offering an alternative to white heteronormative toxic hypermasculinity. Characterization of Korean masculinity as "safe" for that reason would be a liberating critique of misogynistic and toxic masculinity around the world. While I agree with Shimizu's argument, I am wary of embracing some viewers' assumptions of Korean "safe" masculinity as a positive phenomenon because of the real-life consequences that may emerge from such decontextualized assumptions. As I noted in chapter 2, Korean televisual masculinities were developed by Korean women scriptwriters who found fundamental flaws in real-life Korean masculinity (J. S. Cho 2013; N.-J. Yoon 2015). These writers hoped to provide more idealized versions of Korean masculinity through their dramas to problematize the masculine status quo in Korea. In other words, Korean televisual masculinity may appear "safe," but that does not mean that all real-life Korean men are "safe." As with any other country in the world, Korean men embody diverse forms of masculinities; some are gentlemanly and romantic, as reflected in the dramas, but others may be violent and misogynistic. In that case, some fans-turned-tourists may put themselves in dangerous situations by engaging in wanton and carefree acts that they would not participate in in their home countries.

Furthermore, many comments on the forum seemed to imply that the notion of Korean masculine "safety" served less as a liberating method of critique against misogyny and more as a method of perpetuating certain racial assumptions about Korean masculinity. For instance, the comments on Rakuten Viki and Soompi implied that some of the site users, to varying degrees, conformed to Western Orientalist stereotypes surrounding Korean masculinity by calling them "weak" or questioning the size of Korean men's sexual organs.

The simple binary between so-called Western and Korean masculinity was a theme that played out in many Hallyu-related websites and among my Hallyu tourist informants. I suggest such a binary interpretation of Western versus Korean masculinity was a "reality" that the site users whom I observed and my informants produced to fulfill their racialized erotic desires for Korean masculinity. To fulfill their desires, Korean masculinity had to be inherently different from Western masculinity, which my informants were dissatisfied with.

Online Spaces of Korean Drama Fandom as a Mode of "Escape"?

Are the fans I observed in this chapter who used the online Hallyu spaces to meet other like-minded fans and focus on their emotional pleasures and interpretations of Korean television dramas escaping from reality into these spaces? It is hard to claim that my Hallyu tourist informants, who traveled to Korea to fulfill their racialized erotic desires, were escaping from reality. After all, their transnational travel and their dates with Korean men were very much "real." However, the question of escape becomes murkier for the larger group of Korean television drama fans who visit websites where they can find and intimately interact with other fans.

The Korean dramas and fan-made music videos allow viewers to "escape" from their daily problems. For example, a commenter said, "This Korean drama is magic because while you are watching this it gives you a different happiness and you forget all your problems in the meantime . . . just sharing my thoughts," to which another responded, "This couple literally saved my life. I was going crazy with jealousy over this guy (yeah ok I know it sounds stupid) but my friend told me to watch MLFAS (*My Love from the Star*). Their couple chemistry made me forget about that jerk I couldn't get over" (MaknaeCloud 2014). These comments received approvals from other viewers represented by dozens of "likes" to the comment. The comments implied that the commenters could escape from the painful emotions incurred through real-life events by consuming Korean television dramas, which inflicted their minds and bodies with stronger emotions that overrode the real-life grievances they were feeling before watching the dramas.

Their "escape" differs from other forms of "escape" that feminist media and literary scholars have examined regarding romance novels and soap operas. For instance, Janice Radway (1984) analyzes U.S. housewives "escaping" from their house chores in the Harlequin romance novels. However, I contend that the mechanism of "escape" for Radway's subjects and mine are slightly different. These differences are based on the fact that for Radway's informants, "escape" came in the form of printed copies of novels, while my informants' mode of "escape" came through new media. For the housewives in Radway's research, their "escape" was into the literary world of romance novels; they were physically isolated from others, and this physical isolation and immersion into the novels provided them with a sense of escape. For the Hallyu fans who commented on the websites, their "escape" happened on two registers: first, they immersed themselves in the television dramas, and second, they commented about their feelings to the anonymous online community of Hallyu fans; their "escape" was neither isolated nor solitary—it was communal. Their "escape" was an "escape" to another community that understood and empathized with their desires. While the proliferation of streaming websites that prohibit viewer interactions (such as Netflix) has influenced online fan interactions by generating fans who are not organically introduced to the online fan spaces alongside their streaming of Korean television dramas, such streaming platforms have not eradicated the various ways the fans attempt to interact with each other.

The transnational fans of Korean television dramas found multiple online spaces to form transnational connections with one another. They carried out labor to share their love for Korean television dramas with other fans and connect with them online. Since their love for Korean television dramas was still considered a marginal pastime activity in their cultures and home countries, they ventured into the digital world to find others who shared and understood their passion for Korean dramas and Korean men. In this chapter I analyzed three online venues through which transnational fans formed connections with other fans. These digital intimacies fundamentally revolved around their erotic desires for, and fantasies about, Korean men.

Although the type of transnational connections that these online spaces garnered are different from each other, they are similar in that all of them constituted a venue for fans to feel connected to each other and to express their racialized erotic desires. Whether it was the YouTube comment section, Soompi forums, or Rakuten Viki's timed comments, the fans expressed their love for interaction with other like-minded fans. They expounded on their desire for Korean masculinity and the type of romance that they will hypothetically provide. The conversations and debates in these online spaces echo the sentiments of the Hallyu tourists I interviewed for this research. They exemplify the convergence of fantasy and experience that my informants and the site users experienced. Fantasies were not merely incorporated into the viewers' experiences; instead, they created realities by shaping the erotic desires and actions of the fans who used these sites.

The dramas were so effective in (emotionally) "moving" the viewers that some traveled to Korea as Hallyu tourists. They engaged in such tourism to engage with the "realities" they produced about Korean masculinity to satisfy their racialized erotic desires. After all, hearing the crispness of food through television and imagining its texture, albeit inducing "real" physical sensations in the viewers, is a different experience from actually touching, eating, and smelling the food in person. Both are corporeal experiences, but in slightly different ways. This is why my Hallyu tourist informants visited Korea in person after seeing the dramas. If new media could substitute for every physical and emotive human encounter, Hallyu tourism would not exist. In the following chapter I analyze my Hallyu tourist informants' experiences of physical intimacy with Korean men in real life and how this intimacy complicated their perceptions of Korean masculinity.

4

"Korean Men Are So Bad Because They Are Perfect"

• • • • • • • • • • • • • • • • • • • •

Hallyu Tourists' Experiences in Korea

One of the guesthouses where I stayed with my Hallyu tourist informants had a large full-length mirror in the living room for people to check their appearances before going to clubs and bars. Every evening, I would see a slim Korean man named Wu hogging the mirror, carefully applying makeup to his face. He would deftly apply foundation, eyeliner, and eyeshadow before styling his hair with a hair straightener and carefully picking an earring to match his outfit. One day, I asked him, "How are you so good at applying makeup?" He responded, "Well, that's my passion and a job. I like makeup. Of course, I am good at applying makeup." I was not the only one who noticed his makeup skills; some of my Hallyu tourist informants would entrust their faces to him before a night of partying. During some evenings, I would see women from various countries lining up in front of him, waiting for his professional touch to make their faces appear beautiful. Some of my Hallyu tourist informants were infatuated with him. They would ask him out on dates or hook up with him in the clubs. One night, I observed him coming back from his night out with my informants with an oval-shaped bruise on his neck, presumably from one of the Hallyu tourists kissing his neck. He routinely hooked up with the foreign women he met at the clubs.

Contrary to my Hallyu tourist informants who were infatuated with Wu and Korean workers and guests at the hostel who mainly were unbothered by his fascination with makeup, some foreign men could not stand the sight of Wu. For instance, one evening, two men, one from the United States and another from the United Kingdom, sat on the sofa across from the large mirror where Wu was applying makeup to the women's faces. I was seated on the other side of the sofa and could see them exchanging glances and staring at Wu with what appeared to be contempt. After Wu left the guesthouse to go to a party, the man from the United States asked the Hallyu tourists, who were putting the finishing touches to their makeup in front of the mirror, "Why do you like him so much? He's so girly. He wears makeup." One of the women responded, "He wears makeup, and he knows a lot about makeup. What's wrong with that?" The man from the United States responded, "You should be interested in guys like us." As he said this, he raised his arms to the side at a ninety-degree angle as if to flex his biceps. The Hallyu tourists in front of the mirror rolled their eyes and returned to applying makeup. Not getting the responses they wanted from these women, the two men turned to me and said, "Aren't they weird? Liking a man like that?" I awkwardly laughed and said, "I don't think it's weird." The two disgruntled men shook their heads and left the living room to go bar hopping. These two men, who were unfamiliar with Hallyu, could not understand why some of the heterosexual Hallyu tourists desired Korean men, who, by these foreign men's standards, were too effeminate and queer to be attractive to heterosexual women. However, among the Hallyu tourists, their erotic attractions for Wu and Korean men at large were neither deemed questionable nor strange.

The interaction between the two foreign males and my Hallyu tourist informants was marked by their different conceptions of Korean masculinity. The two men were using Western hegemonic masculine conceptions of "appropriate" masculine performances to claim that Wu was "so girly" and, therefore, somehow inferior to them. Hegemonic masculinity is not mainstream statistically; only a few men practice it (Connell and Messerschmidt 2005). Despite this, hegemonic masculinity becomes hegemonic because men who benefit from patriarchy and women complicit in its perpetuation hegemonically subscribe to the ideology (Connell and Messerschmidt 2005). Under such hegemony, certain daily activities become gendered, with applying makeup and paying attention to one's appearance being such gendered activities that those aspiring to Western hegemonic masculinity should refrain from.

The inverse relation between makeup and masculinity is hegemonic in some Western cultures that value male strength and domination of space (Monocello and Dressler 2020). For instance, a case study of some of the most popular Tik-Tok influencers from the United States has demonstrated that "White, cis-gender, heterosexual, and conventionally attractive men" whose focus on their appearances translate to their exercise regimen and not their interest in beauty products are portrayed as ideal masculine men (Foster and Baker 2022, 10). The few who transgress hegemonic masculinity by virtue of their makeup or fashion are interpreted to embody hybrid masculinities that entail both masculine and feminine traits. In effect, they are displaced from hegemonic masculinity due to their hybrid gender performances.

However, there is no clear-cut inverse relation between makeup and ideal masculinity in Korea. Korean men who wear makeup are not deemed "hybrid" because makeup is not associated exclusively with femininity. Multiple Korean scholars contended that in both Korean women's and men's perceptions, men wearing makeup and taking care of their face is not antithetical to hegemonic masculinity (G. Jung 2023; J. Han and Choi 2023). Even men who denounce feminism and other liberal gender politics do not find a paradox in embracing traditional gender ideology and following a cosmetic regimen, because the latter is not deemed to be antithetical to masculinity (Elfving-Hwang 2021, G. Jung 2023). The two male tourists in the above anecdote used their cultural standards of masculinity to judge Wu's masculinity. In that regard, their judgment of Wu was marked by ethnocentrism and anti-Asian sentiments.

In contrast, my Hallyu tourist informants actively rejected such anti-Asian sentiments. While one of the main questions that this book addresses is the question of whether Hallyu perpetuates or problematizes Western Orientalism, I feel confident in saying that none of my informants were anti-Asian racists. Granted, Western Orientalism and anti-Asian racism share some similarities (Bow 2021; C. Han 2021). I agree with C. Winter Han (2021), who argues that assuming only bad people with conscious hate for members of a certain race are racists limits the possibility for society to examine other forms of systemic racism that are not couched in overt hate. In that regard, Western Orientalism is also a form of racism. Often, Western Orientalism and anti-Asian racism culminate in similar outcomes from the perspectives of those at the receiving end of them (Zheng 2016). However, in my view, the difference between Western Orientalism and anti-Asian racism in the contemporary era is the motive and the emotions behind the two phenomena. The former may be based on what appears to be attraction, fascination, or love, while the latter is motivated by and exudes hate. Were my Hallyu tourist informants successfully debunking both anti-Asian racism's hatefulness and Western Orientalism's racialized gendering and sexualizing of Korean masculinity through their desire for Korean men?

I suggest they successfully contested and fought against anti-Asian racism. However, whether they successfully dispelled Western Orientalism needs further discussion. The discourses used by some of my informants in expressing their racialized erotic desires for Korean men and the way they interacted with their Korean dates tell a more complicated story than just a liberating tale of my informants successfully overthrowing Western Orientalism. I found that in their attempts to rework Korean masculinity through Korean television dramas, they sometimes perpetuated new forms of essentialist caricatures of Korean masculinity that failed to unchain gender and sexuality from race.

In other words, Korean television dramas did not necessarily challenge the negative Western stereotypes of Asian masculinity. Instead, they altered some of my informants' points of view so that those same stereotypes now manifested as desirable traits of Asian masculinity. In these tourists' minds, Korean men "dethroned" white men at the top of the masculine hierarchy. However, ironically, such reshuffling of the masculine hierarchy reinforced and normalized the stereotypes associated with Asian masculinity because now, instead of feeling like they were racists or racially prejudiced for calling their Korean dates nonsexual or weak, such sentiments were justified by the logic that they were meant to be compliments. Paradoxically, through the shift in connotations attached to stereotypes of Korean masculinity from negative to positive, such stereotypes come to be readily accepted as a deeply ingrained and "natural" part of Korean masculine identity because they are superficially dissociated from the icky feeling of anti-Asian racism that was historically associated with such essentialist stereotypes. In the following sections I examine how, in debunking Western Orientalist stereotypes of Korean masculinity, some of my Hallyu tourist informants produce another essentialist assumption about Korean men.

Korean Men as Representative of Ideal Masculinity

The Hallyu tourists with whom I did my fieldwork asserted that Korean men offer a kind of romantic love that contrasts with men in their home countries. Elena, a Russian Hallyu tourist, claimed that she loved Korea based on how it was depicted in the dramas. Elena and several other Russian women who participated in my research share a unique positionality in that, unlike many of my informants who were from countries conventionally conceptualized as the "West," such as the United States, Canada, and countries of northern and western Europe, people have opposing notions of whether Russia is a part of the "West." At a certain point, among some Russians, the nation was considered a part of the West (Gvosdev 2007), but more recently, it has distanced itself from the West due to geopolitical reasons (Haslam 2011). It is not the scope of this chapter to closely examine the ongoing scholarly and popular debates regarding whether Russia is a part of the West. I mention this debate to introduce the discussion about "Russian Orientalism." While Russia occasionally considered itself a part of the West, scholars contend that the nation rarely appeared to consider itself a part of the "East" on par with the region comprised of South and East Asia (Kemper 2018; Van Der Oye 2010). Instead, scholars of Russia indicate that the nation developed its version of Orientalism toward these geographic spaces that uncannily echoed Western Orientalism (Kemper 2018; Van Der Oye 2010). According to these scholars, while Russian Orientalism is not an exact replica of Western Orientalism, they share similarities in that they define Asians and their culture as "Other." It is this sense of "Otherness" that I focus on in my analyses of Elena's racialized erotic desires for Korean men.

During my stay at the guesthouse, I often observed Elena lounging on the dark brown sofa in the living room. The sofa faced a large screen that was hooked up to a computer which played a nonstop cycle of K-pop music videos and Korean dramas. One day, while I was sitting on the sofa with Elena, she said, "I watch so many dramas at once. I watch more than five dramas at the same time, so if I watch one a day throughout the week, I can wait for the new episodes easily. Of course, if I find older dramas, I binge-watch them with my mom." Elena's entire week was scheduled around her plans to watch Korean dramas. She beamed with delight while talking about her meticulous weekly plans to keep up-to-date on Korean dramas. When asked what drama she watched recently, Elena stated, "*Descendants of the Sun* was good. I love listening to the original soundtracks [OSTs]. When I feel sad, I just turn on those *Descendants of the Sun* OSTs and I feel happy again. Whenever I hear the songs, it is like me falling in love all over again. Can you play it for me?" I fidgeted with the television remote control to find the requested music video. When a long list of music videos popped up, Elena excitedly jumped up from the sofa and pointed to one. "That one; that one is my favorite."

Elena and I silently listened to the *Descendants of the Sun*'s original soundtrack playing on a loop from the television. She dreamily remarked, "Song Joong-Ki's character [Captain Yu] in *Descendants of the Sun* is so bad because he is so perfect. Korean guys in dramas are so cute! And I guess in real life, too. Russian guys can be caring, but sometimes they say, 'I am too man to do this.' Still, Korean guys don't have that [problem]!"

I asked her, "Do you mean they [Russian men] are less loving?" She responded, "No, I don't think that's it. They definitely love us, but . . . I don't know how to describe it. I think . . . I think they can't show their feelings, and it makes me sad sometimes," she said as she pouted. Romantic gestures exist in different cultures in different shapes. Culturally specific gender roles and marriage and courtship traditions influence how one expresses one's feelings of love (Regis 1997). However, Elena juxtaposed fictive Korean television drama characters with essentialist caricatures of Russian men. She was not the only one to do so; many of my Hallyu tourist informants justified their desire, specifically for Korean men—both fictive and real—by comparing them to men of other ethnicities and races and claiming that Korean men were superior to others.

Do my informants' assumptions of the difference between Korean men and men back in their home countries stem from a fundamental cultural difference that makes Korean men uniquely ideal romantic partners? I do not believe this is the case, because, as I illustrate in the following sections, the discourses of "difference" that my informants were mobilizing in explaining their desires for Korean masculinity as opposed to masculinity from other cultures were equally as fictive and essentialist as the assumed "difference" between the East and the West that facilitated the rise of Orientalism in the first place.

Even though my informants were reworking their conception of Korean masculinity through Korean television dramas, such efforts still focused on two issues that made them similar to Orientalism. The first issue is the persevering attempt to explain Korean men's gender and sexual behaviors through their race as opposed to their individuality, which perpetuates essentialist notions of Korean men's masculine gender and sexual performances. The second issue is the presumption of innate differences rather than a focus on the process through which those differences were created. The project of juxtaposing supposedly preexisting differences between cultures further entrenches those differences (Gupta and Ferguson 1997; Narayan 1998). Cultural differences are not latent; they are created and entrenched through people's juxtaposition of cultures to fulfill their desires to find discrepancies. Simply put, differences are created to satisfy the desire for difference.

Applying such theory to intimate contexts, C. Winter Han argues, "Rather than blur racial boundaries, interracial desires help to create and maintain perceived racial differences through sexual behaviors that are racially marked and marketed" (2021, 105). In other words, interracial desires focused on supposedly preexisting racial differences perpetuate racial stereotypes rather than dissolve them. Just because one desires the racial "Other" does not mean that all sociocultural racial politics are erased through such desire and love. Relatedly, my informants' insistence that there was something different about Korean men versus men of other races and ethnic backgrounds was not founded on the reality of Korean masculinity's fundamental uniqueness; it was a difference produced by my Hallyu tourist informants' desires to find such differences. Their desires produced such differences because they wanted to maintain hope that there were ideal men of their dreams somewhere in this world who would make them feel special, and they believed they found those ideal men in Korea.

Desiring Korean Men's Restrained Sexualities but Making Fun of Their "Small" Penises

In particular, for many of my informants, their assumptions about the difference between "ideal" Korean masculinity and the supposedly less-than-ideal foreign masculinity primarily revolved around the binary categories of romance and sex. While they equated Korean masculinity with romance and restrained sexuality, they claimed that men of other races were sexual and unromantic. For instance, when I asked them about men back in their home countries, many of the anecdotes they provided focused on cases of discomfort they experienced at the pressure they felt to have sex with men they went on dates with in their home countries. When I asked them if they felt such discomfort with their Korean dates, my informants appeared somewhat surprised by even the thought of Korean men's sexual assertiveness and resoundingly said they did not feel such discomfort or fear with their Korean dates because they were simply "not like that."

My informants' struggle to rework Korean masculinity against the grains of Western Orientalism culminated in occasional conversations they had among themselves regarding their Korean men's penis sizes. Such discussions revealed that in their efforts to outline how Korean masculinity differed from that of other races and ethnicities so that they could justify their racialized erotic desires, my informants only had Western Orientalist ideology to fall back on to hyper-emphasize Korean men's supposed uniqueness.

One of the interview sessions on Saturday morning consisted of eight female Hallyu tourists from different parts of the world chatting over breakfast. They did not travel together but became friends by staying in the same hostel and by sharing similar interests in Korean pop culture and Korean men. One by one, they stumbled out of their beds at nine in the morning, many still in their pajamas. They came down from their rooms to the living room area, which also served as a dining room. Small, uniformly designed square tables lined one part of the wall so the guests could take their plates to these tables and eat breakfast. Some women looked visibly tired, with tousled hair and sleepy eyes, while others looked as though they had fallen straight into bed after their night of partying. They had smudged makeup and were still wearing clothes they had worn the night before. Interview questions regarding Korean popular culture that usually sparked the interviews fell flat this time among this tired crowd of women.

However, the quiet interview session turned vociferous, and the women's eyes began to sparkle when one of them broached the topic of her sexual experiences with Korean men.

MJL When did you guys get back home last night?

BRITTANY (UNITED STATES) I think we came around five or six in the morning because we didn't find any guys. Jane, on the other hand . . .

JANE (SWEDEN) Let me tell you something surprising. This Korean guy I met yesterday . . . [at this point, she dramatically lowered her voice and mouthed the words] had the biggest dick.

When she dramatically lowered her voice and leaned into the crowd of listeners, everyone leaned forward in their chair to listen to what she had to say. As Jane said "had the biggest dick," she measured out the length of it in front of her breasts using both of her hands. Other participants laughed gleefully. The quiet and sleepy living room suddenly became noisy because of our group's sudden burst of laughter. Some of the Hallyu tourists laughed so hard at the story that one of them even fell off her chair.

HELEN (DOMINICAN REPUBLIC) Wait, how big did you say it was?!

JANE It was so big and wide that I thought he did something to it. I asked him, and he said no, but I think he did and just didn't tell me. It was surprising because he was Korean. You don't think they have that big of a penis, you know?

BRITTANY I mean, I guess there are always one-in-a-million exceptions. How would he have sex with Korean girls or Asian girls with that big of a penis anyways?

JANE So, I would conclude by saying this. Swedish guys' dicks are like McDonalds. You always know what to expect, so you are decently satisfied. Korean guys' dicks, on the other hand . . . you never know what to expect.

The underlying assumption that all women in this conversation shared was that Asian men were not well-endowed; as one of the tourists stated, the Asian man with a big penis was supposedly a "one in a million exception" to an otherwise not-so-well-endowed majority of Asian men. Jane was so astonished by the Korean man's "atypically" large penis that, without considering the rudeness of the question, she asked the Korean man whether his penis was "real" or if he had surgical procedures done on it to enlarge it. In the above interview, Korean men's sexual organs were contrasted with those of Swedish men. Throughout my fieldwork, I heard numerous stories about their Korean partners' penis from my informants who, unprovoked, excitedly shared their penis stories with me. Some of them seemed to be as fixated on the topic as much as they were on the notion of romantic characteristics supposedly associated with Korean masculinity.

A long history of medical research worldwide has attempted to decipher the correlation between a social construct—race—and a biological trait: the size of sexual organs (Kuhl 2002). I am uninterested in deciphering whether there is a correlation between the two. Instead, I find the way different societies utilized the data about the supposed correlation between race and penis size to be especially relevant to analyzing my informants' discussions and fascinations with Korean men's penises. Western eugenicists used the supposed correlation between race and penis size to claim that penis size is inverse to brain size to justify their claim that Black men were supposedly less intelligent and thereby inferior to white men (Mehler 1989; Horsburgh 1995). In anti-Asian racist discourse, Asian men's supposed effeminacy and presumed sexual deviance were explained in conjunction with their supposedly small penises (Fung 2016). The underlying theme in all of these attempts to associate social constructs of race and gender with biological traits is twofold: one, to use science to justify whatever racial prejudice that the society mobilized to discriminate against people of certain races and ethnicities systematically, and two, to legitimize the desire to differentiate oneself from the racial "Other" by affirming that the differences are biological, and therefore, "natural" rather than representative of the larger society's problematic prejudice.

I do not believe that my informants consciously participated in the discussions of Korean men's penis size to continue the legacy of Western Orientalism or the eugenics movement. Instead, their conversation seemed much more motivated by postfeminist sex positivity and sexual consumerism (Jess Butler 2013). From my view, Korean men and their sexual organs seemed to merely be tools through which some of my informants were exercising their postfeminist empowerment. Similar to postfeminist fictional icons like the women in the U.S. television series *Sex and the City*, they seemed to be deriving pleasure from their own ability to freely talk about men's sexual organs. The primary topic of their conversation—Korean men's penises—provided them with much entertainment, but objectifying it and ridiculing Korean men did not seem to be the main point of this conversation. After all, the loudest and the longest bout of laughter from these women came when Jane referred to the Swedish penis as McDonald's as opposed to when they were talking about Korean men's penis. At the end of their conversation, a couple of the women turned to me and said, "This definitely should go in your book!" Others nodded their heads in agreement. I understood the "this" in their exclamation to me to mean the moment of their postfeminist excitement rather than the case of one Korean man's supposedly large penis. Occasionally, I saw similar moments of postfeminist sex talk that, from a purely non-intersectional gendered perspective, may have been liberating for my female informants but that from an intersectional feminist perspective veered close to echoing Western Orientalist discourses.

However, another reason I doubt my informants were consciously perpetuating anti-Asian racism is that I occasionally observed them displaying a keen awareness of racism when they noticed possible instances of it while they were in Korea. They would be quick to point out the potential racism that motivated the different ways that the Korean convenience store workers would treat them versus their non-white tourist friends. Furthermore, their inspirations for conceptualizing Korean masculine sexuality were not Western Orientalist texts but television dramas produced in Korea.

Granted, it is hard to pinpoint exactly where my informants derived the assumption that Korean men have small penises. I give part of the credit for such an essentialist assumption to Korean television dramas because, before traveling to Korea, other than Western Orientalism or anti-Asian racism, Korean television dramas appeared to be the primary source of my informants' knowledge about Korean masculinity. Seeing as my informants used masculine tropes depicted in the television dramas to deduce other aspects of Korean masculinity, such as their supposed romanticism, emotionality, and loyalty, it is not too far-fetched to think that the dramas' depictions of masculinity that are disassociated from the penis influenced my informants' assumptions about Korean men's penis size. Furthermore, they did not have much personal interaction with Korean men prior to traveling to Korea: none of them had dated diasporic Korean men or other Asian men before traveling to Korea.

Some Korean television dramas my informants watched popularized the trope of "flower boy" or "soft" masculinity, which I discussed in depth in chapter 2. Such masculinities deemphasize the penis. For instance, the "flower boy" implies flora and fauna; it is dissociated with corporeality or meaty flesh. By being described as flower-like, these masculinities are de-linked from the penis. Furthermore, the adjective "soft" in "soft masculinity" is also used to describe their depiction in media as well as their ways of life (S. Jung 2010). The softness as an adjective is an apt image used in contrast to the "rigid" and "macho" masculinity. The word "soft" is reminiscent of the way the nonerect male penis is described; when it is not erect or functioning sexually, it is colloquially referred to as "soft." Although these descriptions apply to the depiction of men in Korean television dramas, they are not always suitable for describing Korean men in real life. Nonetheless, as indicated above, some of my informants appeared to use the characteristics of fictional masculinities featured in Korean television dramas to assume that Korean men at large were not sexually well-endowed.

Whether their inspiration came from television dramas or not, the effect of my informants' discourse on the Korean penis is similar to the impact of anti-Asian racism and Western Orientalism. They attempt to relegate Korean men as the perpetual "Other" who exist outside of my informants' home countries and who are entirely (biologically) different from men in their home countries. My informants did attempt to twist the narrative by essentializing Swedish men's sexual organs alongside that of Korean men by referring to the former as "McDonald's," implying that they are all uniform. I find such attempts to be quite novel in that in Orientalist or anti-Asian racist discourse, Asian men's sexual organs are usually associated with food items, such as "eggrolls," and those in the gay community who are attracted to them are called "rice queens" or "sticky rice," whereas such essentialist food metaphors are not as prevalent for white men's sexual organs or attraction to them (Nguyen 2014; Wu 2018). While jokingly discussing Korean men's penis size, my informants were not using such discourse to effeminize them or to justify their lack of attraction to them, as it has historically been used in anti-Asian racism.

However, neither the essentializing of Swedish masculine sexuality nor the defeminizing of Asian masculinity solves the fundamental problem: the linking of race with gender and sexuality in conceptualizing Korean masculinity. Such a link between race, gender, and sexuality essentializes Korean masculinity. Essentializing other races to the same extent or reframing the linkage between race and sexuality as "not effeminate" is only a partial solution to a bigger problem. My informants' seeming inability to go beyond the notion of Korean men's racial identities informing their gender and sexual performances affirms that their racialized erotic desires share similar veins with Western Orientalism. Both of them associate race with gender and sexuality. My informants rebranded the previously "negative" connotations of Western Orientalist stereotypes to "positively" connotated characteristics. There is no such thing as a "positive" stereotype. Thus, the shift in connotations regarding Korean masculinity does not ultimately liberate it from the chains of racial, cultural, and gender essentialism. The process of reworking their conception of Korean masculinity at times shares similar tropes with conventional Orientalism. Nonetheless, the underlying driving force is their racialized erotic desire that generates "produced realities," which blur the boundaries between fantasy and reality.

Fictional Korean Men Versus Men in Real Life

Sometimes the realities that my informants produced about Korean masculinity based on Korean television dramas effortlessly merged with their experienced realities when they met Korean men who were as romantic and gentlemanly as the characters in Korean television dramas. For instance, my informants would frequently compare the supposed sexual aggression of foreign men to the supposed sexual reserve of Korean men to appraise the latter:

> GRACE (SWITZERLAND) I like going to clubs in Asia and, especially, clubs that do not have many tourists.
> MJL Why is that?
> EMILY (CANADA) I noticed the foreigners are so aggressive. I like going to clubs, mainly with Koreans too.
> GRACE I am not saying the Korean men are weaker. I am not saying that. That is such a bad stereotype [eyeing me] but . . . but they are actually less strong. Foreign guys are more aggressive and much ruder than Korean guys. Even at home, men do not take no for an answer. I had to punch some guys to get

them to stop harassing me. My brothers even taught me how to defend myself because of those kind of men.

EMILY Yeah, foreigners are so rude. The other night, one of them stuck their hand up my dress, and this Korean guy saw it and made that f-cker get off me.

In this instance, my informants' assumptions about Korean men being different and better than men of other races and ethnicities were affirmed by the reality they experienced. Likewise, a number of my informants told me of instances when Korean men "saved" them from foreign men's sexual advances at clubs and bars. Such similitude between their produced realities and experienced realities helped my informants solidify their belief that Korean masculinity is fundamentally different from other masculinities.

However, what happened when my informants' produced realities and their experienced realities did not match or, worse, when the experienced reality directly contradicted the realities that my informants produced after watching Korean television dramas? My informants experienced such dissonance quite often. Unsurprisingly, not all Korean men were always as they are depicted in Korean television dramas; at times, they were violent as opposed to always romantic, gentle, and sexually restrained. Grace was a Swiss tourist. As one of my other informants said, she looked like Kim Kardashian but younger and with lighter skin. I occasionally went out to bars and clubs with her and observed Korean men asking her out on dates. One day, while she was eating lunch with other Hallyu tourists, one of the tourists prodded her about her clubbing the night before, as she had supposedly separated from the rest of the Hallyu tourist group. Grace said,

So, I was at the club with you guys, and there was this Korean guy, totally my type, who was standing next to the bar. So, I started making out with him in the club for like thirty minutes and I thought, yes! I am going to have sex tonight. But when we were leaving the club, I saw him crying! I mean, he wasn't sobbing, but I could see tears on his cheeks, so I asked him in Korean, :Are you ok? Ex-girlfriend problems? Family problems?" But he said never mind, so we were walking, and then this Black guy was walking next to me out of nowhere, and apparently, he was Tanzanian living in Korea, so I said, "Oh cool, my brother is living in Tanzania," and we began talking. He spoke better Korean than me so I asked him if he could ask the Korean guy if he was OK, and the Tanzanian guy and the Korean guy with me exchanged words. I couldn't understand what they were saying, but I could feel that it wasn't really friendly, so I made the Korean guy walk with me to the other side of the road from the Tanzanian guy, and we reached the hostel, right? And I went inside but I felt like something was going to happen. I had that feeling, so I went out again, and the Korean guy and Tanzanian guy were like this.

She imitated them grabbing each other by their collars, and continued,

> I was trying to break them up, saying I don't want any trouble, but the Tanzanian guy actually tried punching the Korean guy, and all of a sudden, out of nowhere, the Korean guy had . . . what do you call them? They are not stones . . . oh, bricks! And he was throwing bricks at the Tanzanian guy, and they were throwing it at each other in the middle of the street! I stepped in the middle and held the Korean guy like this.

Grace swung her arms around in front of her in a hugging motion. Some Hallyu tourists listening to Grace gasped with concern. She said, "The Korean guy actually texted me just now asking me to go on a date with him again." I asked, "Are you going to go? He sounds unstable and dangerous." Grace, without any hesitation, said, "Why not? He doesn't seem dangerous, and he was my type!"

This anecdote locked Grace's Korean love interest and a Black Tanzanian man in fisticuffs. According to Grace, even though the Korean man and Grace were walking side by side on the street when the Korean man displayed a moment of emotionality, the Tanzanian man attempted to insert himself between Grace and the Korean man. He attempted to "steal" Grace away from the crying Korean man, who was temporarily emasculated by his display of emotions. However, when the Tanzanian man swung the first blow, rather than backing down, the Korean man escalated the fight by throwing bricks in return. In this instance, the Korean man displayed a masculinity far from "soft" masculinity akin to the drama heroes. The fight was a racially charged homosocial competition whereby the winner of the fight would "acquire" access to Grace regardless of her preferences or desires. In this instance, the Korean man was neither performing "soft" masculinity nor prioritizing Grace's (the woman's) desires; instead, through the physical altercation, he was asserting hypermasculine behavior that even endangered Grace by creating a situation where she had to intervene in the fight. His homosocial competitive behavior was not dissimilar to the homosocial competition observed in masculinities from other cultures (Fleming et al. 2019; Ringrose, Regehr, and Whitehead 2022).

However, Grace was attracted to the Korean man before the fight, and even after the fisticuffs, she still chose the Korean man over the Tanzanian man. I had a follow-up interview with Grace a couple of days after hearing the story about the brick-throwing incident. She was about to go into the communal shower when I noticed minor reddish-blue marks on her forearm and asked Grace what happened. "Oh, it must have been that guy that I told you about; wait, we can talk after I come out of the shower." She came out of the shower and started blow-drying her hair. The hallway had a mirror on top of a wooden chest of drawers that held miscellaneous beauty products that past hostel guests had left behind. She began talking when she finished blow-drying her hair and styling it with a curling iron. "I'm not sure, but I think it was the guy. You remember the guy I told you about? The one who got in a fight? I went on a date with him yesterday. I think he might have grabbed my wrist or something. I don't think it was even that hard, but I bruise really easily, so this happened." Grace lightly rubbed her wrist. "Why did you give him another chance?" I asked, to which she said:

> Well, I didn't have any other dates planned because another Korean guy canceled on me, and I didn't think he was that dangerous. He was in a mood the other night when he was throwing bricks, you know? So, I wanted to see him when he wasn't drunk. The date was not that great. He was still so possessive and giving me a hard time. He doesn't live in Seoul so he had to take the bus here, and he initially said he had other business in Seoul and he is meeting me in between his other meetings, but when we met he revealed that he didn't have any other plans. He rode the bus for three hours to Seoul just to meet me. That made me feel really pressured to give him something . . . have sex with him, whatever, you know? So, I just told him I had plans with my girlfriends and just came home. He wanted something more, but I didn't feel like it.

Even though the Korean man acted aggressively and possessively toward her, Grace did not condemn his actions. This was surprising because previously, Grace told me that if and when men back home showed remotely coercive behaviors, she fought tooth and nail against them. However, she merely brushed off the Korean man's aggressiveness. It was as if she was implementing different standards of masculine violence for Korean masculinity and masculinity back in her home country.

Although barely discussed by my informants, examples of Korean male forcefulness do exist in Korean television dramas. One popular trope of Korean dramas is the "wrist-grabbing" scene: sometimes, Korean dramas create iconic and symbolic scenes in which two different men in love with the heroine grab each of her wrists. They both grab her wrist and pull her in opposite directions, asserting their power over the heroine, who is emotionally and physically torn and rendered powerless between the two men. Although these scenes are portrayed as romantic (such portrayals are slowly changing with increased awareness in Korea regarding sexual assault), stripped of their rose-tinted effects, they are scenes of abuse whereby the men attempt to physically force the woman to act in certain ways regardless of her desires. Some scholars have critically analyzed such scenes and global audiences' responses to such scenes (Gammon

2023; Schulze 2013). The common theme in these findings is that the audience tried to make sense of it instead of simply condemning such scenes. In particular, Marion Schulze (2013) notes how the Western audience attempted to explain and trivialize the scene's violence by pointing to "cultural differences" between the audience's culture and that of Korea. They mobilized culturally relativist and essentialist discourses of "cultural difference" to justify scenes of violence in ways that align with the Western Orientalist ideology of the fundamental difference between the East and the West.

When some of my informants experienced similar situations in real life, they also attempted to trivialize the situation. Grace kept saying she thought "he doesn't seem dangerous," even though his behavior told a different story. I suggest that Grace's attempt to trivialize potentially dangerous situations that counter her drama-based conception of Korean masculinity is based on her assumption that Korean soft masculinity is equivalent to "safe" masculinity. Joanna Elfving-Hwang (2011) explains that Korean soft masculinity represents "safe" masculinity because they openly behave in an effeminate manner. These men's comfortable adoption of effeminacy makes them appear less hierarchical or patriarchal and thereby "safer" compared to men of other races and ethnicities. Furthermore, Asian men have long been stereotyped as "weak, effeminate, math and science geeks" who are the antithesis of masculine coolness and power (E.-Y. Jung 2010, 234).

Even though soft masculinity is a fictional masculinity created through television dramas and popular music, my informants produced realities through their racialized erotic desires for Korean men. In such produced realities, soft masculinity is equivalent to safe masculinity, which becomes equivalent to "authentic" Korean masculinity that is supposedly different from masculinities in other parts of the world. Hence, mediated and fantastical masculinity becomes representative of an "authentic" Korean masculinity that is fundamentally different from other racial and ethnic masculinities in the minds of my informants.

"Authentic" and "Inauthentic" Masculinities

Tourism, to varying degrees (depending on the type of tourism), is fueled by a desire for authenticity. Such a desire for authenticity generates a tourism industry that focuses on making those desires come true. In other words, the tourism industry produces realities that live up to tourists' desire for difference and authenticity. In conventional Hallyu tourism, tourists from Japan and China would participate in a group tour organized by the tourism industry to provide them with the ultimately "sanitized" experience where they would visit the television drama filming sets and other locations that would cater to their desire for authentically emotive experiences (Y. Oh 2018). Those spaces would be designed to help the tourists feel like they are traveling into the media rather than traveling to Korea (Choe 2016). Other companies that facilitate mediated tourism, such as the *Sex and the City* tour through New York City, also strive to provide a "sanitized" perception of the city that the fans of the show expect to see when they visit (Sadler and Haskins 2005). Furthermore, in countries with a big sex tourism industry, the sex workers alter their appearances and actions to conform to the tourists' desires. As a case in point, some Jamaican men would wear their hair in dreadlocks and pretend to be Rastafarian to cater to tourists' desires (Pruitt and LaFont 1995). In these instances, the preservation of the tourists' desires relies on the tourism industry's efforts to provide a "sanitized" authentic experience for the tourists—and on tourists' efforts to ignore certain aspects of the knowledge that do not conform to their expectations. However, in the case of my Hallyu tourist informants, without a tourism industry to help them sustain their desires for authentic Korean masculinity, they were left to their own devices to maintain their desires. After all, my informants' Korean dates were not sex workers who had financial incentives to cater to the women's desires.

I found that another method that my informants deployed to maintain their belief in Korean masculinity's supposed fundamental difference from the masculinities back in their home countries was to distinguish between "authentic" and "inauthentic" masculinities. They condemned the men who performed what they believed to be "inauthentic" Korean masculinity. Concurrently, they would criticize themselves for not working hard enough to find the "authentic" Korean men. In other words, in my informants' minds, it became the individual men's fault and my informants' fault that their relationship did not turn out to be as romantic as the television dramas. They did not consider the possibility that perhaps their unfulfillable desires that are based on idealized and fantastical masculinities may be the cause of their dissatisfaction with Korean men. I interpreted their desire to maintain their belief in idealized perceptions of Korean masculinity to be indicative of the extent to which they found the normative masculinity and dating culture back in their home countries to be problematic. As I indicated in the previous section, my informants believed that Korean men embody soft masculinity that is safe and either desexualized or sexually restrained. Therefore, when my informants encountered men who were overtly sexual, they accused these men of being "inauthentic."

I interviewed Jessica at a cool, air-conditioned café. Jazz music played in the background, and constant fizzing and clanking from the espresso machines blended into the music. Large slabs of roughly cut wood served as coffee tables and were matched with straw-woven seats. The café created a milieu of laid-back space. Jessica was a Danish woman in her early twenties. When I walked around the streets with her in Seoul, some Koreans unfamiliar with white features openly ogled at her and even told her she looked like a porcelain doll. When discussing Korean television dramas, she frequently told me of her attraction toward Korean culture and men. On one occasion, my questions about the types of dramas she enjoyed turned into a conversation about Korean men.

MJL What exactly are you looking for when you go on dates with Korean men?

JESSICA Mostly a relationship. It is fun to have sex and stuff, but that is kind of like we are using each other. You know? It is not anything emotional or stuff like that. We just use each other, and that is the end. Those things are totally different. If I have someone I really like, sex and all that stuff are not that important. We will be doing a long-distance relationship anyway, so we will not be having much sex. What matters is the heart and feelings and caring about each other enough to keep in contact through long distance.

Jessica espouses the binarism of emotional connection and sex. While she claims that the former is what she truly desires, she trivialized the latter as two people "using" each other to satisfy basic sexual instincts.

She seemed to revel in the idea that some Korean men she interacted with, particularly a guy named Joseph, whom she had a special interest in, appeared to be interested in her as more than a sexual partner because he mostly appeared to be sexually restrained when they met, except for their last few encounters that became sexual. She believed that because of his sexual restraint, they could successfully carry on a long-distance relationship after she returned to her home country. However, Jessica's relationship with Joseph changed when she returned to Denmark. Through follow-up interviews, I found out that, despite her efforts, she soon lost contact with Joseph because he no longer showed any interest in her. Many of my informants had similar experiences: they would return to their home countries expecting to have long-distance relationships with their new Korean boyfriends. However, their hopes would be crushed when the Korean men quickly appeared to lose interest in them now that they were physically distant. According to Jessica, Joseph purportedly blamed his bad English skills for his lack of responses to her messages and phone calls. Considering Jessica's fluency in Korean, his explanation for his lack of responsiveness did not make sense to me. Jessica said, "Some Korean guys are just f-ckboys. Take this advice from a girl who has slept with and tried to date many Korean guys. I know this is not a problem just with Korean guys, but I dated two Korean guys for about three months each, and both relationships ended because our relationship resulted in nothing but sex".

Even though she used to often use Korean words or Korean pronunciations for English words when she was describing Joseph, such as *jalsaenggyeosseo* [handsome] and *romaentikhae* [Korean pronunciation for being romantic], she used the English term "f-ckboys" to describe Joseph now that he disillusioned her. It is also possible that she did not know a Korean version of the term "f-ckboys," such as *baramdungi* or *hosaekan*, because her knowledge of Korean terms was derived from Korean television dramas. These terms do not appear frequently in the dramas compared to positively connoted verbs and adjectives to describe Korean men, such as some of the terms she initially used to describe Joseph. When she was faced with insurmountable evidence of his deviance from soft masculinity, instead of reflecting on whether her assumptions about Korean masculinity were too essentialist, she resorted to claiming that those men who perform masculinities other than soft masculinity were inauthentic Korean masculinities. These "inauthentic" men did not merit the Korean adjectives that she only reserved for "authentic" Korean men.

Although I understood and sympathized with Jessica's anger and sense of betrayal, I also wondered whether the sense of betrayal could be justified. After all, to my knowledge, Joseph did not indicate that he was like a Korean television drama's romantic hero. That was what she assumed. From his perspective, she may have easily been a casual sexual partner whom he could spend time with over the summer without any strings attached. As I analyze in more depth in chapter 5, some of my Korean male informants seemed to treat their Hallyu tourist partners in such ways. If that was the case, Joseph may have felt that communicating with Jessica when she was not residing in Korea made the relationship too serious, and he decided to end it. That does not make his masculinity inauthentic or condemnatory; it just means that he performed a different type of masculinity than soft masculinity, as do many men.

Even as some of my informants expressed their anguish, they seemed to move on from these men fairly quickly. Therefore, I hypothesize that perhaps Jessica and some of my other informants' frustration at "inauthentic" Korean masculinity may not have been anger directed toward the men per se but at the limitations of postfeminist consumerism as a replacement for feminist activism. In other words, even if they may have felt hopeful when they envisioned Korean masculinity as unique from other types of masculinities, felt empowered when they were openly talking about sex and men's penis sizes, and felt invigorated when they met Korean men who lived up to their romantic standards, they may have realized that such moments do not change the pervasiveness of toxic masculinity in each cultural context, including Korea. After all, during the time I was conducting fieldwork, the online clash between Korean radical feminists verging on misandry and anti-feminists verging on misogyny started spilling over to off-line gender wars (Jeong and Lee 2018; G. Jung and Moon 2024). It was revealed after the fact that around the same period as my fieldwork, some young Korean men were using digital technology to sexually victimize women in large numbers in what became known around the world as the Nth Room Incident (G.-S. Kwon and Cho 2020). My tourist informants could not escape the reality that some men choose to perform toxic masculinity, even though they hoped they could escape it by traveling to Korea.

Jessica looked to Korean men as a solution to her dissatisfaction with the supposed male callousness: Korean men were supposed to be romantic, caring, gentle, and overall different from men back home. Therefore, she was especially scathing toward Korean "f-ckboys"—like Joseph—who purportedly prioritized sex over emotional intimacy and thereby provided a challenge to her assumption that Korean men could serve as antidotes to her dissatisfaction with dating culture and masculinity back in her home country. However, she soon met another Korean man after her "breakup" with Joseph. Although Jessica felt disappointed that Joseph shattered her fantasies about Korean masculinity, such disappointment did not deter her from desiring Korean men and seeking them as ideal intimate partners. When I asked her why she pursued Korean men despite repeated experiences with them that disappointed and angered her, she seemed to blame herself for not being able to see through those types of "inauthentic" men: "I think I wasn't trying hard enough. I wasn't able to see that they were lying and believed them too fast. Next time, I'm going to go slower and try harder." Instead of thinking about adjusting her expectations for Korean men, she accused the men of being deceptive and blamed herself for being gullible. While blaming these men for being "fake" and inauthentic, she pursued other romantic relationships with Korean men in hopes that they would be the ones to comply with her produced realities regarding Korean masculinity.

My informants' sense of betrayal at "inauthentic" Korean masculinity and their love for it has less to do with their Korean dates' actions. Instead, their accusations of inauthenticity or expressions of affection toward Korean men were all based on my informants' expectations stemming from the realities they produced through their racialized erotic desires for Korean masculinity. I believe Leslie Bow's observation that "racist love transforms into racist hate with dizzying speed" (2021, 195) most accurately describes the emotional pendulum between condemnation and adoration that my informants felt toward Korean men. Their racialized erotic desires transformed into racialized hatred from one week to another. I suggest that this was possible because the essence of my informants' desires for Korean masculinity relied on their *interpretation* of Korean masculinity and the subsequent reality they produced through their desires that were closer to fantasy than to their experienced reality. In other words, even when my informants' Korean dates did not change their masculine performances, if my informants' interpretations of their behaviors changed concurrently, their desires for Korean men quickly turned into hate. For instance, Jessica interpreted Joseph's not being proactive about sex early in their relationship to mean that he embodied soft masculinity and sexual restraint, so she loved him. Even when their relationship became more sexual, which defied prototypical soft masculine traits, because she interpreted his behaviors as romantic and caring she was able to maintain her affection for him.

However, when he wanted to stop their relationship, she reinterpreted all of his actions to claim that he was an inauthentic "f-ckboy" and to hate him. Her swing of emotion between love and hate for Korean masculinity was entirely dependent on her interpretation of his masculinity based on her knowledge of Korean televisual masculinity, rather than on what he did or did not do. In that regard, I find it imperative to compare my Hallyu tourist informants' interpretations of the mediated Korean masculinity to that of my Korean women informants to compare how their desires are different from each other due to the different ways that Western Orientalism influences their perception of Asian masculinity.

Different Desires of the Korean Women

On numerous occasions throughout my field research, I talked to Korean women about my research. As if they coordinated their responses, most of them, after hearing about my research, scoffed at the Hallyu tourists who traveled to Korea to form intimate relations with Korean men. Some of them claimed to feel sad for the foreign women and their "delusions" about Korean men. One Korean woman I talked to said, "Well, if they expect to find Korean men in real life who are like the drama characters, they are in for a rude awakening. Korean men in real life are nothing like the fictional characters in the dramas." I disagree with her generalized doubts about Korean men because they embody disparate masculinities, and some can embody masculinity quite similar to the drama heroes. However, she reflected sentiments similar to those of Korean drama scriptwriters, many of whom claimed that their dramas were inspired by the discontent they felt with real-life situations and masculinities.

The points at which Korean women and Hallyu tourists derived pleasure from Korean television dramas differed. For my Korean female informants, everyday life in Korea was a place they needed to escape from, while for my Hallyu tourist informants, everyday life in Korea was a place they wanted to flee toward. Much like the women in Janice Radway's (1984) research on Anglophone readers of romance fiction, who claimed they read these novels for a sense of "escape," the Korean women whom I talked to expressed that the pleasure of watching Korean television dramas came from a sense of "escape" into the drama-world. One Korean woman said, "We see Korean men in our everyday lives, from our fathers and brothers to our boyfriends and colleagues. We see too many of them to believe that they are anything like the television drama characters. I watch dramas because they show men who are nothing like men in real life." This sentiment was echoed by other Korean women with whom I did my fieldwork. Since my research focused on exploring Hallyu tourists' consumption of television dramas, I only conducted several cursory interviews with Korean women. However, my Korean female informants' sentiments echoed those found in Youna Kim's (2009) book, which focuses on extensive ethnographic research on Korean women's consumption of television dramas.

According to Youna Kim (2009), depending on the Korean women's class and age, they differed in what types of emotional satisfaction and fulfillment of desire they derived from watching television dramas. Although the details of why and how Korean women in Kim's research viewed television dramas differed, the underlying theme in their motivations was that they used the dramas as a tool for reflexivity to aspire toward dreams of a better life than what they had. In other words, Kim refers to these women's reflexivity through the dramas as "journeys of hope" (2009, 210). According to Kim, dramas facilitate a reflexive journey within oneself to find hope for something better than the status quo. Similarly, my Korean female informants disassociated their lived experiences from the television dramas. None of them racially eroticized Korean masculinity. They could clearly distinguish between the fantasy of the dramas and their lived realities when it came to Korean masculinity. If they were producing romanticized fantasies about masculinity, it seemed to be about non-Korean masculinity. After all, even though many Korean women whom I talked to claimed that they watched Korean television dramas, they were uninterested in talking about it in depth and were more interested in talking about foreign television dramas, such as that of the United States. This led me to wonder whether, similar to how some Hallyu fans fantasize about Korean masculinity, some Korean women do the same with foreign men. While there has not been published literature that specifically examines whether there is such a phenomenon, Korean women in Kim's (2009) research appear to essentialize and fantasize about modern and liberated U.S. women. If such fantasies and essentialist assumptions about U.S. women exist, it is possible that similar essentialist fantasies could exist for U.S. men as well.

After all, Lisa Yuk-ming Leung (2004) claims that transnational audiences tend to engage in further "hyper-reading" of television dramas than local viewers by interpreting the fantastical elements of media texts into reality and incorporating them into their daily lives. Even though Hallyu tourists of different races appeared to participate in such "hyper-reading" of television dramas, only a few were able to experience the privilege of having their hyper-reading be reflected in real life. Unlike some tourists who had the privilege of fantasizing and having at least a fair chance of their fantasies coming true, some non-white Hallyu fans were unable to have such a luxury.

Non-White Hallyu Tourists' Experiences with Racism and White Tourists' Experiences with Racial Prejudice

Unlike conventional sex tourism or romance tourism, whereby tourists from economically affluent countries usually travel to less affluent countries to engage with a sex work industry that caters to their desires, my Hallyu tourist informants did not have the luxury of having their desires being catered to by financially strapped Korean male sex workers who were willing to do anything to satisfy them. Instead, most of the time, the men they were encountering were those who had no incentive, other than satisfying their own racialized erotic desires, to engage with the Hallyu tourists. These were young men, most of whom claimed to be college students (which is unsurprising because a majority of Korean high school students proceed to get a college education, one of the highest percentages among the OECD countries). From my observation, most of them were not looking to earn money by giving the tourists the "boyfriend experience" or having sex with them. Instead, many of these men were highly selective because they paid for much of the dating expenses. Their selectiveness meant that my informants not only had their produced realities occasionally shattered by men who defied their expectations, but they also experienced moments when they were conscious of how they were being subjected to racialized eroticization by some Korean men.

Beth and Bella are Black women from the United States. Over breakfast one day, Beth and Bella confided in me and some other tourists that they planned to create their own YouTube channel; they asked us what topics they should focus on in their videos. One of the tourists suggested, "Maybe something about fashion. You guys are always so fashionable, and you s look like models!" Other women in the vicinity nodded in agreement. Another tourist suggested, "You should make a video about dating Korean men. I think Black-Asian babies are so adorable." Beth laughed and said, "But it is harder to find Korean men interested in you if you are darker than Korean girls because the ideal of beauty here is to be white, so if girls who go opposite of that, they are not popular. I am not saying this to talk about racism or anything or say that we [darker-skinned women] have it hard, but that is just the way it is. Even Southeast Asian girls are not popular here."

Beth brought up the issue of race but attempted to depoliticize it by saying that she was not trying to talk about racism. She presumably tried to depoliticize her comments because most of the other Hallyu tourists who were participating in the conversation were white, and she may not have felt comfortable talking about racism to a group of white women. However, Beth brought up a very significant point about colorism and racism in Korea. Another tourist responded to Beth's comment,

Yeah, I know! My friend is Iranian and Southeast Asian mixed, and she used to love Korea and visit it so often and post pictures on Facebook, but all of a sudden, all of that was erased from her Facebook and Instagram, so I messaged her saying, yo, what's up with that? And she said she had really bad experiences in Korea with racism, and I guess more than that, Korea in real life was not as she expected from the television dramas, and she was disappointed with that, you know? The Korean dramas let her survive the hard times she had in middle school and stuff, and she had a very grand image of Korea, and the reality did not live up to expectations, I guess.

Class, nationality, and gender intersect with racism to form a system of prejudice against certain foreigners in Korea. As I will discuss further in chapter 5, the mutual racialized erotic desire between my Hallyu tourist informants and their Korean dates primarily applied to white tourists. For the non-white tourists, the desires were not necessarily mutual. Instead, similar to Beth, many of them restrained their desires, knowing that those desires would not be met by Korean men.

However, unlike the Iranian woman in the above quote, many of my informants of color did not necessarily give up their racialized erotic desires for Korean masculinity entirely. They knew that they were going to have a more difficult time than their white counterparts, but that did not deter them from the idealized perceptions of Korean masculinity. It is ironic how, even despite non-white tourists having a clear understanding of the trend of colorism or racism in some Korean men's dating preferences, they still coveted these men who racially discriminated against this group of women. Perhaps it was because the racism and the colorism they experienced in Korea felt different from those they experienced back in their home countries.

After all, although white supremacy is part of the reason that non-white Hallyu tourists had a more difficult time finding Korean boyfriends compared to their white counterparts, that did not mean that my white tourist informants were idealized by their Korean dates. As a case in point, even though my white informants were not experiencing the same type of racism in the Korean dating scene as my Black informants, they were still experiencing some form of racial prejudice when some Korean men mistakenly identified them as sex workers.

For example, one day, one of my white informants posed a question to me. She asked, "Do you know what 'Russian' means in Korea?" It was clear from her tone of voice that she already knew the answer but was asking me this question because she wanted to tell me something. Other tourists in the vicinity were also listening to our conversation; their eyes sparkled, and they were smiling as if they knew the answer to the question as well. I asked, "I don't know, what does 'Russian' mean in Korea?" Several of my informants shouted, almost in unison, "It means, 'Are you a prostitute?'" One of them explained, "You know prostitution is illegal in Korea, right? So Korean guys, when we are in clubs, ask us, "Are you Russian?" At first, I didn't know what it meant, but now I know! They were asking if I was a prostitute." One of my informants wondered aloud, "Do they actually want us to be prostitutes, or are they asking because they don't want to engage with us if we are prostitutes?" None of us had an answer to that question. As I discuss in more detail in chapter 5, a significant number of sex workers in Korea are white women from countries like Kazakhstan and Russia (H.-J. Lee 2019), which is why my white informants were sometimes mistaken as sex workers. Women from Russia and Eastern European countries (along with South American and Southeast Asian women) travel to Korea to work in the sex industry because it supposedly guarantees much higher pay than if they were working in the same occupation in their home countries. While the sex workers' transnational travel occurs in drastically different contexts from that of my tourist informants', once they are in bars and clubs in Korea, the Korean men, like the ones that my informants in the above anecdote encountered, could not tell the difference between the two groups of women and treated all of them as de facto sex workers.

My tourist informants' and their Korean dates' mutual racialization of the "Other" and the imposition of it on each other is where they differ considerably from other forms of interracial relationships involving Koreans and non-Koreans with considerably skewed power dynamics that scholars have closely examined. For instance, Joane Nagel (2000) analyzes the Korean prostitution industry in Kansas to argue that the industry runs on a global economy of desire that underlies the global movement of money, people, media, and ideologies. In explaining such an economy of desire, she uses the term "ethnosexual frontiers." Nagel's definition of "ethnosexual" refers to the intersection of ethnicity and sexuality that relies on each other for meaning. Relatedly, she refers to the sexual encounters between the Korean female sex workers and their mostly white male clients as ethnosexual frontiers where people forge sexual links with each other. While the interaction between my tourist informants and their Korean dates could also be seen as ethnosexual frontiers, instead of using that term, I choose to use the term "racialized erotic desire" to refer to my tourist informants' desires. This is because Nagel's concept of ethnosexual frontiers, stemming from the power imbalance between Korean sex workers and foreign male clients, was unsuitable for conceptualizing the relative parity between my tourist informants and their Korean dates. In Nagel's (2000) article, she mobilizes the term "ethnosexual frontier" to refer to a clear power hierarchy between the Korean sex workers and their American male clients, whereby the latter engages in a fantasy of white saviorism and the former fantasizes about being rescued from poverty. As I have indicated thus far in this chapter, such a clear power hierarchy did not exist between my tourist informants and their dates. I mobilize the concept of racialized erotic desires to emphasize that neither my tourist informants nor their Korean dates were the ultimate "victims" or "perpetrators" of racial essentialism. They were mutually navigating the perilous landscape of desire complicated by geopolitical contexts and Orientalism.

It is not just one's race that factors into foreigner-discrimination in Korea; geopolitical factors also function heavily in such discrimination. Some Korean men offensively equated "Russian" nationality with female hypersexuality and availability. Even though not all of my informants were from Russia, due to their phenotypic resemblance to the stereotypical image of Russian women—white with blond hair and blue eyes—they were mistaken for "Russians" or sex workers: in such instances, their whiteness did not grant them the privileges of being white. Instead, they were stigmatized for their "overt" or phenotypic "foreignness." The privileges they assumed they experienced as tourists from developed nations were erased through such exchanges with Korean men when they realized they did not have much privilege over their Korean dates, other than the fact that they were tourists who were temporarily free from the duties and expectations of their daily lives. It seemed as though such exchanges occurred often enough that many of my tourist informants were aware of the hidden meaning of the "Are you Russian?" question.

The above anecdotes reveal that there are multiple axes of racialization between my informants and Korean men. While my non-white informants were subjected to racism through the lack of opportunities to become intimate with Korean men, my white informants were subjected to a form of racialized bias by being perceived as sex workers who are always expected to be sexually available. Here, I find it imperative to emphasize that I do not believe my white tourist informants' practice of going on numerous dates and having sexual relations with many men in Korea was because they were conforming to the stereotypes of Western white women as being sexually "freer" than women of other races and ethnic backgrounds. Such essentialist entwinement between white women's race and sexuality has been promulgated by a paradoxical assemblage comprised, on the one hand, of Western white feminists who aspired to help sexually "liberate" non-Western women by portraying all Western white women as more sexually liberated than non-Western women (Abu-Lughod 2013) and, on the other hand, of patriarchal men in non-white or non-Western cultures who use such essentialist caricatures to warn women within their communities not to be like the "promiscuous" white women (Nader 1989). My white Hallyu tourist informants' relationships with Korean men were not about them conforming to such stereotypes. Instead, they could engage in such relationships because of the geopolitics of desire that made them more erotically desirable to their Korean dates than women of other races.

The racialized experiences of my white informants being perceived as sex workers are relatively new phenomena that came with the rise of Korea's economic status in the twenty-first century. According to Erin Aeran Chung (2019), in contemporary Korea, new racial hierarchies are emerging due to the influx of migrant workers to Korea. The white sex workers in Korea are examples of migrant laborers who are creating new racial hierarchies in Korea

(E. Chung 2019). The nation's system of racial bias is intertwined with colorism, classism, sexism, and prejudice against certain nationalities. Such a system impacted my informants through the Korean concept of *injongchabyeol* [a system of racial prejudice]. Hence, they were not able to impose their assumptions about Korean masculinity onto men who were passive recipients of such impositions. In the following chapter, I will analyze the racialized erotic desires of my Korean male informants and how these men's gender performances were formulated about men of other races as well as through their intimate relations with the Hallyu tourists.

5

"How Can We Compete with Men Like That?"

• •

Korean Men's Perception of
Their Newfound Popularity

"Nuna [elder sister], isn't he so good-looking? How can these foreign guys look like that with their noses and eyes?"[1] The young Korean man who said this to me had short-cropped hair, which is typical for Korean men serving mandatory military service. He wore a black baseball cap to hide his short hair. He had a small, youthful-looking face with round eyes that reflected his youth. His name was Han, and he said he was in his early twenties. He wore a gray sweatshirt and black pants with sneakers. Apart from his hairstyle, he looked like a typical college student. He was a guest at one of the hostels I stayed in for my field research. From my understanding, he was on a short vacation before his military service began. He was staying at the hostel to enjoy his freedom before he had to spend years completing his mandatory military service. I met him for the first time when the hostel arranged a night out for all the guests staying there. The group was mostly Hallyu tourists from various countries, including Canada, the United States, Switzerland, Russia, Singapore, and Turkey. Han and I were the only two Koreans in the group. The Hallyu tourists eyed Han throughout the night; they appeared interested in him, glancing shyly at him while giggling among themselves. We went to a damp and dark club with blazing strobe lights. Scantily clad, sweaty men and women of all nationalities and races were dancing to the blaring beat of K-pop songs. While wading through

a crowd of jam-packed dancing bodies, Han yelled the above sentence in Korean into my ears as he pointed to one of the men in the club.

I was on friendly terms with the man Han pointed out to me; I had become acquainted with him at another hostel where I stayed while doing field research. His name was John, and he was a tourist from the United States. He had light brown and slightly curly hair and shockingly blue eyes. When we first met, John introduced himself to me as a student from the Midwest. Han said, "I mean, this is so unfair. . . . Life is so unfair. How can we compete with men like that?" He shook his head and walked away to get more drinks from the bar. Ironically, Han himself was attractive enough for the Hallyu tourists in our group to be eyeing him with interest. I overheard some foreign women in the bar talking about how cute he was. However, he compared himself to a white man from the United States and considered himself physically inferior to him. At that moment, Han was not competing with John for the attention of any specific woman at the bar, nor were they on hostile terms throughout the night when I introduced them to each other. Nonetheless, Han felt he was in perpetual competition with a man from the United States.

Some Korean masculinity is shaped through—for lack of a better word— "competition" with men of other races; these "competitions" may be imagined, psychological, or physical. In this type of "competition," winning the Hallyu tourists' affection becomes symbolic of one's masculine superiority over the racial "Other." For instance, I went to a crowded club with my Hallyu tourist informants. Two tall Korean men approached the white tourists from behind and began grinding themselves against the tourists. After glancing back and checking out the men, the tourists continued to dance with them. I was standing right next to them and overheard the Korean men telling each other in Korean, "Hold on to your girl and be careful; there are many foreign men around us who may take these girls away from us." While kissing and grinding with the tourists, they would constantly look around, seemingly to "guard" against foreign men's intrusion, and tightly held onto the white tourists' waists. When their friends came along, these two men proudly nodded to their friends. I interpreted their interactions with their friends as an assertion of their masculinity and masculine sexual achievement.

The Korean men whom I talked to and observed were not the only ones who attempted to formulate their masculinity through competition with foreign masculinity. In the mid-1980s, almost forty years before Han compared himself to John and the two tall Korean men at the club guarded against foreign men, Millie Creighton (2009), a white woman researcher, asked a group of Korean men to define their masculinity. They answered, "The one who looks intelligent—he's the Chinese. The one who looks rich—he's the Japanese. And the one who looks sexy—he's the Korean" (Creighton 2009, 11). A critical difference between my anecdote and that of Creighton's is that while the Korean men in the 1980s compared themselves to other East Asian men, Han compared himself to a white U.S. tourist and not to other Asians in the club. Han's point of comparison went beyond the racial boundaries of East Asia. His primary concern was how he would romantically and sexually compete with white Western men for heterosexual (white) women's attention. Such competitiveness was one of the recurring themes I observed among some Korean men I interviewed and observed.

Such cross-racial masculine competition in the Korean context has been extensively examined in relation to militarism. For instance, scholars hypothesized that Korean men felt emasculated by American men during the immediate aftermath of the Korean War as U.S. soldiers established bases around the peninsula (J. Lee 2009; J.-M. Park 2015). Although some scholars have conducted interviews or ethnographic research to examine personal accounts of Korean men and how they perceived their masculinity in relation to Western militaristic masculinity (A. J.-S. Lee 2019; Gage 2013), few have examined Korean masculine performance in relation to Western masculinity in romantic circumstances.

This chapter contributes to the existing body of work that considers Korean masculinity in transnational and interracial contexts by analyzing how Korean masculinity is shaped through erotic encounters with white women. I analyze the interracial and transnational encounters between my Hallyu tourist informants and my Korean male informants through the latter's perspective. I ask: How did my Korean male informants formulate their masculinity in relation to transnational dynamics of race, gender, and sex? How did Hallyu and its transnationality influence masculinity among my Korean male informants? By addressing these questions, I argue that Korean men are not just passive recipients of Hallyu tourists' reworking of Korean masculinity through Korean television dramas. They did not need their images to be reworked by foreign women on their behalf. Instead, they were actively asserting their own perceptions of masculine gender and sexuality in their encounters with my tourist informants. They were active agents who pursued their own racialized erotic desires.

The majority of Korean men whom I interviewed and observed were college students in their early twenties who had close interactions with my Hallyu tourist informants. Some Korean men were in their late twenties or early thirties and worked at the hostels frequented by the Hallyu tourists. I also interviewed non-Korean male tourists whose travels to Korea were not inspired by Hallyu. While they were interested in Korean pop culture and had some knowledge about the topic, they were not avid fans in the same way as the Hallyu tourists. They were backpackers from countries like France, England, the United States, New Zealand, and the Netherlands who were touring different Asian countries. These tourists were also in their twenties, and I deduced from the long duration of their travel—lasting from a month to six months—that they had expendable income and resources to travel around the world for an extended period of time.[2] I examined the foreign men's perspective critically because some expressed overly judgmental and excoriating sentiments about Korean masculinity (as seen in the anecdote at the beginning of chapter 4). Nonetheless, interviewing them was necessary because, as an ethnic Korean woman, I was not always privy to the discussions men had with each other. Often, Korean men would stop talking or filter their conversation when talking to me. Hence, the foreign men's accounts provide some interesting insight into encounters I could not experience. The concept of Korean masculinity stirred strong emotional responses among my Korean male and foreign male tourist informants. Most of these strong opinions revolved around issues of Korean men's racialized sexuality and racialized desires. The men I talked to and observed provided insight into the complex and constant negotiations between Hallyu tourists and their Korean dates to fulfill their disparate racialized desires for one another.

Negotiating Disparate Desires: The "Mutual Gaze" and the Disparate Conceptions of Race

When analyzing the politics of tourism, scholars often look to situations in which the tourists hold more power than the locals. For instance, the tourist's gaze is often interpreted as being politically charged: it judges as well as denigrates and objectifies certain cultures and people, often based on imperialist stereotypes (Werry 2011). However, countering the tourist gaze, the observant gazes of the locals are also judgmental and politically charged; Darya Maoz (2006) calls it the "mutual gaze." According to Maoz, "The gaze does not belong to the tourists only" (2006, 225). She claims that tourism is an elaborate performance centered on the imagined notion of authenticity and that the tourists and locals participate in elaborate performances that shape how they behave in each other's presence. To extrapolate, she argues that the tourists seek and demand "authentic" experiences in the toured spaces because that is what the locals expect of the tourists. Meanwhile, the locals put on a show based on what is expected of them by the tourists.

Although I agree with Maoz's point that the gaze is not one-sided, her argument is premised on a strictly monetary and stage performance-centered approach to tourism. What about tourist experiences that occur off-stage? When money is not a factor, do the locals comply with the tourists' expectations and demands? Could there be nonmonetary reasons that the locals abide by the tourists' expectations? These questions are especially pertinent in the case of Hallyu tourism compared to other researched cases of sex tourism or romance tourism.

Often in sex/romance tourism, the local men in the tourism industry are gigolos. Since they are in the business for money, these gigolos fashion themselves after the tourists' fantasies, form intimate relationships with them, and then ask for expensive gifts and allowances. In comparison, based on my field research, my Korean participants who desired Hallyu tourists were not in these relationships for money. They did not ask for money or gifts from my Hallyu tourist informants. The relationship between Korean men and the Hallyu tourists formed through the "mutual gaze" and expectations about the "Other." While my Hallyu tourist informants "gazed" at Korean men, expecting them to be romantic and sexually reserved, my Korean male informants "gazed" back at the tourists and fantasized about them as sexually promiscuous women. The transnationally intimate encounters between Hallyu tourists and Korean men were clashes (for lack of a better term) between conflicting racialized erotic desires for and expectations of the "Other."

Hallyu tourism does not operate through a lopsided power hierarchy dictated purely by tourists' fantasies. Instead, it has become a site of intimacy fraught with conflicts of interest whereby the tourists and their Korean partners each attempt to make their racialized erotic fantasies come true. Orientalist methods of racialized gendering and sexualizing of the "Other" were not imported to Korea in the same way it is practiced in the West; they were adapted to fit into the narrative of Korea's supposed "pure blood" characteristic serving as the standard against which to judge others. The contemporary Korean system of prejudice operates through the intersection of race, ethnicity, nationality, and other factors: "In other words, *injongchabyeol* is discrimination based on perceived different human categories. This is a flexible type of discrimination that can include, but is not limited to, ethnic, racial, cultural, national, religious, and/or regional (e.g., Southeast Asian) difference. It is based on a multivariate calculation of who belongs and who is valued" (D. Oh 2022, 7).

For instance, some Koreans demonstrate more prejudice and discrimination against other Asians who, in Western racial categories, are lumped together as the same race of people, such as those from China, Southeast Asia, and South Asia and ethnic Koreans from China (*Joseonjok*), than they do for non-Asians with darker skin colors (M. Han 2022; E. Lee and Miyose 2022). Such discrimination occurs due to a mix of classicism and xenophobia. Hence, rather than identifying the Korean men who participated in my research as engaging in "racist" behavior in the sense that the term is understood in the United States, I suggest that they were engaging in Korean-centric conceptions of hierarchies that accounted for not only one's racial identity, but also that of one's nationality, class, gender, and sexuality.

Although my tourist informants and Korean male informants embraced slightly different conceptions of racial hierarchies, they were similar in their use of race to draw contrasts between "us" and the "Other." My informants' (both the Hallyu tourists' and Korean men's) racialized desires stemmed from comparing discourses of "Western" gender norms to that of Korea and exaggerating the differences between the "Western" and Korean cultures. Akhil Gupta and James Ferguson posit: "As an alternative to this [culturally essentialist] way of thinking about cultural difference, we want to problematize the unity of the 'us' and the otherness of the 'other,' and question the radical separation between the two that makes the opposition possible in the first place" (1992, 14). "Us" and the "other" are not inherently/naturally distinctive entities. Nationhood and culture take disparate forms depending on the unique difference-making relations they were exposed to. Hence, cultural differences result from difference-making connections rather than something immutably demarcating the spatial, ideological, or cultural boundary between "us" and "other." Both my Korean male and Hallyu tourist informants' erotic desires derived from transnationally difference-producing encounters; the supposed cultural differences between the "West" and Korea are inflected by "cross-cultural" contacts across time, cultures, and spaces. My focus in this chapter pertains to the difference-making set of relations between Korean men and Hallyu tourists that formulated my Korean male informants' racialized erotic desires for white women.

Erotic touching and contact come to dismantle and, at the same time, reaffirm notions of (racial) differences. Touching, which can be interpreted as a form of contact, acts as a boundary-forming activity and trespassing of those boundaries. The act of touching and contact, whether symbolic, literal, physical, emotional, violent, or amicable, complicates the concept of "difference"; those touching and being touched come to contemplate the fundamental meaning of the difference (Holland 2012). While they are touching or being intimate, two people of different backgrounds may feel "at one" with each other through their corporeal and emotional intimacy, but, at the same time, their physical, experiential, and cultural differences are rearticulated through such erotic "touching." Racialized erotic desires stemming from the discourses of cultural differences between Korea and the "West" drew the Hallyu tourists and Korean men whom I observed into intimate relationships. In other words, the encounters and relationships were built on the realities they produced about each other to satisfy their desires. These transnational intimacies (which can also be seen as a form of touching/contact) made racial and cultural boundaries between Korea and the "West" ever more permeable through the potential of interracial marriage and reproduction but, at the same time, they reaffirmed certain essentialist fantasies of cultural and racial differences.

My Korean male and Hallyu tourist informants forged transnational intimacies despite their different linguistic and cultural understandings of love. This is not to say that only two cultural conceptions of love—that of Korea and the Hallyu tourist's "native" culture—were in operation in these intimate encounters. After all, the supposed "Korean" cultural notion of love and that of the Hallyu tourist's cultures were created through cross-sections of various culturally, historically, and situationally affected notions of love. Certain ideals of love are universalized through transnational media and influence the ideas and practices of love in other cultures. Hollywood romantic comedies, Bollywood films, and Mexican telenovelas—screened and consumed all over the world—are a few examples of transnational media that disseminate culturally inflected ideologies of love to their transnational viewers. While these mediatized ideologies of love may influence their viewers' expectations and behaviors, this does not mean that fictionalized ideologies of love are reflective of real-life romantic practices of the people living in the United States, India, or Mexico. Korean dramas are another example of transnational media that transnationally disseminate certain fictionalized ideologies of love, which were then interpreted and drawn upon by my Hallyu tourist informants in multiple ways. These romantic Hallyu dramas depict heterosexual romantic love occurring between "soft" masculine men willing to do anything for love and women who do not have to do anything extraordinary to become the recipients of such unconditional love. Such depictions of love created intimate contact zones between my Korean men and Hallyu tourist informants that, depending on circumstances, functioned to both satisfy individuals' racialized erotic desires and, at other times, bitterly disappoint them.

Overcoming Discrimination in the Dating Scene

While the idealized depictions of Korean masculinity in the television dramas helped my Korean male informants experience popularity among my Hallyu tourist informants, some of them were still grappling with their newfound popularity. Their long-term exposure to traditional forms of Orientalism that, before Hallyu, disseminated unfair portraits of Asian men as less-than-ideal erotic partners seemed to have detracted from their self-esteem. Based on my observation, it seemed as though some of my informants were in disbelief that there were foreign women who were attempting to rework Orientalist stereotypes of Korean masculinity and who desired Korean men as intimate partners. For instance, when I met Jung, he was a twenty-eight-year-old Korean man who spoke enough English to communicate with the Hallyu tourists but not enough to engage in a lengthy conversation with them. He was tall and lanky. I met him at a birthday party for one of my Hallyu tourist informants. He was invited to the party by the Hallyu tourist because she thought he was handsome (an opinion that she kept whispering to me throughout the party).

While all the Hallyu tourists were getting drinks at the bar, I stood beside Jung outside on the patio because neither of us was fond of drinking. Our conversation took place in Korean as we stood, looking into the crowded bar through a large window Jung said to me, "Look inside. It's all foreigners and then some Korean girls who are obsessed with sleeping with foreigners." I looked inside, and indeed, the bar was filled with people who appeared to be foreigners and a small group of fashionably dressed Korean women. There were some Korean men, but they seemed to keep to themselves. After a moment of silence, Jung turned his face toward me and remarked, "Korean guys have it hard because they are so unpopular, especially in places like these. You, as an Asian [*dongyang*] girl, can go into the club right now and attract any foreign guy you want. Any foreign guy in the room would go for you if you approached them." He tilted his head to stare off into space and said to me, "But, for example, if I go in there and try to get foreign girls, there is maybe a one in ten chance that I will get some. Asian girls, you can even go to clubs in foreign countries too, and they will love you because you are seen as exotic and all, but I bet I will be so unpopular in the clubs in the U.S. or Europe. I bet some of them would not even let me in because I am an Asian man." He looked down at his feet for a while before reverting his gaze to the bar. Jung believed that by virtue of being Asian, he, along with many other Korean men, was unpopular among U.S. and European women.

From Jung's perspective, there was a distinct difference between Korean women's and men's experiences with racialized erotic desires based on Orientalism. According to Jung, Korean/Asian women were globally desirable because they were perceived as "exotic" beauties. It is due to the feminization of Asia, which renders Asian women as desirable and hyper-feminine figures while portraying Asian men as effeminate and emasculated subjects. Thus far, both popular and scholarly discourse have extensively analyzed how Asian men's supposed femininity makes them unpopular in both the heterosexual and the queer dating scene in the West; many online dating profiles in the United States even boldly state "no Asians" (Nguyen 2014). Jung was aware of such anti-Asian discrimination even though he did not use the term to describe his thoughts. He was feeling bitter and despondent due to the racialized erotic desires that supposedly made Korean men unappealing as intimate partners for Western women.

Jung's observation of his unpopularity was especially ironic because he was invited to a Hallyu tourist's birthday party due to her desire for him. I questioned Jung's statements, asking him, "Is that really true? I feel like you guys may be more popular than you think, what with Korean dramas and K-pop. Don't you think so?" Jung replied, "Maybe a little, I don't know. But all I know is that we are still not as popular as that guy," pointing to a white man jovially chatting inside the bar with a glass of beer in his hands, "or that guy," pointing to a Black man perched on a stool. I asked, "Why do you think so?" He answered, "I don't think so, I know so. That's just the way it is. You wouldn't understand [because] you are an Asian girl. So, to come back to your question about why we use the phrase *saranghae* so much, that is my long-winded answer." He smiled sheepishly and looked around the patio at all the people standing around us. He was responding to my question: Some of my tourist informants complain that Korean men say "I love you" without actually feeling love. Do you think that is the case?

Jung claimed that Korean men performed romantic masculinity because that is the one quality through which they could "compete" against men of other races. He seemed to be implying that Korean men performed romantic and "soft" masculinity so they could be competitive in the multiracial dating scene composed of foreign male backpackers and Hallyu tourists. By Jung's logic, romance seemed to be a tactic rather than simply an emotional state or a communication method across language barriers. Korean men's gender and sexual performances did not fit into the neat category of Orientalized objects. They did not passively accept the problematic stereotypes derived from anti-Asian hate, and neither did they blindly accept the positively connoted stereotypes that the tourists imposed on them. Instead, I interpreted Jung's comment to mean that Korean masculinity co-opted romantic and gentle imagery—derived from the tourists' reworking of racial stereotypes through Korean television dramas—to fight against anti-Asian racist stereotypes. However, rather than attempting to dismantle the stereotypes by disassociating race from gender and sex, Jung argued that Korean men reaffirmed such connections so that they could work to their benefit. While elite Korean men from the Japanese colonial period claimed that Koreans needed to become Westernized in order to maintain their competitiveness (Y.-H. Chung 2006; J. Cho 2021a), Jung and other Korean men in the twenty-first century were not attempting to become Western. Instead, they were trying to distinguish themselves as uniquely different from Western masculinity through romantic performances.

I find Youjeong Oh's (2018) argument of the Hallyu tourism industry's chimerical nature to be particularly relevant to analyzing my Korean male informants' gender performances. Oh argues that Hallyu tourism is chimerical because it creates places by erasing space's political and historical contexts and overlaying it with fantastical and utopian images of modernity and developmentalism. In some ways, I find some of my Korean male informants' deliberate performance of romantic masculinity to be similarly chimerical as the Hallyu tourist destinations that Oh analyzes. After all, as I will discuss later in this chapter, Korean men's performance of soft masculinity was not representative of how these men perform their gender and sexuality outside of their relationships with foreign tourists.

However, the difference between Oh's analyses of chimerical tourist destinations that erase the historical context of places and my Korean male informants' performance of certain forms of idealized masculinities is that the latter were historically contextualized; they were not erasing history through adaptations of Hallyu-inspired "soft" masculinity. Their performance of romantic masculinity was a reaction against the historical dominance of Orientalist stereotypes. Hollywood films have been some of the media that effectively disseminated Orientalist stereotypes around the world. In them, Asian men were (and to some extent, still are) rarely portrayed sexually and are imputed with no sexual drive whether they are characterized as wimps, martial arts contenders, foreigners, or silent victims (Chua and Fujino 1999; E.-Y. Jung 2010). These were the types of American media that my tourist informants claimed to have consumed throughout their lives before they began consuming Korean media.

Celine Parreñas Shimizu (2012) complicates the scholarly critique of Hollywood by posing a counter-reading to scholarship that critiques Hollywood for its desexualized and effeminate portrayal of Asian American men. While acknowledging such stereotypes, Shimizu argues that Asian American male depictions in Hollywood movies show that there are *other ways* of being masculine through intimacy, emotionality, and vulnerability: she calls it "ethical masculinity." She claims that stereotypically effeminate images of Asian men in Western popular culture and the racialized interpretations of them by Western critics should not merely be cast off as racist. Instead, Shimizu suggests that feminists should uphold these depictions of Asian masculinity as ways to challenge hypermasculinity and patriarchy.

Although Shimizu's reinterpretation of Hollywood movies provides a novel feminist theoretical framework, the radical potential of reinterpreting Hollywood/Western media seemed to have eluded Korean men like Jung. Embracing "alternative" masculinity did not result in the liberating potentials that Shimizu envisioned. My informants embraced the soft masculinities as a means of competition within the existing system of heteropatriarchy rather than seeing it as a means to erect their own system of values and norms surrounding masculine gender performances. While it is easy for me to say that erotic desires driven by racial essentialism are problematic, I must also acknowledge that some Korean men were willing to be essentialized if it gave them a chance to be popular. For instance, Jung envied Asian women's popularity that was driven by Orientalist conceptions of their racialized gender and sexuality rather than finding a problem with it.

Jung's perspective on his global unpopularity contrasted with what I observed daily in the hostels as I interacted with the Hallyu tourists. Some Hallyu tourists with whom I worked even preferred Korean men as intimate partners above men of other races, ethnicities, and nationalities. Some specifically came to Korea because they were attracted to Korean men. In extreme cases, some dreamed of marrying a Korean man and living in Korea. I witnessed a few instances of Hallyu tourists leaving the hostel to go and live with a Korean man in his apartment. I was unable to conduct extensive interviews with these women since I did not have time to recruit and screen them for my research before they left the hostel to live with their partners. On their last days at the hostel, I observed some women giddily packing their bags and confiding in other Hallyu tourists. The other Hallyu tourists were simultaneously jealous and concerned; they expressed envy and, in the same breath, told the women who were moving out to hurry back to the hostel at the first sign of trouble from the Korean men. I even heard of a Hallyu tourist from Russia who became pregnant during her trip to Korea and married the Korean man with whom she had intimate relations. According to the hostel workers who told me her story, starting on the first day of her stay in Korea, the Russian tourist said she wanted to marry a Korean man. Thus, her story of pregnancy and marriage was narrated by others as a story of "fulfilling her dreams" rather than a one-night stand gone wrong. The disjuncture between Jung's accounts of Korean men's unpopularity and my observation of their popularity indicated that Orientalism significantly impacted how my Korean informants conceptualized their masculinity. However, instead of merely feeling despondent, many of my informants actively attempted to debunk Orientalist stereotypes through various means.

Mobilizing "I Love You" for Competitive Edge and to Overcome Language Barriers

As Jung noted, the erotic phrase *saranghae* (I love you) played a significant role in mediating the relationship and the power dynamics between my Korean male informants and my tourist informants. *Saranghae* [사랑해] is a phrase that the heroes in Korean dramas state during the climax of the dramas. For example, Kim Shin, the hero of *Guardian, The Lonely and Great God* (analyzed in chapter 2), tells the heroine that he loves her just before sacrificing himself for her sake. The dramas use the phrase as a symbol that emphasizes the depth of the hero's love for the heroine. Even though Kim's love is already made evident through his acts of sacrifice, the phrase becomes a punchline that verbally drives the message home. Similarly, in the television dramas *Descendants of the Sun* and *My Love from the Star*, the protagonists verbally profess their love near the drama's finale. In these dramas, the heroes' declaration of *sarang* [사랑, love] for the heroines comes after all the episodes that emotionally build up to the moment. Due to the significance of the phrase *saranghae* in Korean dramas, the most popular debate among the Hallyu tourists I interviewed pertained to the meaning of the phrase. The unconditional love associated with the term in the dramas was critical to their reworking of Orientalist stereotypes of Korean masculinity through Korean television dramas. They used the unconditionality and loyalty attached to the phrase to generate certain assumptions about Korean masculinities that inspired them to travel to Korea to find Korean boyfriends.

However, in reality, the phrase lent itself to disparate uses, some detached from the emotionality associated with the phrase in the fictional dramas. Michael was a Korean man in his early thirties. He sported a trendy asymmetrical haircut in which one side of his hair was considerably longer while the other side was almost shaven off. He meticulously styled his hair with wax every day so that the longer hairs would be combed back and textured with wax. He spoke fluent English. He invited some of his friends to the party at our hostel. We were all seated in a circle in the lounge area. Since the space was small, everyone was sitting very close to each other. Three Korean men were in the group, two of whom were Michael's friends. There were also Hallyu tourists from various countries, including Sweden, Switzerland, the United Kingdom, the United States, Canada, and Hong Kong. The women far outnumbered the men at this party. In the middle of the circle was a small table brimming with bottles of alcohol and light snacks. While only a few guests were eating the snacks—consisting of peanuts, saltine crackers, and chips—the alcohol was disappearing very rapidly. Michael sat next to me while his two friends sat on his other side. Speaking in Korean, Michael told one of his friends, "Pick one you like and say 'I love you.'" When I heard this, I turned toward them to observe their conversation.

One of Michael's friends, a Korean man with a long, narrow face and tanned skin, was staring at a woman seated directly across from him in the circle of people. She was a Hallyu tourist from Switzerland with platinum blond hair and very pale skin. She wore a plaid miniskirt that barely covered her bottom and a cut-off top with platform shoes and knee-high socks. Noticing that he was eyeing the woman, the hostel owner told his friend to say "I love you" to flatter her. When he noticed me observing them, Michael turned to me and said in Korean, "You know, this guy always gets the best-looking girls. At one of the guesthouse parties we went to a while ago, he scored with two of the hottest French girls that I have ever seen in my life. And I'm being serious! They were the most beautiful women I have seen in my entire life. I think it is his looks. He looks so cheesy that when he says *saranghae,* he sounds really serious. Girls fall for that stuff."

Michael's friend finally approached the Swiss tourist by moving to a seat closer to her. Throughout the night, I observed him showering her with compliments and saying "I love you" in English and Korean. When everyone else got up to go bar hopping at the end of the party, they disappeared together, presumably to spend the night together.

In this case, Michael and his friends used "I love you" as a catchphrase to capture women's interests. They actively incorporated the phrase in their efforts to pursue white Hallyu tourists. Michael did not state whether "two of the hottest French girls" that his friend had sex with were white. However, earlier in the night, during a casual conversation, both Michael and his friend listed white Hollywood stars like Scarlett Johansson and Chloe Moretz as their ideal women, so I deduced from this conversation, as well as from Michael's friend's attraction to the white Swiss woman, that the two French women were most likely also white. In this regard, Michael and his friend's erotic desires were very much racialized; they did not use the phrase "I love you" to pursue just any Hallyu tourist; they specifically used it to appeal to the white Hallyu tourists.

Some foreign male backpackers whom I spoke with claimed Korean men were performing "fake" masculinity in their mobilization of "love." One evening, the lounge area of the guesthouse was abuzz with excitement as multiple women were going in and out of the lounge on dates with Korean men. One woman was busy preparing herself for a movie date with a man she met on Tinder. She was in the lounge with a big hand mirror and cosmetics bag, meticulously applying makeup to her face. In the meantime, another Hallyu tourist walked into the lounge, disgruntled from a dissatisfactory date. Many more women were sitting around immersed in their phones and swiping left or right on pictures of Korean men on Tinder. The bright lights of their cell phones lit their mesmerized faces. They occasionally looked up from their phones to exchange comments about their success or progress in securing a hot date for the night. Observing the buzz of motions and emotions, a male tourist sitting next to me nudged my arm. He was a short French tourist with deep-set brown eyes, a dark stubbly beard, and curly hair poking out from under a blue baseball cap that he had on backward. Wearing a colorful and flowery Hawaiian-style shirt, he was casually sipping on a can of Korean beer. "I'm Fred, what's your name?" he asked me. After I responded, we went about asking each other the typical introductory questions that people at the guesthouse usually asked: name, countries they have visited, the country they were from, how long they are staying in Korea, and their upcoming destinations. Fred told me he lives in France and came to Korea for three weeks—he had planned on staying just one week in Korea but liked the country so much that he extended his stay. He said he planned to go to Japan and Southeast Asia when he grew tired of Korea.

After learning about my research on the relationship between Korean television dramas and tourism, Fred was eager to tell me his observations on Hallyu tourism. He was very opinionated. In a loud and sharp voice, Fred argued:

Korean men in dramas or K-pop are so dandy and harmless-looking. But in reality, they are not like that. When I first came to Korea, some Korean guys . . . who, I guess, did language exchange in the U.S. and thought they were hipsters now, were like, "Yo man, hey, what's up," and all that f-cking shit. They were all acting fake American cool, you know what I mean, right? You are from America, you can understand. They say, "Oh, let's go to the club with us. You know foreign girls we can f-ck?" They just want to f-ck foreign girls to check it off of their list.

Fred made a checkmark in the air with his fingers. "Korean guys want to brag about f-cking foreign girls. They literally go," Fred poked me with his elbow and, while imitating the Korean guys' accented English, said, "Oh, you f-ck Korean girls, eh? You introduce me to some foreign girls." Looking at my confused face, Fred elaborated, "I mean, they think that because I am a foreign guy in Korea who likes to party, I must have had sex with many Korean girls. They are saying, um . . . they are saying it is their turn to have some fun. It's like, I had my go with the Korean chicks; they want their shot with foreign women to make it fair or whatever."

Fred spoke as if all these thoughts were in his mind the whole time, and he finally had a willing listener in me. "They refer to women like a piece of meat you can f-ck just to complete your checklist. I would never treat women the way Korean guys do because French men would never treat women like that. Never!" Fred was emphatic in his disgust. He took a swig of beer and continued, "And because Korean guys look so cute and clean, the foreign girls let their guard down. Going on dates with guys can be dangerous, especially in another country, but look at all these women going on dates with Korean guys they barely know."

Fred thought the Hallyu tourists had no reservations about going on dates with Korean men because they felt safe with Korean men due to their androgynous appearance and the discourses surrounding their romantic attitudes. However, from Fred's perspective, this sense of safety was misguided because men cannot be androgynous and "soft" while desiring women. This ignores the various forms of masculinity that exist in different cultures. In Korea, some behaviors typically associated with effeminacy in the West, such as applying makeup and being sensitive and emotional, are not necessarily associated with being gay (Elfving-Hwang 2011). Furthermore, whether the soft masculine performances of Korean men can be interpreted as "fake" depends on how and to what extent one can define gender performances as "real" or "fake." After all, as Judith Butler (2004) contends, all genders are formulated through performative acts. If that were the case, there is no reason why Korean men's gender performances should be seen as less genuine than the socially learned gender performances of other heterosexual men. Many foreign male tourists who were uninvolved in the Hallyu fandom scene were disgruntled that the Hallyu tourists desired and felt safe around Korean men. Another male tourist seated next to me during Fred's interview session contributed his thoughts: "I mean, do Korean men even do housework after getting married? I heard they don't. There is proof that they are fake gentlemen."

I found these foreign men's arguments deeply problematic and often wondered if such claims were driven by their jealousy at the popularity of Korean men in Korean clubs and bars. I describe and analyze such discourse in this section not to perpetuate such problematic discourse of Korean masculinity but to question what it means to refer to certain masculine performances as fake and how such rhetoric risks echoing anti-Asian racism.

Just because some Korean men choose to use the phrase "I love you" to their benefit does not mean that their masculinity is deceptive. Based on my interviews with my Korean male informants, I found that while some of them may have used "I love you" for other purposes besides expressing their emotions, not all were intentionally deceptive. In other words, even though some of my Korean male informants used "I love you" as a "tactic" to make themselves appealing to white women, it is essential to acknowledge that such examples do not indicate that all Korean men had ulterior motives when they were saying "I love you" to my Hallyu tourist informants. Just because a particular performance and discourse of love do not always coincide with a Western understanding of love and its expressions does not mean its status as love should be denied. Romance and sex are intertwined with the politics of race and modernity; for a long time, those with Eurocentric conceptions of romance held onto the belief that only the modernized Western cultures and their inhabitants knew love (Jankowiak 1997). However, in their unique form, romantic love can be found in non-European cultures. Some Korean men's expression of "I love you" may at times be interpreted as a phrase that they use for sexual gains, but it could very well be their interpretation of what love means.

There are no standards to measure the emotion of love. I had a chance to interview my Korean acquaintance Jay, who inspired me to think about the cultural differences of love. After hearing about my research, he told me his thoughts. Jay said, "From the Korean perspective, we say 'I love you' (saranghae) when we reach this much feeling for another person." Jay held his left hand up to his chin. "But in some cultures, like my ex-girlfriend's culture, people say 'I love you,' and the sentence has a much more serious and deeper meaning than it does in Korea. They say love when they have this much feeling," he said as he lifted his right hand over his head. He emphasized the gap between his two hands by vigorously waving them up and down in front of my eyes. According to his interpretation, it is not that Korean men do not "love" foreign women; it is that the word "love" (sarang) in Korea is different from how it is used in some other cultures. According to him, Koreans use the phrase "I love you" and the concept of love more "lightly" than in some other cultural contexts. Although I do not have a way to verify whether his interpretation is accurate, I believe it could be one of multiple explanations for some of my Korean male informants' romantic gestures toward their foreign dates.

At times, the Korean men's "I love you" served as a form of mutual understanding between the Hallyu tourists and Korean men who had almost nothing in common, including language. For example, some of my Korean male informants said that *saranghae* was the only way they could get their erotic intentions across to Hallyu tourists who had varying degrees of Korean fluency. Three Korean men and I sat down in a guesthouse lounge at a long conference table that also served as a dinner table. They were each in complicated romantic situations: Yoon had a crush on a Japanese tourist, Park was in a relationship with a German tourist, and Sean was in an on-and-off relationship with a Korean woman but was having sex with foreign tourists.

PARK The thing about dating foreign girls is that you cannot predict anything.
MJL What do you mean?
PARK I mean, when I am dating Korean girls, I know their pattern. I know why they behave a certain way. I can see whether they are pissed or happy, or turned on based on how they act. But when you are interested in or dating a foreigner, that's not the case.
YOON I agree 100 percent. I cannot tell what that Japanese girl is thinking . . . what she thinks of me. . . . I would have known by now if she were Korean.
SEAN Don't be so definitive about that. Look at my ex-girlfriend. She is Korean, and I can't tell what that b-tch is feeling or thinking most of the time.
YOON But it is easier with Korean girls, though! You can fight it out in Korean and stuff, but with foreign girls, we can only say "I love you" and go from there. That is like the one phrase that all girls want to hear, right? It is what they expect us to say. But anything more complicated than that is just impossible with the language barrier and everything.[3]

Here, the phrase "I love you" was used to mediate the potential miscommunications and misunderstandings arising from cultural and language differences. *Saranghae* became the sole phrase that my Korean male informants and their Hallyu tourist partners could comprehend when the latter did not understand Korean or when the Korean men had limited English skills.

The Hallyu tourists whom I interviewed were not naïve women; they were able to decipher men who performed "soft" masculinity for untoward purposes and those who did to strike up a conversation. For example, many Hallyu tourists told me anecdotes about "creepy Korean men" who were so hungry for sex that they became nuisances to the tourists by pestering them for sex. In some of the hostels I stayed in during my fieldwork, there seemed to be at least one Korean man who stayed there to pester the female Hallyu tourists. At first glance, these men would appear romantic and considerate because they would buy the tourists food and take care of their various needs, but once one became more acquainted with such men, one would realize that these men would indiscriminately attempt to have sex with any foreign tourist; some of them even displayed sexually predatory behavior. Whenever these men attempted to engage my Hallyu tourist informants in conversation, my informants would secretly share exasperated glances with each other, roll their eyes, and whisper about these Korean men behind their backs. My Hallyu tourist informants would warn each other about these men's identities so that their fellow Hallyu tourists could guard themselves against these men's "fake romantic" advances.

Fred and other foreign male backpackers' claims that the Hallyu tourists are naïve in falling for "fake" masculine performances, rather than acknowledging that the Hallyu tourists may be as knowledgeable and situationally aware as them, indicates signs of paternalistic protectionism. Therefore, rather than interpreting the dynamic between my tourist informants and their Korean dates as fake or deceptive, I find that it was a mutually beneficial relationship where they derived racialized erotic satisfaction from each other. Their relationships went beyond the binary scope of the deceiver and the deceived or the Orientalizing versus the Orientalized. They constantly negotiated the power dynamic in their encounters to satisfy their racialized erotic desires. Furthermore, much like my tourist informants, who traveled to Korea in part due to their dissatisfaction with masculinity and dating culture in their home countries, my Korean men informants' racialized erotic desires were also complicated by their relationships with Whiteness and Korean femininity.

The Juxtaposition of White Women and Korean Women in Korean Men's Racialized Desires

While Jung lamented the unpopularity of Korean men due to Orientalism, he also made an interesting remark about how he believed Korean men treated foreign women more trivially than Korean women. Jung noted, "Korean guys probably say 'I love you' and approach *seo-yang yeojadeul* (literally, Western women) more easily than Korean women because there are no consequences. I mean, the foreign women stay in Korea for maybe a few weeks at most. If Korean guys say 'I love you' to them and don't mean it, they can pretend and have fun for a few weeks without any long-term duties attached to it. If they approach Korean girls, they have to think about the people they may know in common, their reputation, and other long-term relationship issues, even marriage, maybe." Jung's statement highlights the dominant stereotype some Korean men hold of Western (mainly white) women as sexually available. Although I have not heard my informants use such terms, some Koreans would use derogatory and sexist slang to refer to white women. For instance, the term *baekma* literally refers to white horses. Alternatively, and colloquially, it equates white women to horses because both can be "ridden" by men whenever they desire (Cheng 2021). Their consent is unnecessary because they are supposedly available at the whims and desires of their riders (in this case, Korean men). It is a sexually violent conception of white women that assumes that they are hypersexual and sexually available. In this regard, the Korean men whom Jung was referring to in his comment and those using terms such as *baekma* complicate the power dynamic between themselves and white women. Although they were aware of and attempted to resist Orientalist stereotypes through the performance of romanticism,, their performances presumed the "ease" with which they thought they could woo the women who Orientalized them. The sexual objectification of white femininity culminated in some Korean men asking my tourist informants whether they were sex workers. As I noted in chapter 4, several white women tourists informed me that in clubs, Korean men often asked them in a roundabout way if they were sex workers. By virtue of their racialized bodies in Korea, white Hallyu tourists were not only deemed sexually available but literally conflated with the foreign sex workers in Korea.

I specifically say "white" Hallyu tourists for two reasons: first, based on my field research, only the white Hallyu tourists were conflated with sex workers, and, second, from my observation, few Korean men specifically or exclusively expressed erotic desires for women of color. Furthermore, assuming that market demands influence market supply, the vast "supply" of white sex workers in contemporary Korea indicates Korean men's erotic fantasies for white women (Cheng 2021). The non-white Hallyu tourists had very different racialized erotic experiences in Korea compared to white Hallyu tourists. My white tourist informants would have an abundance of dates and would have men approach them on the streets and in subway stations, but I often saw my non-white informants not receive as much attention as their white counterparts.

One day, I accidentally became privy to a discussion between two men that provided some perspective about how some Korean men conceptualize white tourists as being positioned in direct contrast to Korean women. I plopped down on a dank brown vinyl sofa that faced a pool table. Next to the pool table were several plastic chairs and round tables littered with beer cans and soju bottles.[4] Dart and pinball machines were lining the walls adjacent to the pool table. Two white women were playing pool. I was absentmindedly observing the women playing pool when I inadvertently overheard two Korean men talking on a couch adjacent to mine. "That one is a nine and a five . . . and that one is a two and an eight." "No, that short girl is more like a ten and a seven!" The two men were speaking Korean but seemed to be using some coded language. They spoke freely in front of me, presumably because they thought that I did not understand Korean. After listening to their conversation for a while, I finally realized what they were saying: they were numerically evaluating the two women playing pool as if they were judges in a beauty pageant. The first number represented the points they gave to the women's breasts, while the second number referred to how appealing their hips and legs were. One of them said, "That short girl has enough of everything. I guess it's more than enough. Those kinds of breasts do not exist among Korean girls. What is that, like a D cup? Korean chicks don't have that kind of body." The woman they were talking about leaned over the pool table, very much engaged in her game of pool and unaware that these two Korean men were evaluating her. The other man responded, "Yeah, they are pretty amazing. On the other hand, that tall girl over there has nothing to show on top and everything on the bottom. God gifted her with amazing hips but no breasts. That's sad." They were silent for a while, observing the women in front of them. "Who would you go for?" "The tall one, definitely. Those kinds of legs are something you can only get in those *seoyang* [Western] chicks."

The two women who were Hallyu tourists were not fluent in Korean, so they were not fully cognizant of the fact that they were the subjects of this lewd conversation. The short woman approached one of the Korean men sitting on the sofa and said: "Play together!" He smiled and stood up to join their pool game. He did not attempt anything sexual while playing pool with her, and he behaved and talked innocently, as though he had not just sexually objectified her. These Hallyu tourists presumably saw this Korean man as one of the romantic and gentlemanly men they imagined they would find in Korea.

In their sexually explicit conversation, the two Korean men were explicitly comparing *seoyang* (Western) women with Korean women; the *seoyang* women were seen as embodying certain traits lacking in Korean women. Some of the Korean men I observed and those I interviewed used such binary categorization between Western and Korean women. In this particular discourse, white women's bodies were idealized as opposed to the less-than-ideal bodies of Korean women who—according to them—lacked big breasts and glamorous legs. In the conversation between the two Korean men, white Hallyu tourists were caricatured, objectified, and sexualized in comparison to an equally simplistic perception of Korean women.

Tourists' gender plays a significant factor in the amount of privilege and respect awarded to them in transnational relationships. While German male tourists in Denise Brennan's research (2001) could freely roam around in the Dominican Republic and be respected by the locals due to their wealthy white male status, female tourists do not experience as much privilege as their male counterparts. For example, in Paulla Ebron's (1997) research on romance tourism in the Gambia, while the white female romance tourists were treated with respect to their faces, when they were absent the locals talked about their supposed promiscuity and haplessness. In these discourses, Western white women were deemed to be foolish and sexually promiscuous. These discourses define white women as sexually indiscriminate and, therefore, morally reprehensible. Similarly, in the above case of Korean men judging the Hallyu tourists' bodies, the tourists were not experiencing much of the privilege of being tourists. This was because of a combination of their gender and the lack of economic privilege they have in Korea, an OECD country.

My informants' comparison between white women and Korean women did not end at the physical/aesthetic level; they extended to the comparison of these two groups of women's supposedly different sexual behaviors. In one particular interview session, my informants' preconceptions of *seoyang* (Western) women's "promiscuity" were directly contrasted to Korean women's (my own) supposed virtuousness. After a particularly wild night of partying, Michael shuffled back to the hostel the following day. He plopped down on the sofa where I was interviewing a British male tourist named Ben. Michael said, "Speaking of yesterday . . ." He paused as he quickly eyed and contemplated me sitting on the other side of the couch. He said in Korean, "I am sorry for what I am about to say. It seems like an inappropriate topic to raise in front of a lady." I assured him I would not take offense at what he was about to say. He lowered his voice considerably and said, almost in a whisper, "Did you hear the Swedish girls talking last night and this morning?" Ben nodded his head and said, "Yeah, they were really . . ." Michael completed his sentence, "I think the word you are looking for is 'wild.' Some of these Western girls are just so wild." I asked, "About what?" Michael responded, "I just ask them how was your night, and they go into detail like, 'Oh, we went to X club and met some Korean guys and had sex. It was OK, but she had more fun than me,' they say!"

Michael snorted and continued, "Based on the tone of their voice, they sound like they are saying, 'Oh, she had more fun than me; next time, I am going to do more extreme stuff and have more fun sex than her!' Even guys don't say all those things in detail when talking to other guys, but these girls are telling me, a guy, about how they had all this wild sex. These Western girls . . . they have sex, they talk about sex."

Ben agreed enthusiastically, "Yeah, I am so surprised that they share all that with us guys. When I listen to them talking, sometimes I am just amazed [at the amount of private sexual details they share]! The things they do and say . . . Korean girls would never do something like that, would they?" He looked at me to agree with his rhetorical question. Just in time, a guest hauled her luggage out of the tiny elevator connected to the hostel, and Michael jumped up to help. Our interview halted for a few minutes, and the hiatus saved me from having to answer Ben's question.

Michael, a Korean man, and Ben, a British tourist, shared their mild disdain toward Swedish Hallyu tourists' open sexuality. Even though Ben was from Britain, he fervently agreed with Michael regarding his simultaneous astonishment and disdain for the supposed overt sexuality of the Swedish Hallyu tourists. Ben even juxtaposed the Swedish women's behaviors with that of "virtuous" Korean women who would supposedly never flaunt and discuss their sexuality in such a way. In these two men's discourses, "Korean femininity" and "Western femininity" were pitted against each other to affirm Orientalist and essentialist ideologies of cultural difference. Although Ben seemed to compliment Korean women's virtues, what he said was not necessarily a compliment. Ben merely drew on the Orientalist stereotype of Asian femininity to demean Western female sexuality.

Asian women and Western white women are frequently juxtaposed against each other to promote the male notion of how "proper" women should act. Amy Sueyoshi (2018) analyzed the emergence of the Asian "geisha" stereotype in the United States. According to Sueyoshi, this stereotype gained popularity in the United States in juxtaposition to white women's feminist movements in the nineteenth century. These feminist movements called for women to become physically strong and financially independent. The mainstream U.S. media juxtaposed geisha stereotypes with this "new" white middle-class womanhood; the media embraced the geisha trope as the ideal femininity brimming with docility and subservience—qualities supposedly lacking in the new white womanhood that was being touted by women's rights movements. Hence, in the nineteenth-century United States, racialized desires for East Asian women were formulated in juxtaposition to—and in competition with—white femininity. In the context of Hallyu tourism, my Korean male informants' racialized erotic desires for white women were likewise formulated through their comparison to Korean femininity.

In such ways, discourses of racialized erotic desires were formulated through a difference-making set of relations that create imagined binaries between the "East" and the "West." As a case in point, when discussing the allegedly unbridled sexuality of the Swedish tourists, Ben referred back to me, a Korean woman, to affirm the discourse of docile and virtuous Asian feminine sexuality that can be contrasted to the discourse of uncontrollable sexuality of Western women. Here, Ben was using culturally essentialist ideology regarding romance and sexuality to contrast the West with Korea to create a patriarchal ideal of how women should act. Such binary ideology is disseminated through media. Gina Marchetti (1994) claims that when Hollywood films portray interracial relationships between the West and Asia, the romantic heroes—who are undoubtedly white—are depicted as rescuing the Asian heroines from their own cultures through the power of love. Asian women in these films are depicted as sacrificing themselves for love, while Caucasian women in these same movies are depicted as independent and dangerous. Binary constructions of Eastern and Western sexuality/romance have historically contrasted Asian women with Western women to make two points: first, that Asian women are oppressed in their culture and prevented from the liberating experiences of love, and second, that Western white women are too liberal and sexual compared to the "docile" and "innocent" Asian women.

Such comparisons echo larger essentialist and racist discourses surrounding romance and sex. According to Caren Kaplan (2001), even some Western feminists ascribe to such essentialist ideologies of love. In analyzing Hillary Clinton's transnational travel to North Africa as a first lady amid Bill Clinton's sex scandal, Kaplan points to how the U.S. news media and Clinton herself imparted all forms of gender-based problems onto the non-Western "Other." Meanwhile, the domestic (U.S.) issues that disturbed Hillary Clinton—Bill Clinton's infidelity and the U.S. media's sexist attacks against her—were swept under the rug. As an extension of such tactics to "outsource patriarchy" onto other cultures (Grewal 2013), some Western feminists (Kaplan calls them "global feminists") employ discourses of non-Western women's romantic and sexual "oppression" while pointing to Western cultures as pinnacles of gender equality and female liberation. My male informants also adhered to such binary discourses that juxtaposed Western women with Korean women—however, they used the same logic in reverse to criticize Western women's supposed promiscuity. Their critique of Western women's supposed promiscuity did not mean that they viewed Korean women in a more favorable light.

While Michael viewed Western women as sexually promiscuous, concurrently, he defined Korean women as emotionally needy. When he returned from helping the guest, Michael plopped down on the sofa again, and the conversation turned to his critique of Korean women. He said, "Ugh, Korean girls. . . . I don't like how Korean girls need to constantly text. When I go three days without texting them, they are like, 'Why didn't you text me during those three days?' It somehow becomes all my fault! But I say, 'Why didn't YOU text me during that time?' You know? And they say guys should text first and all that nonsense, but see. . . . It isn't all my fault."

After taking a breath from his rant, he looked my way and said, "Sorry for saying that about Korean women in front of you." I told him I did not take offense. He then continued: "Korean girls worry and text too much. They want proof of love every three seconds and make themselves out to be something more than even our mothers are in our lives. For example, the boyfriend was at her house twenty minutes ago, but she makes the boyfriend text every minute he is walking back home. Nothing happened in between leaving her home twenty minutes ago and arriving at his home. That's just psycho stuff that normal Korean girls do!"

Ben nodded his head in agreement, and encouraged by the gesture, Michael went on, "Neither of us has to worry about each other that much! We lived just fine on our own before we met each other. For the past ten years, I haven't even told my mom where I am and whether I ate lunch or what I had for dinner!

Why do I have to inform my girlfriend when I don't even do that for my mom? My current girlfriend doesn't do that. She is fine, but I wonder if it is because I told her I don't like that or she is just that kind of cool, unconventional Korean girl." "Oh, so you told her not to do that?" I asked, to which he replied proudly, "Yes, I specifically told her not to nag me, or we have to break up." Michael's dissatisfaction with Korean women's "clinginess" is juxtaposed with his discourse of the Hallyu tourists, who are supposedly not as emotionally demanding or controlling of their male love interests.

According to Michael's discourse, Western women are desirable because they do not demand as much emotional commitment as Korean women do in relationships. The Hallyu tourists, in particular, do not even get a chance to be "clingy" because they are in Korea only briefly as tourists. They became the primary "targets" for some of my Korean male informants because they already desired Korean men due to Korean television dramas. My Korean male informants' desires resonated with what Elizabeth Bernstein (2007) calls "bounded intimacy." Bernstein theorizes about "bounded intimacy" in the context of relationships between sex workers and their customers. She argues that these relationships are not strictly sexual or emotional; instead, they are "bounded intimacy," at once sexual and emotional, transient and stable, fungible and durable. Some of the Korean men whom I observed seemed to want this type of "bounded intimacy" with white women because of the masculine prestige associated with dating and having sex with white women.

These Korean men did not see their relationships with the Hallyu tourists as lasting ones that could turn into long-distance relationships and marriages. Nonetheless, many of them treated the Hallyu tourists as lovers and girlfriends during the duration of their stay in Korea. Some Hallyu tourists left Korea after being satisfied and fulfilled by such short-term intimate relationships. In contrast, others left Korea, hoping that upon their next trip to Korea, they would be able to find something more long-lasting. Their level of satisfaction differed based on the depth of their racialized erotic desires.

In this chapter I examined the racialized erotic desires of my Korean male informants for two reasons. First, through a critical analysis of their desires, I wanted to emphasize the constant negotiations of power that they engaged in with my tourist informants. Such negotiations went beyond simple binaries of the Orientalizer versus Orientalized, or the empowered versus the disempowered. The Korean men whom I spoke to and observed were not merely passive recipients of my tourist informants' racialized erotic desires and their reworking of Korean masculinity through television dramas. Instead, they had their own racial conceptions and essentialisms that they mobilized in their relations with the tourists to reject Orientalism. Second, I wanted to emphasize that while they were, at times, successful at outmaneuvering Orientalist conceptions of Korean masculinity that used race as a predetermining factor to presume

Korean men's gender and sexual performances, at other times they were unable to escape the pervasiveness of Orientalism, as can be seen from some of my informants' cognitive dissonance about their newfound popularity. As a result, some of my informants would resort to problematic essentialisms of their own whereby they would respond to the tourists' essentialization of Korean masculinity with their essentialization of white femininity. While I found my tourist informants' reworking of Orientalism through Korean television dramas limited in its liberating potential for only succeeding in creating positively connoted stereotypes of Korean masculinity while failing to delink race from gender and sexuality, I didn't find my Korean male informants' tactics to be particularly liberating either. They were engaging in racialized erotic desires that, while having an abundance of liberating potentials for problematizing gender and sexual norms, were limited by the historical and cultural contexts within which they were situated.

Epilogue

• •

Upon my return to the United States from Korea in 2018, I could feel the ubiquity of Korean popular culture in my everyday life. Though I witnessed its global impact during my fieldwork, I did not realize how big K-pop would become. After 2018, the cultural phenomenon seemed to become global on a whole other scale. In this epilogue, I outline some of the Hallyu-related events that occurred after my fieldwork and conceptualize the significance of the racialized erotic in the phenomenon's increasing cross-cultural interconnectedness.

Although most of this book was dedicated to analyzing the global popularity of Korean television drama series, other aspects of Hallyu, such as films and beauty, merit discussion. Starting in 2018 with the film *Burning*, directed by Lee Chang Dong, followed by Bong Joon Ho's *Parasite* in 2019 and Park Chan Wook's *Decision to Leave* in 2022, Korean films began to be nominated for, shortlisted, and even awarded global film awards. In 2019 Bong won the Palme d'Or, the top prize at the Cannes Film Festival, with his film *Parasite*. While many Korean directors and actors had been recognized at Cannes in previous years, *Parasite* was the first Korean film to win the festival's top prize. The film again made history in 2020 by becoming the first non-English-language film to win the Best Picture Award at the Academy Awards. While Korean films' recent feats at the global film festivals could be signs of their superior quality compared to older Korean films, I believe that this success may also be a sign of the mainstream Western culture finally taking Korean popular culture seriously.

Language barriers have been a factor in Korean popular culture's inability to be taken seriously for its literary and artistic merit. However, this seems to be changing. During his speech at the Golden Globes, where *Parasite* won Best Motion Picture for Foreign Language Films, Bong said, "Once you overcome the one-inch-tall barrier of subtitles, you will be introduced to many more amazing films" (NBC 2020). Commentators at major news outlets such as the *New York Times*, *Chicago Tribune*, and CNN applauded Bong for his statement encouraging cultural open-mindedness and cross-cultural connections.

Arguably, Korean films and television dramas were overcoming the barrier of subtitles well before 2020. Nonetheless, Bong's comment emotionally touched many mainstream viewers as an eloquent request for open-mindedness to other cultures. YouTube clips of his speech garnered millions of views, with people in different languages commenting about how touched they were by his words. Likewise, Korean media live-streamed the Academy Award ceremonies, anticipating Bong's success. In the aftermath of his win, the Korean broadcast companies uploaded documentaries of Bong on their YouTube channel, as if they had predicted and prepared for his win. Based on Korean media reactions, Bong's ability to be recognized by the mainstream global award ceremonies was not interpreted as a lucky break but as a recognition that was a long time coming for the Korean film industry.

Films were not the only entertainment forms that overcame the language differences to capture mainstream attention outside the Korean peninsula post-2018. Korean author Han Kang won the Nobel Prize in Literature in 2024. K-pop groups like BTS and Black Pink performed on mainstream American television programs such as *Jimmy Kimmel Live*, *Good Morning America*, the American Music Awards, Billboard Awards, and *The Late Show with Stephen Colbert*. These mainstream media seemed to be in the process of accepting the idea that Korean idols had significant fandom and influence in the American entertainment music industry.

At times, I was amazed to see Korean cultural products in places around the United States where I least expected to see them. As I roamed the Natick Mall in Massachusetts in 2020, I saw posters, CDs, cups, and other items with pictures of BTS and Black Pink on them. In 2020, at the CVS pharmacy in Los Angeles (the last place where anybody would think they would be taken aback), I was taken aback when I saw an entire section dedicated to Korean beauty products. The "K-Beauty" section (so the large label in the aisle proclaimed) featured various Korean face masks and moisturizers. Around the same time, the multinational beauty retailer Sephora created a designated section for K-beauty products in its stores and on its website. Concurrently, the K-beauty regimen, referring to a multi-step skincare routine that supposedly is the key to Korean women's fine skin, became a trend that many YouTubers and social media influencers experimented with and advocated. Korean cultural products came to occupy a space within American stores and have become some individuals' daily skincare routine.

Not only has Korean culture become part of individuals' daily routine, but individuals also consume it literally. Korean food became popular through a YouTube trend called *mukbang* [먹방], a Korean term that refers to entertainment programs featuring people eating large amounts of food. It started on Korean internet broadcasting websites. Some internet broadcasters shared their recorded shows on YouTube, and it became a sensation that people worldwide picked up. The concept of *mukbang*, as well as Korean food featured in the YouTube videos, became famous around the world. The term became a proper noun that is now recognized by non-Koreans.

Perhaps due to the mainstreaming of Korean popular culture, its audience has become more diverse. For instance, an academic I met at a conference who taught at American prisons told me that her students, incarcerated non-Korean men aged forty-five and older, were avid Korean television drama fans who, after finding out she is also a fan, wanted to talk about the dramas with her. The middle-aged men in prison are far from the demographic of the Hallyu tourists whom I interviewed for this book, who were primarily heterosexual ciswomen in their early twenties who were able to roam around the world freely. One theory does not explain all of the diverse fans' desires and attractions to Hallyu and to Korean television dramas. The diverse demographic of Korean television drama consumers and their presumably diverse motivations for consuming Hallyu dramas indicate that there is much work to be done in the future to explore why and how Korean television dramas and other Hallyu products cut across different national and cultural backgrounds of people all over the world.

Even though the reasons for fans' attraction to Hallyu dramas or pop culture at large may be elusive, the outcome of their attraction is clear: the creation of a high-profit industry. Global conglomerates began focusing on the lucrative potential of the Korean television drama industry. Global streaming platforms such as Netflix, Amazon Prime, and Disney+ began to feature an increasing number of Korean television dramas on their platforms. These platforms also began to fund the production of Korean television dramas. Netflix announced in 2023 that it will spend $2.5 billion throughout the next few years to produce Korean television dramas. In 2023 Disney+ helped fund the production of the most expensive Korean television drama to date, titled *Moving* (2023), which had a production budget of roughly $45 million.

On the Korean side, the Korean nation and the Korea-based corporations embraced Hallyu's global mainstream success and affiliated themselves with the phenomenon. A few years ago, I noticed that when I boarded a Korean Airlines flight from the United States to Korea and vice versa, BTS's song "Dynamite" blared from the plane speaker to greet passengers as they found their seats. Unlike the flight safety announcements on other airlines that usually feature flight attendants or paid actors instructing the passengers, Korean

Airlines featured K-pop idols dancing to upbeat tunes as they instructed the passengers on flight safety. The camera would sometimes show a close-up of the idols' beautiful faces and pan out to take a panoramic shot of their muscular bodies. In 2024 the Korean government announced that it would allocate 8.7 percent of the national budget to support the Korean culture and tourism industry (Kim 2023). This means that the total budget for the culture and tourism sector for 2024 will be 1.77 trillion won (approximately $1.3 billion). Specifically, the government vowed to dedicate 1.36 trillion won (approximately $1 billion) to attracting foreign tourists to Korea. Hallyu is front and center in branding Korea as a global nation. From the moment one steps on a Korean Airlines flight to Korea and throughout their travel, they are surrounded by the government's careful plans to enhance foreign tourists' presence in Korea through Hallyu.

The government expends attention and funding to facilitate Hallyu tourism because Hallyu fans are forces to be reckoned with. As indicated in this book, Hallyu fans are not passive couch potatoes; they are mobile and actively challenge social norms. Their presence is noticeable in politics, where they use their digital savviness to make their values of diversity and inclusion known. Many fans acquire digital skills as a result of their fandom, such as getting tickets for K-pop concerts that sell out almost as soon as tickets are available or using hashtags to share images of their favorite Korean celebrities via social networking sites. During the 2020 U.S. presidential election, the fans used such skills to oppose the racist, xenophobic, and otherwise hateful sentiments that specific subsections of the population were toting. Hallyu fans who disliked the hateful rhetoric decided to take matters into their own hands, appropriating the racist hashtags on social media. While using the hashtags, the Hallyu fans began posting photos of their favorite Hallyu stars and, hence, effectively severed one means of communication among disparate racist circles. Furthermore, they participated en masse to get tickets to Trump rallies around the United States so that Donald Trump's actual followers could not go to the rallies to root for him. As a result, some of the rallies were held in quite empty arenas or were canceled (Andini and Akhni 2021). Hallyu fans' involvement in politics goes beyond the United States; scholars have noted their collective mobilization against problematic cultural norms and politics in countries including Poland, Indonesia, and Thailand (Andini and Akhni 2021; Trzcińska 2020).

Based on these examples, it seems like Hallyu's potential is very bright. However, there is some precarity involved in Hallyu's global success because the disparate desires—erotic or otherwise—that comprise Hallyu and its fandom sometimes clash and result in calamitous outcomes for everyone involved. The demise of a popular Korean television drama streaming platform, Dramafever, indicates the logistical precarity of Hallyu dramas. Before 2018 the most prominent Korean drama streaming sites in the United States were Dramafever and Rakuten Viki. However, Dramafever shut down overnight in 2018 without warning, leaving many fans who relied on the website for Korean drama consumption befuddled. Other online fan spaces were plastered with questions from the fans asking whether Dramafever's shutdown was temporary or permanent. No one seemed to have an answer. The murky situation became messier when a former executive of Dramafever sued its parent company, Warner Bros., for wrongful termination. Chung Chang, the former president of Dramafever, stated that Warner Bros.' claim that it had to shut down the popular website due to possible copyright infringement issues is false and that the corporation was motivated by its anti-Asian bias (Perman 2019). Chang claimed that he was personally subjected to many racially insensitive and discriminatory instances in Warner Bros. board meetings and that such instances indicated the company's anti-Asian mindset, which worked against the preservation of Dramafever (Perman 2019). While I do not have knowledge of what drove Chung Chang and Warner Bros. to make the decisions they did, it seems as though they lost out on a lucrative opportunity to be one of the pioneers in Korean drama streaming. The subscribers and the fans lost a reliable website where they could access various Korean television dramas. The messy and abrupt closure of Dramafever is symbolic of what could happen to Hallyu at large when disparate desires clash and refuse to work with each other.

Is Hallyu just a phase driven by ephemeral desires? On the one hand, at nonacademic venues where the participants were primarily Hallyu fans, they asked me questions about the disparity between fictional Korean masculinity and that in real life. The fans who have already been to Korea and those who anticipated going to Korea someday to find Korean boyfriends shared their experiences and expectations regarding Korean men. I sensed that these conversations were tinged with hope that there weren men somewhere in the world who were romantic and caring rather than patriarchal and sexually demanding. To them, Hallyu was not merely a phase; it was a phenomenon that deeply impacted their conceptions of gender and erotic desires. On the other hand, at some academic conferences I encountered skeptics who believed Hallyu was a phase. For instance, after I presented a paper at a conference, a middle-aged woman in the audience raised her hand and asked, "How old are your research subjects?" When I responded that they were in their early twenties, the audience member said, "Oh, that is why they are so naïve. They are living in a dream world. They'll grow out of it." This comment presumed that Hallyu was just a phase for my informants, who, the person believed, would presumably grow out of their love for Korean television dramas when they grew older.

I cannot predict the future and cannot foretell Hallyu's future. All I can do is look to the past to anticipate Hallyu's future trajectory. Admittedly, since the era of silent films, and perhaps before that, the West has been fascinated with the East, and vice versa. During the silent film era, Sessue Hayakawa, a Japanese American actor, became a heart-throb for many U.S. viewers; he was dark, mysterious, dangerous, and therefore sexually appealing (Miyao 2007). His fame not only spoke to the West's Orientalist fascination with the "East" and its people but also to the geopolitical situations that influenced how the mainstream U.S. audience perceived him as a double-faced, mysterious, and dangerous man who may appear gentlemanly on the outside but is beast-like in private (Peng 2022). Perhaps the K-pop idols BTS and Hallyu celebrities and their transnational fandom are contemporary, larger-scale, and more global variations of the Sessue Hayakawa phenomenon in the United States that occurred over a hundred years ago. Heterosexual women's continuous search for alternative masculinity through fictional stories of the racial and ethnic "Other" indicates the irrevocable entwinement between erotics and race.

However, Hallyu and the fandom surrounding Sessue Hayakawa are also somewhat different, which makes it harder to predict Hallyu's future. Hayaka-wa's popularity among the U.S. audience arose from them consuming locally produced Hollywood depictions of Asian American men. Such media was tinged with racist overtones., Hallyu, in contrast, is a transnational media phenomenon whereby the fans are consuming and fantasizing about depictions of Korean men that were produced in Korea. Relatedly, the critical difference between Hayakawa's career and that of many Korean celebrities is that the former experienced a considerable dip in popularity when he shifted from starring in silent films to films with sound. In contrast, Korean celebrities and popular culture have overcome the language barrier in ways that Hayakawa's slight accent was unable to in the early 1900s. They became transnationally popular by acting and singing in Korean and in Korean media. They are rarely maligned for speaking accented English. Hallyu's transnationality provides it with the potential to problematize gender, sexual, and racial assumptions in one cultural context with media from another culture.

While I cannot make a definitive statement as to whether Hallyu will last longer than other phases of the West's interests in Asian cultures, I can say that I empathized with my informants in multiple regards and that their racialized erotic desires should not merely be cast off as a trivial "phase" that people go through and move away from. My informants were wholly immersed in the fictional worlds; that does not make them naïve. Neither does the government's efforts to use Hallyu dramas to rebrand the national image nor my Korean male informants' reworking of Korean masculinity through television dramas make them manipulative. In the introduction to this book, I state that the stories I analyze are stories of desire. I want to reiterate that point here, at the end of the book, to emphasize my view that the phenomenon, while not having reached its liberating potential to debunk geopolitical, racial, and gendered norms in

Korea and beyond due to the legacy of Orientalism and nationalism within which it operates, can still be categorized as something more than a mere "phase" of naïve or deceptive individuals. My informants' desires were fueled by problems with gender and sexual norms that they experienced to be real and attempted to rework through Korean television dramas. As I have argued, transnational Korean television dramas create mediated erotic connections that attempt to rework the binaries of the powerful versus powerless, Orientalizer versus the Orientalized, and the desiring versus desired subjects.

Acknowledgments

I am thankful to many people I've met in academia. As an undergraduate student at Williams College, I was inspired to pursue academia thanks to the mentorship of professors Christopher Bolton and Helga Druxes. As a graduate student at UCLA, I learned research and pedagogy from many scholars, but I especially want to thank Purnima Mankekar, Lieba Faier, Elizabeth Marchant, and John Caldwell. Purnima and Lieba have especially taken time out of their busy schedules to help me make sense of my research, and I am eternally grateful for their generosity and constructive feedback. Staff at UCLA Gender Studies, Jenna Miller-Von Ah, Richard Medrano, Van Do-Nguyen, and Samantha Hogan were instrumental in helping me figure out the logistics of grad-student life. I am thankful for Stephanie Chang's friendship, which lasted beyond our days at UCLA.

Once I acquired my PhD, I traveled cross-country in my pursuit of full-time jobs, where I met wonderful colleagues who helped me while I was wondering whether there was a place for me in academia. I met Elena Creef, Rosanna Hertz, Jennifer Musto, and Xan Chacko at Wellesley College. I remember our end-of-semester campfires and impromptu get-togethers full of food and laughter. I started my visiting lecturer position during COVID-19. While it could have been a difficult situation, the faculty's goodwill helped me overcome any anxieties I may have had about teaching in ballrooms and chapels modified into classrooms to accommodate the six-feet distancing requirement. At Indiana University, Bloomington, Seung-kyung Kim in East Asian Languages and Cultures, Stephanie Andrea Allen, Sara Friedman, Colin R. Johnson, Meredith Lee, Stephanie A. Sanders, Brenda R. Weber, Cynthia Wu in the Department of Gender Studies, and Sonia Song-Ha Lee and Sylvia Martinez at the Center for Research on Race and Ethnicity in Society greeted me with open arms from the moment I accepted the postdoctoral fellowship. I am very grateful that I was able to make acquaintance with these folks because their combined academic brilliance, down-to-earth personalities, and helpful mentorship during the short time we spent together in Bloomington helped shape my vision for what kind of academic I wanted to be in the future.

I am fortunate to now teach at Occidental College, where I have met many supportive colleagues. During my first year as a Mellon Postdoctoral Fellow, Leila Neti organized programs and provided mentorship so that I could make the best out of the fellowship. The get-togethers with Leila, Sohaib Khan, and Season Blake, my postdoc cohort, were awesome. Department of Asian Studies colleagues Alexander F. Day, Amy Holmes-Tagchungdarpa, Yurika Wakamatsu, Jingyi Li, and Meimei Zhang fostered a great sense of community over all the meals that we had together. I would also like to thank all my colleagues on the fourth floor of Johnson Hall. Our weekly lunches make my day. I thank Romy Corona for the awesome food you sometimes bring and for all the logistical issues you take care of on my behalf. Jane Hong, Yumi Pak, and Heather Lukes have provided a lot of their time to answer my teaching and research-related questions, and I am grateful for their generosity. I also want to thank my thirteen colleagues who began their career at "Oxy" along with me during the 2023–2024 academic year.

There are many people whom I feel grateful to for helping me with the publication of this book. I am indebted to all my research participants for sharing their precious time to help me with my research. Nicole Solano at Rutgers University Press was so supportive of my book project. I was feeling insecure about my work, but her affirmations and excitement helped me finish my manuscript. I am thankful for the anonymous reviewers who provided constructive feedback that helped me think more deeply about the topic at hand. I also thank the copy editor, Michelle Asakawa, indexer Amron Lehte, and the cover design team who helped during the last stretch of the production process. I thank all my family and relatives who supported me throughout the book-writing process. Last, I thank all the readers who have picked up this book for taking interest in the subject.

Earlier versions of chapters 2 and 4 were published in the journals *Feminist Formations* and *Journal of Tourism and Cultural Change* as well as in a chapter of the anthology *The Rise of K-Dramas: Essays on Korean Television and Its Global Consumption.*

Notes

Introduction

1 I am using the Revised Romanization of Korean.

Chapter 1   Mouth Agape and Ecstatically Screaming

1 I translated the post from Korean to English. I am responsible for all translations from Korean to English in this book henceforth.
2 Since her performance in *The Jewel in the Palace* (2003), she did not star in any other television drama until *Saimdang: Memoir of Color* (2017).

Chapter 2   Romance and Masculinity in Korean Television Dramas

1 Chungdamdong is an affluent part of Seoul. "Chungdamdong daughter-in-law" is a popular term to refer to women who are prototypically feminine and docile. The term is used to refer to women who have the appearance and characteristics that make them suitable to be daughters-in-law to rich families that live in Chungdamdong.
2 Even though my informants occasionally mentioned classic Hallyu dramas like *The Jewel in the Palace* (2002) or *Winter Sonata* (2002), most of them seemed to have already moved beyond such dramas, which have already been thoroughly studied and analyzed in Hallyu scholarship (Han and Lee 2008).
3 For instance, the KCSC is responsible for blocking harmful websites including pornographic sites. In Korea all pornographic materials and websites are banned. If one attempts to access such content, one will be redirected to a KCSC website that warns about the dangers of harmful content and the penalties for accessing such media.
4 I translated the rules from Korean to English.

Chapter 5   "How Can We Compete with Men Like That?"

1 The Korean man was not actually related to me by blood. In Korean, *nuna* (elder sister) is an honorific term that younger men use to address older women.

2 These tourists were thrifty and resourceful in their travels; they would work part-time at hostels to fund their travel, stay at hostels rather than hotels, and take the cheapest transportation available (i.e., boats and buses rather than airplanes). However, the fact that they could afford to spend several months traveling, as opposed to holding a steady job, indicates that they were not in financial situations where they had to support their families or worry about long-term financial plans.

3 I am responsible for translating the Korean dialogue in this chapter to English.

4 Soju is a Korean traditional hard liquor.

References

Abelmann, Nancy. 2003. *The Melodrama of Mobility: Women, Talk, and Class in Contemporary South Korea*. Honolulu: University of Hawaii Press.

Abu-Lughod, Lila. 2002. "Do Muslim Women Really Need Saving? Anthropological Reflections on Cultural Relativism and Its Others." *American Anthropologist* 104 (3): 783–790.

Abu-Lughod, Lila. 2013. *Do Muslim Women Need Saving?* Cambridge, MA: Harvard University Press.

Ahmed, Sara. 2014. *Cultural Politics of Emotion*. Edinburgh: Edinburgh University Press.

Ahn, Ji-Hyun. 2015. "Desiring Biracial Whites: Cultural Consumption of White Mixed-Race Celebrities in South Korean Popular Media." *Media, Culture & Society* 37 (6): 937–947.

Anderson, Crystal S. 2020. *Soul in Seoul: African American Popular Music and K-pop*. Jackson: University Press of Mississippi.

Andini, Amalia Nur, and Ghaziah Nurika Akhni. 2021. "Exploring Youth Political Participation: K-pop Fan Activism in Indonesia and Thailand." *Global Focus* 1 (1): 38–55.

Ang, Ien. 1985. *Watching Dallas: Soap Opera and the Melodramatic Imagination*. New York: Routledge.

Ang, Ien. 2007. "Melodramatic Identifications: Television Fiction and Women's Fantasy." In *Feminist Television Criticism: A Reader*, edited by Charlotte Brunsdon and Lynn Spigel, 235–246. New York: McGraw-Hill Education.

Appadurai, Arjun. 1996. *Modernity at Large: Cultural Dimensions of Globalization*. Minneapolis: University of Minnesota Press.

Bae, Michelle S. 2011. "Interrogating Girl Power: Girlhood, Popular Media, and Postfeminism." *Visual Arts Research* 37 (2): 28–40.

Bae, Yeon-Ho. 2019. "After the Song-Song Couple Divorce, the Number of Visitors to the *Descendants of the Sun* Filming Set in Taebaek City Plummet [송송 커플 이혼 이후... 태양의 후예 태백세트장 방문객 '뚝']." *Yonhap News*, September 5. https://www.yna.co.kr/view/AKR20190905104200062.

Baudinette, Thomas. 2021. *Regimes of Desire: Young Gay Men, Media, and Masculinity in Tokyo*. Ann Arbor: University of Michigan Press.

Baxandall, Rosalyn, and Linda Gordon. 2002. "Second-Wave Feminism." In *A Companion to American Women's History*, edited by Nancy A. Hewitt, 414–430. Malden, MA: Blackwell.

Bennett, Lucy. 2014. "Tracing Textual Poachers: Reflections on the Development of Fan Studies and Digital Fandom." *Journal of Fandom Studies* 2 (1): 5–20.

Berlant, Lauren. 2008. *The Female Complaint: The Unfinished Business of Sentimentality in American Culture*. Durham, NC: Duke University Press.

Bernstein, Elizabeth. 2007. *Temporarily Yours: Intimacy, Authenticity, and the Commerce of Sex*. Chicago: University of Chicago Press.

Bibigo. 2014. "CJ Bibigo Spreads Positive Images of Korean Food at American Hallyu Event, 'KCON 2014' [CJ 비비고, 미국 'KCON 2014' 현장에서 한식 홍보]." CJ Cheiljedang, accessed August 12, 2024. http://m.bibigo.com/kr/news-detail?cPage=4&seq=17.

Bibigo. 2015. "CJ Bibigo Spreads Positive Images of Korean Food at American Hallyu Event, 'KCON 2015' [CJ 비비고, 미국 한류행사 'KCON 2015'에서 한식 알리다]." CJ Cheiljedang, accessed August 12, 2024. http://m.bibigo.com/kr/news-detail?cPage=3&seq=21.

Boellstorff, Tom. 2003. "Dubbing Culture: Indonesian Gay and Lesbi Subjectivities and Ethnography in an Already Globalized World." *American Ethnologist* 30 (2): 225–242.

Botorić, Vlada. 2022. "Periphery Fandom: Contrasting Fans' Productive Experiences Across the Globe." *Journal of Consumer Culture* 22 (4): 889–907.

Bow, Leslie. 2021. *Racist Love: Asian Abstraction and the Pleasures of Fantasy*. Durham, NC: Duke University Press.

Brennan, Denise. 2001. "Tourism in Transnational Places: Dominican Sex Workers and German Sex Tourists Imagine One Another." *Identities Global Studies in Culture and Power* 7 (4): 621–663.

Bury, Rhiannon. 2017. "Technology, Fandom and Community in the Second Media Age." *Convergence* 23 (6): 627–642.

Busse, Kristina. 2015. "Fan Labor and Feminism: Capitalizing on the Fannish Labor of Love." *Cinema Journal* 54 (3): 110–115.

Butler, Jess. 2013. "For White Girls Only?: Postfeminism and the Politics of Inclusion." *Feminist Formations* 25 (1): 35–58.

Butler, Judith. 2004. *Undoing Gender*. New York: Routledge.

Cartwright, Ashleigh. 2022. "A Theory of Racialized Cultural Capital." *Sociological Inquiry* 92 (2): 317–340.

Cha, Na Young, Claire Shinhea Lee, and Ji Hoon Park. 2016. "Construction of Obedient Foreign Brides as Exotic Others: How Production Practices Construct the Images of Marriage Migrant Women on Korean Television." *International Journal of Communication* 10 (2016): 1470–1488.

Chalaby, Jean K. 2005. "Deconstructing the Transnational: A Typology of Cross-Border Television Channels in Europe." *New Media & Society* 7 (2): 155–175.

Channel A. 2014 [채널A 뉴스TOP10]. "Former President Park Jung-Hee's Visit to West Germany in 1964 [1964년 박정희 前 대통령 서독 방문 영상 공개_채널A_뉴스TOP10]." YouTube, March 19. https://www.youtube.com/watch?v=iNyplH5GrJc.

Cheng, Sealing. 2011. *On the Move for Love: Migrant Entertainers and the U.S. Military in South Korea*. Philadelphia: University of Pennsylvania Press.

Cheng, Sealing. 2021. "The Male Malady of Globalization: Phallocentric Nationalism in South Korea." *Current Anthropology* 62 (S23): S79–S91.

Cho, A-Ra. 2016. "President Park Says Song Joong-Ki Is a 'Real Patriot' and That *Descendants of the Sun* 'Increases One's Sense of Patriotism' [朴대통령, 송중기에 "진짜 애국청년" ... '태후'엔 "애국심 고취 효과"]." *Asia Business Daily*, April 11. http://cm.asiae.co.kr/article/2016041116204523149.

Cho, Grace M. 2006. "Diaspora of Camptown: The Forgotten War's Monstrous Family." *Women's Studies Quarterly* 34 (1/2): 309–331.

Cho, Jinhyun. 2021a. "Constructing a White Mask Through English: The Misrecognized Self in Orientalism." *International Journal of the Sociology of Language* 2021 (271): 17–34.

Cho, Jinhyun. 2021b. "English Fever and American Dreams: The Impact of Orientalism on the Evolution of English in Korean Society." *English Today* 37 (3): 142–147.

Cho, Jung Sun. 2013. SBS "Goddess of Marriage" Writer Jung Sun Choi Interview. In *Television Writers' Monthly*, edited by Mi-Hye Choi. Korea: Korea TV & Radio Writers Association.

Cho, Uhn. 2004. "Gender Inequality and Patriarchal Order Reexamined." *Korea Journal* 44 (1): 22–41.

Choe, Youngmin. 2016. *Tourist Distractions: Traveling and Feeling in Transnational Hallyu Cinema*. Durham, NC: Duke University Press.

Choi, Doing-Uk. 2019. "KCON Captured Global Attention ... 8 Year Cumulative Attendance Passed the 1 Million Mark [지구촌 홀린 케이콘 ... 8년 누적관객 100만 명 넘었다]." *Korea Economics Daily*, August 19. https://www.hankyung.com/life/article/2019081927411.

Choi, Hyaeweol. 2014. "Constructions of Marriage and Sexuality in Modern Korea." In *Routledge Handbook of Sexuality Studies in East Asia*, 87–100. New York: Routledge.

Choi, Seokmoo. 2005. "A Critical Reflection upon Korean High School English Readings: Power Relations and Orientalism." *English Teaching* [영어교육] 60 (4): 517–532.

Choi, Soo-Jin. 2021. "Netflix Achieved Success Through *Squid Game* but Is Criticized for Its Stubbornness During a Government Audit ['오징어게임'으로 대박난 넷플릭스, 국감에선 '배짱 장사' 비판]." *Korea Economic Daily*, October 6. https://www.hankyung.com/article/2021100067973g.

Chon-Smith, Chong. 2014. "Yellow Bodies, Black Sweat: Yao Ming, Ichiro Suzuki, and Global Sport." *Journal for Cultural Research* 18 (4): 291–314.

Chua, Peter, and Dune C. Fujino. 1999. "Negotiating New Asian-American Masculinities: Attitudes and Gender Expectations." *Journal of Men's Studies* 7 (3): 391–413.

Chung, Erin Aeran. 2019. "Creating Hierarchies of Noncitizens: Race, Gender, and Visa Categories in South Korea." *Journal of Ethnic and Migration Studies* 46 (12): 1–18.

Chung, Yong-Hwa. 2006. "The Modern Transformation of Korean Identity: Enlightenment and Orientalism." *Korea Journal* 46 (1): 109–138.

Connell, Raewyn W. 1995. Masculinities. Berkeley: University of California Press.

Connell, Raewyn W., and James W. Messerschmidt. 2005. "Hegemonic Masculinity: Rethinking the Concept." *Gender & Society* 19 (6): 829–859.

Couldry, Nick. 2005. "On the Actual Street." In *The Media and the Tourist Imagination: Converging Cultures*, edited by David Crouch, Rhona Jackson, and Felix Thompson, 60–75. New York: Routledge.

Couldry, Nick. 2007. "On the Set of *The Sopranos*: "Inside" a Fan's Construction of Nearness." In *Fandom: Identities and Communities in a Mediated World*, edited by Jonathan Gray, Cornel Sandvoss, and C. Lee Harrington, 139–148. New York: NYU Press.

Creighton, Millie. 2009. "Japanese Surfing the Korean Wave: Drama Tourism, Nationalism, and Gender via Ethnic Eroticisms." *Southeast Review of Asian Studies* 31:10–38.

Cresswell, Tim. 2010. "Towards a Politics of Mobility." *Environment and Planning D: Society and Space* 28 (1): 17–31.

De Certeau, Michel. 2014. "Reading as Poaching." In *Readers and Reading*, 150–163. New York: Routledge.

Deleuze, Gilles, and Félix Guattari. 1983. *Anti-Oedipus*. Minnesota: University of Minnesota Press.

Deleuze, Gilles, and Félix Guattari. 2004. *Anti-Oedipus: Capitalism and Schizophrenia, Bloomsbury Revelations*. London: Bloomsbury.

Demetriou, Demetrakis Z. 2001. "Connell's Concept of Hegemonic Masculinity: A Critique." *Theory and Society* 30 (3): 337–361.

Desmond, Jane. 1999. *Staging Tourism: Bodies on Display from Waikiki to Sea World*. Chicago: University of Chicago Press.

Diaz Pino, Camilo. 2021. ""K-pop Is Rupturing Chilean Society": Fighting with Globalized Objects in Localized Conflicts." *Communication, Culture and Critique* 14 (4): 551–567.

Diederich, Inga Kim. 2021. "Blood of the Nation: Medical Eugenics, Bio-Nationalism, and Identity Formation in Cold War South Korea." PhD diss., University of California, San Diego.

Doolan, Yuri. 2021. "The Camptown Origins of International Adoption and the Hypersexualization of Korean Children." *Journal of Asian American Studies* 24 (3): 351–382.

Dwyer, Tessa. 2012. "Fansub Dreaming on ViKi: "Don't Just Watch but Help When You Are Free."" *Translator* 18 (2): 217–243.

Ebron, Paulla. 1997. "Traffic in Men." In *Gendered Encounters: Challenging Cultural Boundaries and Social Hierarchies in Africa*, edited by Maria Grosz-Ngate and Omari Kokole, 223–244. New York: Routledge.

Edensor, Tim. 2009. "Tourism and Performance." In *The Sage Handbook of Tourism Studies*, edited by Tazim Jamal and Mike Robinson, 543–557. Thousand Oaks, CA: Sage.

Elfving-Hwang, Joanna. 2011. "Not so Soft After All: Kkonminam Masculinities in Contemporary South Korean Popular Culture." Seventh KSAA Biennial Conference.

Elfving-Hwang, Joanna K. 2021. "Man Made Beautiful: The Social Role of Grooming and Body Work in Performing Middle-Aged Corporate Masculinity in South Korea." *Men and Masculinities* 24 (2): 207–227.

Eng, David L. 2001. *Racial Castration: Managing Masculinity in Asian America*. Durham, NC: Duke University Press.

Fedorenko, Olga. 2022. "*Squid Game*'s Foreigners: Orientalism, Occidentalism, Sub-imperialism." *Communication, Culture & Critique* 15 (4): 538–539.

Fleming, Paul J., Clare Barrington, Suzanne Maman, Leonel Lerebours, Yeycy Donastorg, and Maximo O. Brito. 2019. "Competition and Humiliation: How Masculine Norms Shape Men's Sexual and Violent Behaviors." *Men and Masculinities* 22 (2): 197–215.

Foster, Jordan, and Jayne Baker. 2022. "Muscles, Makeup, and Femboys: Analyzing TikTok's "Radical" Masculinities." *Social Media Society* 8 (3): 1–14.

Fung, Anthony. 2016. "Redefining Creative Labor: East Asian Comparisons." In *Precarious Creativity: Global Media, Local Labor,* edited by Michael Curtin and Kevin Sanson, 200–214. Oakland: University of California Press.

Gage, Sue-Je L. 2013. "'We're Never Off Duty': Empire and the Economies of Race and Gender in the U.S. Military Camptowns of Korea." *Cross-Currents: East Asian History and Culture Review* 1 (6): 121–153.

Gammon, Thi. 2023. "'Isn't It a Bit Rough?': Vietnamese Audience Reception of Wrist-Grabbing in Korean Television Dramas, Feminist Consciousness, and Fantasy." *Sexuality & Culture* 27:1599–1618.

Garcia, Cathy Rose A. 2010. "Founder of Largest English K-pop Site Soompi." *Korea Times,* November 12.

Gibson-Graham, Julie-Katherine. 1996. "Querying Globalization." *Rethinking Marxism* 9 (1): 1–27.

Gledhill, Christine. 1992. "Speculations on the Relationship Between Soap Opera and Melodrama." *Quarterly Review of Film & Video* 14 (1–2): 103–124.

Graburn, Nelson H. H. 1983. "Tourism and Prostitution." *Annals of Tourism Research* 10 (3): 437–443.

Gray, Jonathan, Cornel Sandvoss, and C. Lee Harrington. 2007. "Introduction: Why Study Fans?" In *Fandom: Identities and Communities in a Mediated World,* edited by Jonathan Gray, Cornel Sandvoss, and C. Lee Harrington, 1–18. New York: NYU Press.

Grewal, Inderpal. 2013. "Outsourcing Patriarchy: Feminist Encounters, Transnational Mediations and the Crime of 'Honour Killings.'" *International Feminist Journal of Politics* 15 (1): 1–19.

Griffin, Rachel Alicia. 2014. "Pushing into Precious: Black Women, Media Representation, and the Glare of the White Supremacist Capitalist Patriarchal Gaze." *Critical Studies in Media Communication* 31 (3): 182–197.

Gupta, Akhil, and James Ferguson. 1992. "Beyond 'Culture': Space, Identity, and the Politics of Difference." *Cultural Anthropology* 7 (1): 6–23.

Gupta, Akhil, and James Ferguson. 1997. "Culture, Power, Place: Ethnography at the End of an Era." In *Culture, Power, Place: Explorations in Critical Anthropology,* 1–29. Durham, NC: Duke University Press.

Gvosdev, Nikolas K. 2007. "Russia: 'European but Not Western'?" *Orbis* 51 (1): 129–140.

Han, C. Winter. 2021. *Racial Erotics: Gay Men of Color, Sexual Racism, and the Politics of Desire.* Seattle: University of Washington Press.

Han, Hee-Joo, and Jae-Sub Lee. 2008. "A Study on the KBS TV Drama *Winter Sonata* and Its Impact on Korea's Hallyu Tourism Development." *Journal of Travel & Tourism Marketing* 24 (2–3): 115–126.

Han, Ji Soo, and Joo Hee Choi. 2023. "Women's Non-traditional Gender Role Attitudes and Acceptance of Men's Color Makeup in South Korea." *Journal of Gender Studies* 32 (6): 575–587.

Han, Min Wha. 2022. "Reframing the Difference of Co-ethnic Other in Japan: An Analysis of Representations and Identifications in the South Korean Documentary Film *Uri-Hakkyo.*" In *Mediating the South Korean Other: Representations and Discourses of Difference in the Post/Neocolonial Nation-State,* edited by David C. Oh, 178–196. Ann Arbor: University of Michigan Press.

Han, Woori, Claire Shinhea Lee, and Ji Hoon Park. 2017. "Gendering the Authenticity of the Military Experience: Male Audience Responses to the Korean Reality Show *Real Men.*" *Media, Culture & Society* 39 (1): 62–76.

Hanich, Julian, Winfried Menninghaus, and Steve Wilder. 2017. "Beyond Sadness: The Multi-emotional Trajectory of Melodrama." *Cinema Journal* 56 (4): 76–101.

Haslam, Jonathan. 2011. *Russia's Cold War: From the October Revolution to the Fall of the Wall.* New Haven, CT: Yale University Press.

Hesse, Barnor. 2007. "Racialized Modernity: An Analytics of White Mythologies." *Ethnic and Racial Studies* 30 (4): 643–663.

Hoang, Kimberly Kay. 2015. *Dealing in Desire: Asian Ascendancy, Western Decline, and the Hidden Currencies of Global Sex Work.* Oakland: University of California Press.

Hobbs, Jeffrey Dale, Piengpen Na Pattalung, and Robert C. Chandler. 2011. "Advertising Phuket's Nightlife on the Internet: A Case Study of Double Binds and Hegemonic Masculinity in Sex Tourism." *Sojourn: Journal of Social Issues in Southeast Asia* 26 (1): 80–104.

Holland, Eugene W. 2002. *Deleuze and Guattari's Anti-Oedipus: Introduction to Schizoanalysis.* London: Routledge.

Holland, Sharon Patricia. 2012. *The Erotic Life of Racism.* Durham, NC: Duke University Press.

Holmlund, Chris. 2005. "Postfeminism from A to G." *Cinema Journal* 44 (2): 116–121.

hooks, bell. 2000. *All About Love: New Visions.* New York: Harper Collins.

Horsburgh, Beverly. 1995. "Schrodinger's Cat, Eugenics, and the Compulsory Sterilization of Welfare Mothers: Deconstructing an Old/New Rhetoric and Constructing the Reproductive Right to Natality for Low-Income Women of Color." *Cardozo Law Review* 17:531.

Huang, Shuzhen, and Daniel C. Brouwer. 2018. "Negotiating Performances of "Real" Marriage in Chinese Queer Xinghun." *Women's Studies in Communication* 41 (2): 140–158.

Hyun, Jaehwan. 2019. "Blood Purity and Scientific Independence: Blood Science and Postcolonial Struggles in Korea, 1926–1975." *Science in Context* 32 (3): 239–260.

Iwabuchi, Koichi. 2010. "Undoing Inter-national Fandom in the Age of Brand Nationalism." *Mechademia* 5 (1): 87–96.

Iwashita, Chieko. 2008. "Roles of Films and Television Dramas in International Tourism: The Case of Japanese Tourists to the UK." *Journal of Travel & Tourism Marketing* 24 (2–3): 139–151.

Jang, Sun-Wook. 2021. "Gwang-Ju's K-pop Star Street Project Becomes Bigger in Scale [판 커지는 광주 'K팝 스타 거리']." *Kukmin Ilbo*, August 30. http://news.kmib.co.kr/article/view.asp?arcid=0924206894&code=11131423&cp=nv.

Jankowiak, William. 1997. "Introduction." In *Romantic Passion: A Universal Experience?*, edited by William Jankowiak, 1–20. New York: Columbia University Press.

Jeffreys, Sheila. 2003. "Sex Tourism: Do Women Do It Too?" *Leisure Studies* 22 (3): 223–238.

Jenkins, Henry, III. 1988. "*Star Trek* Rerun, Reread, Rewritten: Fan Writing as Textual Poaching." *Critical Studies in Media Communication* 5 (2): 85–107.

Jenkins, Henry. 2006. *Convergence Culture: Where Old and New Media Collide.* New York: NYU Press.

Jenkins, Henry. 2007. "Afterword: The Future of Fandom." In *Fandom: Identities and Communities in a Mediated World*, edited by Jonathan Gray, Cornel Sandvoss, and C. Lee Harrington, 357–364. New York: NYU Press.

Jenkins, Henry. 2019. "'Art Happens Not in Isolation, but in Community': The Collective Literacies of Media Fandom." *Cultural Science Journal* 11 (1): 78–88.

Jenkins, Henry, Sam Ford, and Joshua Green. 2013. *Spreadable Media: Creating Value and Meaning in a Networked Culture*. New York: NYU Press.

Jeong, Euisol, and Jieun Lee. 2018. "We Take the Red Pill, We Confront the DickTrix: Online Feminist Activism and the Augmentation of Gendered Realities in South Korea." *Feminist Media Studies* 18 (4): 705–717.

Jin, Dal Yong. 2016. *New Korean Wave: Transnational Cultural Power in the Age of Social Media*. Chicago: University of Illinois Press.

Jin, Dal Yong. 2020. "Comparative Discourse on J-pop and K-pop: Hybridity in Contemporary Local Music." *Korea Journal* 60 (1): 40–70.

Jo, Hang-Jae. 2013. "Television Melodramas and Nationalism in Early Korea: An Analysis of *Madam*, *The Road*, and *Step Mother*." In *Korean Television Drama History and the Periphery* [한국의 텔레비전 드라마: 역사와 경계], edited by Korean Association for Broadcasting & Telecommunication Studies, 12–166. Seoul: Culture Look.

Jones, Angela. 2019. "The Pleasures of Fetishization: BBW Erotic Webcam Performers, Empowerment, and Pleasure." *Fat Studies* 8 (3): 279–298.

Jun, Helen Heran. 2011. *Race for Citizenship: Black Orientalism and Asian Uplift from Pre-emancipation to Neoliberal America, Nation of Newcomers*. New York: NYU Press.

Jung, Eun-Young. 2010. "Playing the Race and Sexuality Cards in the Transnational Pop Game: Korean Music Videos for the U.S. Market." *Journal of Popular Music Studies* 22 (2): 219–236.

Jung, Gowoon. 2023. "Men Who Wear Make-up: Young Korean Men's Masculinity Management in the Neoliberal Korea." *Critical Sociology* 49 (7–8): 1269–1288.

Jung, Gowoon, and Minyoung Moon. 2024. ""I AM A FEMINIST, BUT . . ." Practicing Quiet Feminism in the Era of Everyday Backlash in South Korea." *Gender & Society* 38 (2): 216–243.

Jung, Jin-Woo. 2020. "'BTS Mandatory Military Service Extension Bill' Passes the National Defense Committee . . . It Is Their Right, Not a Privilege" ['BTS 병역연기법' 국방위 문턱 넘었다...."특혜가 아닌 권리"]." *JoongAng Ilbo*, November 20. https://news.joins.com/article/23925726.

Jung, Joon-Young. 2012. "Racism of 'Blood' and Colonial Medicine-Blood Group Anthropology Studies at Keijo Imperial University Department of Forensic Medicine [피의 인종주의와 식민지의학: 경성제대 법의학교실의 혈액형인류학]." *Korean Journal of Medical History* [의사학] 21 (3): 513–549.

Jung, Sun. 2010. *Korean Masculinities and Transcultural Consumption: Yonsama, Rain, Oldboy, K-pop Idols*. Hong Kong: Hong Kong University Press.

Jung, Yoon-Mi. 2022. "The Success of Drama 'Extraordinary Attorney Woo' Was Not a Happenstance? [빈틈없는 드라마 우영우 신드롬은 우연이 아니었다?]." *Broadcast Media Writers* [방송작가] 199 (October). http://www.ktrwawebzine.kr/page/vol199/view.php?volNum=vol199&seq=2. Broadcast Media Writers [방송작가].

Kang, Dredge Byung'chu. 2017. "Eastern Orientations: Thai Middle-Class Gay Desire for 'White Asians.'" *Culture, Theory and Critique* 58 (2): 182–208.

Kang, Laura Hyun Yi. 2020. *Traffic in Asian Women*. Durham, NC: Duke University Press.

Kang-Nguyen, Dredge Byung'chu. 2019. "The Softening of Butches: The Adoption of Korean 'Soft' Masculinity Among Thai Toms." In *Pop Empires: Transnational and*

Diasporic Flows of India and Korea, edited by S. Heijin Lee, Monika Mehta, and Robert Ji-Song Ku. Kindle. Hawaii: University of Hawaii Press.

Kaplan, Caren. 1996. *Questions of Travel: Postmodern Discourses of Displacement.* Durham, NC: Duke University Press.

Kaplan, Caren. 2001. "Hillary Rodham Clinton's Orient: Cosmopolitan Travel and Global Feminist Subjects." *Meridians* 2 (1): 219–240.

Kelsky, Karen. 1999. "Gender, Modernity, and Eroticized Internationalism in Japan." *Cultural Anthropology* 14 (2): 229–255.

Kemper, Michael. 2018. "Russian Orientalism." In *Oxford Research Encyclopedia of Asian History*, Article e-297. Oxford: Oxford University Press.

Kim, Bang-Hyun, and Jin-Ho Park. 2019. "Why Are People Flocking to *Descendants of the Sun*'s Taebaek Filming Location and Song Joon-Ki's House in Daejeon? ['태양의 후예' 태백세트장, 대전 송중기 태어난 집에 방문객 몰리는 까닭은?]." *JoongAng Daily*, July 1. https://www.joongang.co.kr/article/23512747#home.

Kim, Bo-Hwa, Jae Kyung Lee, and Hyunjoon Park. 2016. "Marriage, Independence and Adulthood Among Unmarried Women in South Korea." *Asian Journal of Social Science* 44 (3): 338–362.

Kim, Bum-Suk. 2022. "Why Is There a Controversy Surrounding the Actors' Korean Speaking Skills That Are Only Comprehensible Through Netflix Subtitles? [넷플릭스 자막 켜야 들리는 청력 테스트 배우들 논란,왜?]." *Newsen*, September 26. https://www.newsen.com/news_view.php?uid=202209260018571610.

Kim, Daisy Y. 2017. "Resisting Migrant Precarity: A Critique of Human Rights Advocacy for Marriage Migrants in South Korea." *Critical Asian Studies* 49 (1): 1–17.

Kim, Dong-One, Johngseok Bae, and Changwon Lee. 2018. "Globalization and Labour Rights: The Case of Korea." In *Globalization and Labour in the Asia Pacific*, edited by Chris Rowley and John Benson, 133–153. London: Routledge.

Kim, Ha Neul. 2019. "A Critical Study on the Acceptance of Foreign TV Program in Young Korean Generation: Focusing on the Possibility of Naming 'Patriotic Narcissism' [한국 청년세대의 외국인 예능 프로그램 수용에 관한 비판적 연구]." MA thesis, Hanyang University.

Kim, Hyelin. 2023. "Ministry's 2024 Budget of KRW 6.9T Targets Content, Tourism." Korea.net. https://www.korea.net/NewsFocus/policies/view?articleId=237831#:~:text=The%20budget%20for%20supporting%20industries,and%20improving%20the%20tourism%20deficit.

Kim, Hyun-Suk. 2019. "K-Culture Rocks Manhattan . . . 55,000 Visitors in Two Days [맨해튼 뒤흔든 'K컬처'. . . 이틀새 5만5000명 열광]." *Korea Economic Daily*, July 8. https://www.hankyung.com/life/article/2019070896661.

Kim, Jae Kyun. 2015. "Yellow over Black: History of Race in Korea and the New Study of Race and Empire." *Critical Sociology* 41 (2): 205–217.

Kim, Jodi. 2009. "'An Orphan' with Two Mothers: Transnational and Transracial Adoption, the Cold War, and Contemporary Asian American Cultural Politics." *American Quarterly* 61 (4): 855–880.

Kim, Joon K., Vincent Basile, Jesus Jaime-Diaz, and Ray Black. 2018. "Internal Orientalism and Multicultural Acts: The Challenges of Multicultural Education in Korea." *Multicultural Education Review* 10 (1): 3–17.

Kim, Joong Won. 2022. "The Possessive Investment in Honorary Whiteness?: How Asian and Asian Americans Reify a Transnational Racial Order Through Language." *Ethnic and Racial Studies* 45 (1): 173–191.

Kim, Kyung Hyun. 2021. *Hegemonic Mimicry: Korean Popular Culture of the Twenty-First Century*. Durham, NC: Duke University Press.

Kim, Minjeong. 2014. "South Korean Rural Husbands, Compensatory Masculinity, and International Marriage." *Journal of Korean Studies* 19 (2): 291–325.

Kim, Nadia Y. 2006. "'Patriarchy Is so Third World': Korean Immigrant Women and 'Migrating' White Western Masculinity." *Social Problems* 53 (4): 519–536.

Kim, Sang-Hwa. 2015. "Is It a Goose That Lays Golden Eggs or Is It a Money Sucking Waste? [황금알 낳는 거위 vs 돈 먹는 애물단지?]." *Seoul News*, January 17. http://www.seoul.co.kr/news/newsView.php?id=20150117005004.

Kim, Sangkyun. 2010. "Extraordinary Experience: Re-enacting and Photographing at Screen Tourism Locations." *Tourism and Hospitality Planning & Development* 7 (1): 59–75.

Kim, Sangkyun, and Chanwoo Nam. 2016. "Hallyu Revisited: Challenges and Opportunities for the South Korean Tourism." *Asia Pacific Journal of Tourism Research* 21 (5): 524–540.

Kim, Suk-Young. 2020. *K-pop Live: Fans, Idols, and Multimedia Performance*. Redwood City, CA: Stanford University Press.

Kim, Yoon-Yang. 2022. "Explore and Explore Again Says tvN Series *Our Blues* Writer Hee Kyung Noh [탐구하고 또 탐구하라 tvN <우리들의 블루스> 노희경 작가]." *Broadcast Media Writers* [방송작가] 199 (October). http://www.ktrwawebzine.kr/page/vol199/view.php?volNum=vol199&seq=1.

Kim, Youna. 2009. *Women, Television and Everyday Life in Korea: Journeys of Hope*. London: Routledge.

Kim, Youna. 2013. *The Korean Wave: Korean Media Go Global*. London: Routledge.

KOCCA (Korea Creative Content Agency). 2011. 방송영상콘텐츠 제작시설 실태와 운영개선방안 [Broadcasting Video Contents Production Facility Status and Operation Improvement Plan]. Seoul: KOCCA.

KOCCA (Korea Creative Content Agency). 2014. "U.S. Consumers of Korean Content: Summary of Results Pertaining to Television Drama (year 14, vol. 22) [미국] 한국콘텐츠 미국 소비자조사-드라마 결과 요약 (14년 22호)]." Los Angeles: KOCCA.

Korea Communications Standards Commission. 2017. *Regulation on Broadcasting Standards* [방송심의 관한 규정]. Seoul: Korea Ministry of Government Legislation.

Korea Culture and Tourism Institute. 2023. Entry to Korea Tourism Statistics [입국 관광통계]. Seoul: Korea Culture and Tourism Institute and the Ministry of Culture, Sports and Tourism.

Korea Tourism Organization. 2013. Korea Tourism Market Research [한류관광시장 조사 연구]. Korea Tourism Organization, accessed May 25, 2017. http://kto.visitkorea.or.kr/kor/notice/data/report/org/board/view.kto?id=421648&rnum=2.

KOTRA. 2017. "The Current State and Future Prospects of Korea's Cultural Content Industry." Korea Trade-Investment Promotion Agency, accessed June 9. http://english.kotra.or.kr/kh/index.html.

kpopfan. 2017. "[MV] Ailee—I Will Go to You Like the First Snow (Goblin OST). The End." YouTube, January 22. https://www.youtube.com/watch?v=FHCTBn9DULw.

Kuhl, Stefan. 2002. *The Nazi Connection: Eugenics, American Racism, and German National Socialism*. Oxford: Oxford University Press.

Kuhn, Annette. 1999. "Women's Genres: Melodrama, Soap Opera and Theory." In *Feminist Film Theory: A Reader*, edited by Sue Thornham, 146–156. New York: NYU Press.

Kwon, Gwang-Soon, and Yu-Mi Cho. 2020. "The Nth Room Perpetrator Who Boasted of Crimes to Jo Joo-bin, Caught Because of His Desire to Show Off [조주빈에 범죄 자랑한 n번방 원조, 그 과시욕에 덜미 잡혀]." *Chosun Ilbo*, July 13. https://www.chosun.com/site/data/html_dir/2020/05/12/2020051200146.html.

Kwon, Insook. 2000. "A Feminist Exploration of Military Conscription: The Gendering of the Connections Between Nationalism, Militarism and Citizenship in South Korea." *International Feminist Journal of Politics* 3 (1): 26–54.

Lacan, Jacques, Jacques-Alain Ed Miller, and Russell Trans Grigg. 1993. "The Seminar of Jacques Lacan, Book 3: The Psychoses 1955–1956." Translation of the seminar Lacan delivered to the Société Française de Psychoanalyse over the course of the academic year 1955–1956.

Lee, Alex Jong-Seok. 2019. "Manly Colors: Masculinity and Mobility Among Globalizing Korean Men." *Kalfou* 6 (2): 199–230.

Lee, Claire Seungeun. 2021. "Contested Everyday Cultural Citizenship: 'Mixed Race' Children and Their Ethnicized Citizenship in South Korea." *Ethnic and Racial Studies* 44 (7): 1231–1249.

Lee, Euna, Seung-kyung Kim, and Jae Kyung Lee. 2015. "Precarious Motherhood: Lives of Southeast Asian Marriage Migrant Women in Korea." *Asian Journal of Women's Studies* 21 (4): 409–430.

Lee, Eunbi, and Colby Y. Miyose. 2022. "Narratives of Marginalized Otherness in Migrant Women: The South Korean Films Rosa and Thuy." In *Mediating the South Korean Other: Representations and Discourses of Difference in the Post/Neocolonial Nation-State*, edited by David C. Oh, 85–102. Ann Arbor: University of Michigan Press.

Lee, Hyun-Jin. 2019. Foreign Sex Workers Increased 24% Last Year Due to the Influx of Illegal Migration to Korea [지난해 외국인 성매매 종사자 24% 뛰어 취업 목적의 불법체류자 유입] *Korean Economic Daily*, April 23.

Lee, Jin-kyung. 2009. "Surrogate Military, Subimperialism, and Masculinity: South Korea in the Vietnam War, 1965–73." *Positions: East Asia Cultures Critique* 17 (3): 655–682.

Lee, Kyung-Jin. 2020. "Goyang City Will Build a Theme Park and Arena at K-Culture Valley [고양 'K-컬처밸리'에 테마파크-아레나 조성]." *Dong-A Ilbo*, August 12. https://www.donga.com/news/Society/article/all/20200812/102409385/1.

Lee, Kyung-Jin. 2022. "Goyang K-Culture Valley Will Have a State of the Art Performance Hall [고양 K컬처밸리에 최첨단 공연장 짓는다]." *Donga Ilbo*, December 2. https://www.donga.com/news/Society/article/all/20221202/116804104/1.

Lee, Kyung-Tak. 2016. "Sensational KCON . . . A Place to Experience the Popularity of Hallyu That Transgresses Race [케이콘 열광의 도가니 . . . 인종 초월한 한류 열풍 실감]." *Digital Today*, July 26. https://www.digitaltoday.co.kr/news/articleView.html?idxno=71148.

Lee, Mary. 2008. "Mixed Race Peoples in the Korean National Imaginary and Family." *Korean Studies* 32 (1): 56–85.

Lee, Min Joo. 2020. "Touring the Land of Romance: Transnational Korean Television Drama Consumption from Online Desires to Offline Intimacy." *Journal of Tourism and Cultural Change* 18 (1): 67–80.

Lee, Min Joo. 2022. "Aspirational Interraciality and Desirable Whiteness: South Korean Media Depictions of Interracial Intimacies Between White Women and 'Cosmopolitan' South Korean Men." In *Mediating the South Korean Other:*

Representations and Discourses of Difference in the Post/Neocolonial Nation-State, edited by David C. Oh, 27–45. Ann Arbor: University of Michigan Press.

Lee, Min Joo. 2023. "'Korean Women All Make Bad Wives': Misogyny and Nationalism in Online Discourses Promoting Interracial Relationships Between Korean Men and White Women." *Men and Masculinities* 27 (1): 42–60.

Lee, Mun-Woong. 2023. "Head of Household" [가장 (家長)]." In *Encyclopedia of Korean Culture* [한국민족문화대백과사전], edited by the Academy of Korean Studies. Sungnam, South Korea: Academy of Korean Studies.

Lee, Myeoung-hyun. 2020. "The Existence Patterns and Meanings of Narratives of Returning Ladies [환향녀 서사의 존재 양상과 의미]." *East Asian Ancient History* [동아시아고대학] 60:9–40.

Lee, Sangjoon, and Abe Markus Nornes. 2015. *Hallyu 2.0: The Korean Wave in the Age of Social Media*. Ann Arbor: University of Michigan Press.

Lee, Sung-Oh. 2018. K-Culture Valley Acquires Gyeonggi Province Urban Planning Organization's Approval [K-컬처밸리, 경기도 도시계획심의 통과]. *Goyang Newspaper*, accessed January 1, 2019.

Lee, Yeon-Hwa, and Jae Kyun Kim. 2024. "The Peculiar Consensus and Racial Unconscious in Migration Scholarship on Korea." *Critical Sociology* 51 (2): 1–20.

Leung, Lisa Yuk-ming. 2004. "Ganbaru and Its Transcultural Audience: Imaginary and Reality of Japanese TV Dramas in Hong Kong." In *Feeling Asian Modernities: Transnational Consumption of Japanese TV Dramas*, edited by Koichi Iwabuchi, 89–106. Pokfulam: Hong Kong University Press.

Li, Jinying. 2024. *Anime's Knowledge Cultures: Geek, Otaku, Zhai*. Minneapolis: University of Minnesota Press.

Lie, John. 2012. "What Is the K in K-pop? South Korean Popular Music, the Culture Industry, and National Identity." *Korea Observer* 43 (3): 339–363.

Lim, Timothy. 2010. "Rethinking Belongingness in Korea: Transnational Migration, 'Migrant Marriages' and the Politics of Multiculturalism." *Pacific Affairs* 83 (1): 51–71.

Lollypip. 2016. "Descended from the Sun." Dramabeans, accessed June 2020. http://www.dramabeans.com/shows/descended-from-the-sun/.

Lorde, Audre. 2006. "The Uses of the Erotic: The Erotic as Power." In *Sexualities and Communication in Everyday Life: A Reader*, edited by Karen E. Lovaas and Mercilee M. Jenkins, 87–91. Thousand Oaks, CA: Sage.

Lothian, Alexis. 2015. "A Different Kind of Love Song: Vidding Fandom's Undercommons." *Cinema Journal* 54 (3): 138–145.

Louie, Kam. 2012. "Popular Culture and Masculinity Ideals in East Asia, with Special Reference to China." *Journal of Asian Studies* 71 (4): 929–943.

Lukács, Gabriella. 2020. *Invisibility by Design: Women and Labor in Japan's Digital Economy*. Durham, NC: Duke University Press.

Lyan, Irina, and Alon Levkowitz. 2015. "From Holy Land to 'Hallyu Land': The Symbolic Journey Following the Korean Wave in Israel." *Journal of Fandom Studies* 3 (1): 7–21.

Maetawinz. 2013. "[Drama 2013–14] You Who Came from the Stars / My Love from Another Star ★." Online Forum. Soompi, accessed June 2020. https://forums.soompi.com.

MaknaeCloud. 2014. "[You from Another Star] Do Min Joon & Cheon Song Yi: Love Story." YouTube, accessed June 20, 2018. https://www.youtube.com/watch?v=JiMzpnY5Ph8.

Mankekar, Purnima. 2013. "Television and Embodiment: A Speculative Essay." *South Asian History and Culture* 3 (4): 603–613.

Mankekar, Purnima, and Louisa Schein. 2013. "Mediation and Transmediations: Erotics, Sociality, and 'Asia.'" In *Media, Erotics, and Transnational Asia*, edited by Purnima Mankekar and Louisa Schein, 1–32. Durham, NC: Duke University Press.

Maoz, Darya. 2006. "The Mutual Gaze." *Annals of Tourism Research* 33 (1): 221–239.

Marchetti, Gina. 1994. *Romance and the "Yellow Peril": Race, Sex, and Discursive Strategies in Hollywood Fiction*. Berkeley: University of California Press.

Marks, Laura U. 1998. "Video Haptics and Erotics." *Screen* 39 (4): 331–348.

McHugh, Kathleen A. 2001. "South Korean Film Melodrama and the Question of National Cinema." *Quarterly Review of Film & Video* 18 (1): 1–14.

Mehler, Barry. 1989. "Foundation for Fascism: The New Eugenics Movement in the United States." *Patterns of Prejudice* 23 (4): 17–25.

Mimiko, Nahzeem Oluwafemi. 2013. "From Insularity to Segyehwa: The Political Economy of Globalization in Korea." In *Korea and Globalization*, edited by James B. Lewis and Amadu Sesay, 61–78. London: Routledge.

Min, Pyong Gap. 2003. "Korean 'Comfort Women': The Intersection of Colonial Power, Gender, and Class." *Gender & Society* 17 (6): 938–957.

Ministry of Culture, Sports and Tourism. 2019. *2018 Contents Industry Statistics Report* [*2018* 콘텐츠산업 통계조사 보고서]. Edited by Department of Policy on Cultural Industry [문화산업정책과].

Miyao, Daisuke. 2007. *Sessue Hayakawa: Silent Cinema and Transnational Stardom*. Durham, NC: Duke University Press.

Modleski, Tania. 1982. *Loving with a Vengeance: Mass-Produced Fantasies for Women*. London: Routledge.

Molen, Sherri L. Ter. 2014. "Hallyu for Hire: The Commodification of Korea in Tourism Advertising and Marketing." In *The Global Impact of South Korean Popular Culture: Hallyu Unbound*, edited by Valentina Marinescu, 107–122. Lanham, MD: Lexington Books.

Monocello, Lawrence T., and William W Dressler. 2020. "Flower Boys and Muscled Men: Comparing South Korean and American Male Body Ideals Using Cultural Domain Analysis." *Anthropology & Medicine* 27 (2): 176–191.

Moon, Seungsook. 2005a. *Militarized Modernity and Gendered Citizenship in South Korea*. Durham, NC: Duke University Press.

Moon, Seungsook. 2005b. "Trouble with Conscription, Entertaining Soldiers: Popular Culture and the Politics of Militarized Masculinity in South Korea." *Men and Masculinities* 8 (1): 64–92.

Mulvey, Laura. 2009. "Visual Pleasure and Narrative Cinema." In *Media and Cultural Studies: Keyworks*, edited by Meenakshi Gigi Durham and Douglas M. Kellner, 393–404. Malden, MA: Blackwell

Nader, Laura. 1989. "Orientalism, Occidentalism and the Control of Women." *Cultural Dynamics* 2 (3): 323–355.

Nagel, Joane. 2000. "States of Arousal/Fantasy Islands: Race, Sex, and Romance in the Global Economy of Desire." *American Studies* 41 (2/3): 159–181.

Narayan, Uma. 1998. "Essence of Culture and a Sense of History: A Feminist Critique of Cultural Essentialism." *Hypatia* 13 (2): 86–106.

NBC. 2020. "*Parasite*: Best Motion Picture, Foreign Language—2020 Golden Globes." YouTube, January 5. https://www.youtube.com/watch?v=mX3obZolXoU.

Nemoto, Kumiko. 2009. *Racing Romance: Love, Power, and Desire Among Asian American/White Couples*. London: Rutgers University Press.

Nguyen, Tan Hoang. 2014. *A View from the Bottom: Asian American Masculinity and Sexual Representation*. Durham, NC: Duke University Press.

Nye Jr., Joseph S. 2008. "Public Diplomacy and Soft Power." *Annals of the American Academy of Political and Social Science* 616 (1): 94–109.

Oegukeen. 2012. "Dating Korean Guy." Soompi, accessed June 2020. https://forums .soompi.com.

Oh, Chuyun. 2015. "Queering Spectatorship in K-pop: The Androgynous Male Dancing Body and Western Female Fandom." *Journal of Fandom Studies* 3 (1): 59–78.

Oh, David C. 2020. "Representing the Western Super-Minority: Desirable Cosmo-politanism and Homosocial Multiculturalism on a South Korean Talk Show." *Television & New Media* 21 (3): 260–277.

Oh, David C. 2022. "Introduction." In *Mediating the South Korean Other: Representa-tions and Discourses of Difference in the Post/Neocolonial Nation-State*, edited by David C. Oh, 1–26. Ann Arbor: University of Michigan Press.

Oh, Ingyu. 2011. "Torn Between Two Lovers: Retrospective Learning and Melancho-lia Among Japanese Women." *Korea Observer* 42 (2): 223–254.

Oh, Myung-Hwan. 2015. *Drama Humanities 50* [드라마 인문학 50]. Advancement of Broadcasting Culture. Korea: Tree and Forest Publisher [나무와 숲].

Oh, Youjeong. 2018. *Pop City: Korean Popular Culture and the Selling of Place*. Ithaca, NY: Cornell University Press.

Ok, Ki-Won. 2020. "When the Construction for Seoul Arena Is Complete, I Want to Invite BTS as Opening Performers ["서울아레나 완공되면 첫 공연 '방탄소년단' 초청하고 싶다"]." *Hankyoreh*, July 7. http://www.hani.co.kr/arti/area/capital/961156 .html.

Pande, Raksha. 2015. "'I Arranged My Own Marriage': Arranged Marriages and Post-colonial Feminism." *Gender, Place & Culture* 22 (2): 172–187.

Park, Chang Gun. 2015. "The Globalization of Kim Young-Sam Government and Shaky Relationship Between Korea and Japan [김영삼 정부의 세계화와 흔들리는 한일관계: 외환위기를 둘러싼 정치경제적 균열]." *Journal of Japan Studies* [일본연구논총] 42:59–83.

Park, Eun-Ryung. 2017. SBS "Saimdang, Light's Diary" Writer Park Eun-Ryung Interview. edited by Yoon-Yang Kim. Korea: Korea TV & Radio Writers Association.

Park, Hyun Ok. 1996. "Segyehwa: Globalization and Nationalism in Korea." *Journal of the International Institute* 4 (1).

Park, Jeong-Mi. 2015. "A Historical Sociology of the Korean Government's Policies on Military Prostitution in U.S. Camptowns, 1953–1995: Biopolitics, State of Exception, and the Paradox of Sovereignty Under the Cold War [한국 기지촌 성매매정책의 역사사회학, 1953–1995 년: 냉전기 생명정치, 예외상태, 그리고 주권의 역설]." *Studies of Korean Society* [한국사회학] 49 (2): 1–33.

Park, Jin-Hyung. 2020. "[Interview While Going to Work] Funding Young Musicians . . . The Largest National Online Song-Writing Contest [[출근길 인터뷰] 청년 음악인 지원 . . . 국내 최대규모 온라인 창작경연대회]." *Yonhap News*, November 26. https://www .yonhapnewstv.co.kr/news/MYH20201126006100641.

Park, Ju Young. 2020. "Dangerous Memories: War, Chastity, and the Politics of Divorce in 17th Century Korea [병자호란 직후 속환부녀(贖還婦女)의 이혼 문제]." *Humanities Journal* 58:193–235. https://doi.org/10.37981/hjhrisu.2020.08.58.193.

Park, Min-shik. 2016. "My Love from the Star as Profitable as Exporting 20 Thousand Cars ['별그대' 쏘나타 2만대 효과 . . . 잘 만든 드라마가 경제에 '효자']." *Korea Times*, November 11. http://www.hankookilbo.com/v/125e6671692e4ad094596af1e663262f.

Park, You-me. 2016. "The Crucible of Sexual Violence: Militarized Masculinities and the Abjection of Life in Post-crisis, Neoliberal South Korea." *Feminist Studies* 42 (1): 17–40.

Pascoe, C. J., and Jocelyn A Hollander. 2016. "Good Guys Don't Rape: Gender, Domination, and Mobilizing Rape." *Gender & Society* 30 (1): 67–79.

Peng, Xin. 2022. "Anna May Wong and Sessue Hayakawa: Racial Performance, Ornamentalism, and Yellow Voices in *Daughter of the Dragon* (1931)." *Camera Obscura* 37 (2): 1–29.

Perman, Stacy. 2019. "Former DramaFever Executive Sues Warner Bros. Alleging Anti-Asian Discrimination." *Los Angeles Times*, March 6. https://www.latimes.com/business/hollywood/la-fi-ct-dramafever-lawsuit-20190306-story.html.

Pile, Steve. 2010. "Emotions and Affect in Recent Human Geography." *Transactions of the Institute of British Geographers* 35 (1): 5–20.

President Moon Jae-in's Blue House [문재인정부청와대] (@TheBlueHouseKR). 2021. "'Huge Congratulations and Thank You to BTS' AMA Award.' We Convey a Message from President Moon Jae-in. ["BTS의 AMA 대상 수상에 큰 축하와 감사를 보냅니다." 문재인 대통령의 메시지를 전합니다.]" Twitter (now X), November 22. https://x.com/TheBlueHouseKR/status/1463010511482593286.

Pruitt, Deborah, and Suzanne LaFont. 1995. "For Love and Money: Romance Tourism in Jamaica." *Annals of Tourism Research* 22 (2): 422–440.

Pyke, Karen D., and Denise L. Johnson. 2003. "Asian American Women and Racialized Femininities: 'Doing' Gender Across Cultural Worlds." *Gender & Society* 17 (1): 33–53.

Radway, Janice A. 1984. *Reading the Romance: Women, Patriarchy, and Popular Literature*. Chapel Hill: University of North Carolina Press.

Regis, Helen A. 1997. "The Madness of Excess: Love Among the Fulbe of North Cameroun." In *Romantic Passion: A Universal Experience?*, edited by William Jankowiak, 141–151. New York: Columbia University Press.

Ringrose, Jessica, Katilyn Regehr, and Sophie Whitehead. 2022. "'Wanna Trade?': Cisheteronormative Homosocial Masculinity and the Normalization of Abuse in Youth Digital Sexual Image Exchange." *Journal of Gender Studies* 31 (2): 243–261.

Rivers-Moore, Megan. 2016. *Gringo Gulch: Sex, Tourism, and Social Mobility in Costa Rica*. Chicago: University of Chicago Press.

Rosart. 2017. "Every Time I Get Lost, You Will Find Me. Kim Shin & Eun-tak." YouTube, January 11. https://www.youtube.com/watch?v=M06vlSVZMLs.

Sadler, William J., and Ekaterina V. Haskins. 2005. "Metonymy and the Metropolis: Television Show Settings and the Image of New York City." *Journal of Communication Inquiry* 29 (3): 195–216.

Said, Edward W. 1985. "Orientalism Reconsidered." *Cultural Critique* (1): 89–107.

SBS News. 2016. "[VIDEOMUG] President Park's Exceptional Love for Descendants of the Sun? . . . She Mentions the Drama Again on Her Trip to Iran [[VIDEOMUG] 박 대통령의 남다른 '태양의 후예' 사랑? . . . 이란 순방서 또 언급 / SBS]." YouTube, May 3. https://www.youtube.com/watch?v=DsmCNG5BYng.

Schulze, Marion. 2013. "Korea vs. K-Dramaland: The Culturalization of K-Dramas by International Fans." *Acta Koreana* 16 (2): 367–397.

Seo, Yoo-Jin. 2018. "Decrease in Car Tax Extended 6 More Months, K-pop Arena Hopefully Boosts Hallyu Tourism [승용차 개별소비세 인하 6개월 연장 . . . K팝 공연장 마련 '한류 관광' 띄운다]." *JoongAng Ilbo*, accessed January 1, 2019.

Shim, Hoon. 2012. "Our Distorted Multi-Culturalism: Narrative Analysis of Multi-Cultural People in KBS Human Documentary with Holistic-Content Reading and Categorical Format Reading." *Korean Journal of Journalism & Communication Studies* 56:184–209.

Shimizu, Celine Parreñas. 2012. *Straitjacket Sexualities: Unbinding Asian American Manhoods in the Movies*. Palo Alto, CA: Stanford University Press.

Shin, Gi-Wook. 2006. *Ethnic Nationalism in Korea: Genealogy, Politics, and Legacy*. Palo Alto, CA: Stanford University Press.

Shin, Hyunjoon. 2009. "Have You Ever Seen the Rain? And Who'll Stop the Rain?: The Globalizing Project of Korean Pop (K-pop)." *Inter-Asia Cultural Studies* 10 (4): 507–523.

Shin, Jeeweon. 2016. "Hyphenated Identities of Korean Heritage Language Learners: Marginalization, Colonial Discourses and Internalized Whiteness." *Journal of Language, Identity & Education* 15 (1): 32–43.

Shin, Kwang-yeong. 2006. "Korea's Globalization [한국의 세계화]." *Culture and Science* [문화과학] 47:200–215.

Sobchack, Vivian. 1990. "The Active Eye: A Phenomenology of Cinematic Vision." *Quarterly Review of Film and Video* 12 (3): 21–36.

Song, Minzheong. 2015. "Global Online Distribution Strategies for K-pop: A Case of 'Gangnam Style.'" *Broadcasting and Communication* [방송과 커뮤니케이션] 16 (2): 85–121.

Soompi. 2024. "About Soompi." https://www.soompi.com/about.

Starosielski, Nicole. 2015. "Fixed Flow: Undersea Cables as Media Infrastructure." In *Signal Traffic: Critical Studies of Media Infrastructures*, edited by Lisa Parks and Nicole Starosielski, 53–70. Chicago: University of Illinois Press.

Strain, Ellen. 2003. *Public Places, Private Journeys: Ethnography, Entertainment, and the Tourist Gaze*. New Brunswick, NJ: Rutgers University Press.

Sueyoshi, Amy. 2018. *Discriminating Sex: White Leisure and the Making of the American "Oriental."* Chicago: University of Illinois Press.

Sun, Meicheng. 2020. "K-pop Fan Labor and an Alternative Creative Industry: A Case Study of GOT7 Chinese Fans." *Global Media and China* 5 (4): 389–406.

Swisher, Kara. 2013. "Exclusive: Japan's Rakuten Acquires Viki Video Site for $200 Million." AllThingsD, accessed April 7, 2020. https://allthingsd.com/20130901/exclusive-japans-rakuten-acquires-viki-video-site-for-200-million/.

Taylor, Jacqueline Sánchez. 2001. "Dollars Are a Girl's Best Friend? Female Tourists' Sexual Behaviour in the Caribbean." *Sociology* 35 (3): 749–764.

Torchin, Leshu. 2002. "Location, Location, Location: The Destination of the Manhattan TV Tour." *Tourist Studies* 2 (3): 247–266.

Törnqvist, Maria. 2012. "Troubling Romance Tourism: Sex, Gender and Class Inside the Argentinean Tango Clubs." *Feminist Review* 102 (1): 21–40.

Trzcińska, Julia. 2020. "K-pop Fandom as a Left-Wing Political Force? The Case of Poland." *Culture and Empathy* 3 (3–4): 119–142.

Tsing, Anna. 2000. "The Global Situation." *Cultural Anthropology* 15 (3): 327–360.

Ueno, Chizuko. 1997. "In the Feminine Guise: A Trap of Reverse Orientalism." *US-Japan Women's Journal: English Supplement*, no. 13: 3–25.

Urry, John, and Jonas Larsen. 2011. *The Tourist Gaze 3.0*. Thousand Oaks, CA: Sage.

Van Der Oye, David Schimmelpenninck. 2010. *Russian Orientalism: Asia in the Russian Mind from Peter the Great to the Emigration*. New Haven, CT: Yale University Press.

Vares, Tiina. 2018. "'My [Asexuality] Is Playing Hell with My Dating Life': Romantic Identified Asexuals Negotiate the Dating Game." *Sexualities* 21 (4): 520–536.

Werry, Margaret. 2011. *The Tourist State: Performing Leisure, Liberalism, and Race in New Zealand*. Minneapolis: University of Minnesota Press.

Wilkinson, Eleanor. 2014. "Love in the Multitude? A Feminist Critique of Love as a Political Concept." In *Love: A Question for Feminism in the Twenty-First Century*, edited by Anna Jonasdottir and Ann Ferguson, 237–249. London: Routledge.

Williams, Erica Lorraine. 2013. *Sex Tourism in Bahia: Ambiguous Entanglements*. Chicago: University of Illinois Press.

Williams, Linda. 1991. "Film Bodies: Gender, Genre, and Excess." *Film Quarterly* 44 (4): 2–13.

Wong, Y. Joel, Jesse Owen, Kimberly K. Tran, Dana L. Collins, and Claire E. Higgins. 2012. "Asian American Male College Students' Perceptions of People's Stereotypes About Asian American Men." *Psychology of Men & Masculinity* 13 (1): 75.

Wu, Cynthia. 2018. *Sticky Rice: A Politics of Intraracial Desire*. Philadelphia: Temple University Press.

xFictionShadowMV3 xKBS. 2016. "Descendants of the Sun MV—'I Miss You' (Shi Jin x Mo Yeon)." YouTube, July 21. https://www.youtube.com/watch?v=BTRGDWm3txo.

Xiang, Ying, and Seong Wook Chae. 2022. "Influence of Perceived Interactivity on Continuous Use Intentions on the Danmaku Video Sharing Platform: Belongingness Perspective." *International Journal of Human–Computer Interaction* 38 (6): 573–593.

Ya, E. S. 2005. "A Research on Continuous Improvement of Hallyu Tourism as a New Cultural Tourism." *Journal of Korea Tourism Policy* 11 (3): 57–77.

Yonhap News. 2016. "It Finished with a 38.8% Rating . . . What Did *Descendants of the Sun* Leave Behind? [38.8%로 종영 . . . '태양의 후예'가 남긴 것들]." *Hankyeorae News*, April 15. http://www.hani.co.kr/arti/culture/entertainment/739852.html.

Yoon, Go-Eun. 2016. "*Descendants of the Sun* Exported to 27 Countries . . . Increasing Popularity of the Drama [태양의 후예 27개국 수출국가 계속 늘어나]." *Yonhap News*, October 1.

Yoon, Go-Eun. 2017. "The Drama *Guardian* Reaches 20.5% Ratings in VOD . . . Even Without Export to China, the Drama Is Garnering Profits [도깨비 20.5% VOD 흥행기록 깼다 . . . 중국 없이도 흑자]." *Yonhap News*, January 22. http://www.yonhapnews.co.kr/bulletin/2017/01/20/0200000000AKR20170120178800033.HTML.

Yoon, Nan-Joong. 2015. TVN "Hogu's Love" Writer Nan-Joong Yoon Interview. Edited by Sun-Mi Kim. Korea: Korea TV & Radio Writers Archive.

You, Hyun-Kyung, and Lori A McGraw. 2011. "The Intersection of Motherhood and Disability: Being a "Good" Korean Mother to an 'Imperfect' Child." *Journal of Comparative Family Studies* 42 (4): 579–598.

YozohhhCH8. 2014. "Kim Soo Hyun—Promise FMV (You Who Came from the Stars OST)." ENGSUB Rom Hangul. YouTube, March 23. https://www.youtube.com/watch?v=Jfco9C1bR34.

Yu, Sojin. 2023. "Migrant Racialization in South Korea: Class and Nationality as the Central Narrative." *Ethnic and Racial Studies* 46 (10): 2089–2110.

Zhao, Jamie J. 2021. "Blackpink Queers Your Area: The Global Queerbaiting and Queer Fandom of K-pop Female Idols." *Feminist Media Studies* 21 (6): 1033–1038.

Zheng, Robin. 2016. "Why Yellow Fever Isn't Flattering: A Case Against Racial Fetishes." *Journal of the American Philosophical Association* 2 (3): 400–419.

Zizek, Slavoj. 1992. *Looking Awry: An Introduction to Jacques Lacan Through Popular Culture*. Cambridge, MA: MIT Press.

Index

About the Author

MIN JOO LEE is an assistant professor in the Department of Asian Studies at Occidental College. Her research focuses on the gendered and racial perspectives of Korean media and fandom. She has researched topics including cross-dressing in Korean television dramas, interracial couples–turned–YouTube influencers comprising Korean men and foreign women, global fans of Korean popular culture, and the politics surrounding digital technology and sexual consent.